Buying a Computer For Dummies, 2006 Edition

P9-DHI-756

Cheat Sheet

The Five Steps to Buying a Computer

1. Decide what you want your computer to do.
2. Find the software that will get you the result you want.
3. Find the hardware to run your software.
4. Shop for service and support.
5. Buy that computer!

Words of Wisdom

- Don't dwell on brand names, but rather on a solution to your software problem.
- Ignore part numbers: It's an 80GB hard drive, not an 80ZRc4012C-x.
- Avoid untested technology. Unless you see an item in numerous computer ads, it's probably not worth getting.
- Software drives the hardware. Without software to take advantage of a fancy computing device, the device is useless.
- For the best deal, buy stuff just under the leading edge of technology. Rather than the latest, largest, and fastest, get the second or third item from the top. You get a good deal and still get good technology.
- Most computers have a useful life of about four years. After that, buying a new computer is cheaper than upgrading your existing model.

Where to Spend Extra Money

Buy a faster microprocessor. Nothing beats a fast microprocessor. Also, because a fast microprocessor is the most difficult item to upgrade later, you should spend more money here first.

Maximize your memory! Ensure that as much memory as possible is in one bank.

Get a larger hard drive. Although you can easily add more storage later, most folks typically underestimate their storage needs. Too much space is great!

Jumbo-size your monitor. Those 19-plus-inch screens are dreamy. Go LCD!

Don't Forget to Buy These Items Too

- A mousepad
- A wristpad
- A power strip or surge protector or UPS
- A printer cable
- Paper for your printer
- Extra printer toner or ink
- Antivirus software
- Extra CD-R discs
- Internet access
- A roll of paper towels
- A nice reference book, such as PC For Dummies, 10th Edition (published by Wiley, Inc.)

For Dummies: Bestselling Book Series for Beginners

Buying a Computer For Dummies, 2006 Edition

Cheat Sheet

Important Questions to Ask a Potential Dealer (and Some Ideal Answers)

Q: Where do you fix your computers?

A: Right here or in your home or office!

Q: Can I phone up someone to ask questions?

A: Sure! At any time. Here's our 800 number!

Q: Do you offer classes?

A: Yes, we have our own classroom, and classes are free to anyone who buys our computers!

Types of Support

Vanilla: You pay not only for the phone call but also for the support.

Chocolate: You pay only for the phone call.

Carob: You get free support for 90 days, but you pay for the phone call; after that, you pay for the support and the phone call.

Fudge: Free phone call; free support; no time limit.

Hardware Tips and Suggestions

- ✔ Get an LCD monitor over a standard CRT model. Although an LCD monitor is more expensive, it's better on your eyes, uses less power, and may end up lasting longer than a CRT monitor.
- ✔ If possible, try to get a PC with the USB 2.0 standard, which has support for faster external devices, such as hard drives, CDs, and DVDs.
- ✔ The DVD recording standard hasn't been officially set yet. If you plan to record DVDs, buy whichever type of drive your recording software supports.
- ✔ If you buy a laptop, I strongly suggest buying an extended warranty.
- ✔ Double-check to confirm that you're not buying refurbished equipment, unless that's what you want to buy.
- ✔ Optical mice last longer than their mechanical ("ball") cousins.
- ✔ Try to get an ink printer with separate ink cartridges, one for each ink color.

Important Phone Numbers and Information

My dealer's phone number: _____

My dealer's support number: _____

My dealer's Web page address: _____

My dealer's e-mail address: _____

My computer's make and model number: _____

My computer's serial number: _____

Date of purchase: _____

For Dummies: Bestselling Book Series for Beginners

Buying a Computer

FOR

DUMMIES®

2006 EDITION

Buying a Computer

FOR

DUMMIES®

2006 EDITION

by Dan Gookin

WILEY

Wiley Publishing, Inc.

Buying a Computer For Dummies®, 2006 Edition

Published by
Wiley Publishing, Inc.
111 River Street
Hoboken, NJ 07030-5774

www.wiley.com

WILEY

About the Author

Dan Gookin has been writing about technology for 20 years. He has contributed articles to numerous high-tech magazines and written more than 100 books about personal computing technology, many of them accurate.

He combines his love of writing with his interest in technology to create books that are informative and entertaining, but not boring. Having sold more than 14 million titles translated into more than 30 languages, Dan can attest that his method of crafting computer tomes does seem to work.

Perhaps Dan's most famous title is the original *DOS For Dummies,* published in 1991. It became the world's fastest-selling computer book, at one time moving more copies per week than the *New York Times* number-one best seller (although, because it's a reference book, it could not be listed on the *NYT* best seller list). That book spawned the entire line of *For Dummies* books, which remains a publishing phenomenon to this day.

Dan's most recent titles include *Laptops For Dummies*; *PCs For Dummies,* 10th Edition; *Troubleshooting Your PC For Dummies*, 2nd Edition; *Power Excel & Word;* and *eBay Photos That Sell.* He also maintains the vast and helpful Web site www.wambooli.com.

Dan holds a degree in communications and visual arts from the University of California, San Diego. He lives in the Pacific Northwest, where he enjoys spending time with his four boys in the gentle woods and on the temperate blue lakes of Idaho.

Publisher's Acknowledgments

We're proud of this book; please send us your comments through our online registration form located at www.dummies.com/register/.

Some of the people who helped bring this book to market include the following:

Acquisitions, Editorial, and Media Development

Project Editor: Rebecca Whitney

Acquisitions Editor: Gregory Croy

Technical Editor: James F. Kelly

Editorial Manager: Jodi Jensen

Media Development Supervisor: Richard Graves

Editorial Assistant: Amanda Foxworth

Cartoons: Rich Tennant
(www.the5thwave.com)

Composition Services

Project Coordinator: Kathryn Shanks

Layout and Graphics: Carl Byers, Andrea Dahl, Stephanie D. Jumper, Barry Offringa

Proofreaders: Leeann Harney, Jessica Kramer, Carl William Pierce, TECHBOOKS Production Services

Indexer: TECHBOOKS Production Services

Publishing and Editorial for Technology Dummies

　　Richard Swadley, Vice President and Executive Group Publisher

　　Andy Cummings, Vice President and Publisher

　　Mary Bednarek, Executive Acquisitions Director

　　Mary C. Corder, Editorial Director

Publishing for Consumer Dummies

　　Diane Graves Steele, Vice President and Publisher

　　Joyce Pepple, Acquisitions Director

Composition Services

　　Gerry Fahey, Vice President of Production Services

　　Debbie Stailey, Director of Composition Services

Contents at a Glance

Table of Contents

Introduction

· ·

Welcome to *Buying a Computer For Dummies* — a book which assumes that you know *nothing* about a computer but are strangely compelled to buy one. If that's you, you have found your book!

This book is not a buyer's guide. In it, you won't find endless boring lists of prices and products and useless part numbers. Instead, this book assumes that you need a computer for some reason. You'll discover that reason and then read about how to find software to carry out that task. From there, you'll match hardware to your software and end up with the computer that's perfect for you.

Because this is a *For Dummies* book, you can expect some lively and entertaining writing — not boring computer jargon. Nothing is assumed. Everything is explained. The result is that you'll have your own computer and *enjoy* the buying process.

About This Book

Buying a computer is a five-step process, which this book fully explains. Along the way, you'll read about computer hardware and software and fill in some worksheets that help you configure a computer just for you.

The five steps to buying a computer are outlined in Chapter 1. Based on that information, the book is divided into several parts, each of which occurs at a different stage in the buying process:

Part I overviews the entire process.

Part II discusses computer hardware and software: what it is and why you need it.

Part III details the buying process: where to buy, how to read a computer ad, and how to find service and support before the sale.

Part IV deals with setting up your new computer.

Part V is the traditional *For Dummies* "Part of Tens" — various lists for review or to help you get on your way.

And Just Who Are You?

Let me assume that you're a human being who wants to own a computer. You probably don't have one now, or, if you do, it's very, *very* old and you desire a new one. Other than that, your experience with a computer is very limited. You have heard the jargon and know some brand names, but that's about it. If that's you, this is your book.

This book concentrates on buying a computer, which can be a PC, Macintosh, handheld, laptop, or game console. Although all the information applies to buying *any* computer, the main thrust involves buying a desktop computer.

Icons Used in This Book

 Lets you know that something technical is being mentioned. Because the information is technical and written primarily as nerd trivia, you can freely skip it if you want.

 Flags useful information or a helpful tip. When you're visiting the computer store, for example, make sure that you leave with the same number of children you had when you arrived.

 Something to remember, like all computers need monitors, or else you'll never see what it is you're doing.

 Oops! Better watch out. You have lots of warnings to heed when you're buying a computer. This icon lets you find them right quick.

Where to Go from Here

Steadily grab this book with both hands, and start reading at Chapter 0. Then continue reading. Occasionally, you may be asked to visit a computer store or find a computer advertisement. Do so when asked. Fill in the worksheets that are offered. Then get ready to go out and buy yourself a computer.

Part I
Understanding the Whole Ordeal

The 5th Wave — By Rich Tennant

"I just can't keep up with the cosmetics industry. That woman we just passed has a makeup case with a screen and keyboard."

In this part . . .

Buying a computer can be an ordeal. It's scary! Every
year, there are fresh terms, different options, and
spanking-new technology. Stuff that was the latest and
greatest with last year's computer is outdated and no
longer available. It changes that fast.

Now there are two things you can do to avoid the ordeal.
The first is to go into denial, visit some huge, impersonal
store, buy the computer-in-a-box, and pray that you have
exactly what you need. The second thing you can do is
bone up on what's important and what *you* need in a computer. The idea is to understand the computer-buying
process, which is what you'll find in this part of the book.

Ordeal? Nope! Prepare to kiss your fear and doubt goodbye and get a computer that's just right for you.

Chapter 0

Some Questions to Get Out of the Way

In This Chapter

▶ Quick questions you may be pondering

▶ Nothing more

In my years of explaining to folks how to buy the best computer, one just for them, I inevitably encounter *the questions*. These are the burning issues, those topics you have buzzing around in your head. They're important questions, and I'm sure that you don't want to wade through several pages of this book to find the answer, so I present the questions — and my spiffy answers to them — right here and right away.

"Just Tell Me Which Type of Computer I Need!"

I can't do that without knowing what you'll be using the computer for. Everyone is different, and everyone has different reasons for owning a computer. To get the best computer, the one you need and don't have to upgrade or pour more money into over time, you have to work with me.

Now, it's true: You can get by with just about any computer. But, why settle for something less than what you need? This book shows you how to find a computer especially for you.

Think of it like a car. You may say "I want a new car." Which type of car? A sedan? A truck? How big of an engine do you want? What about good gas mileage? Do you want to pay extra for power seats or heated outside mirrors? And — most important — what *color* do you want? Computers are more complex than cars, so you have even more personal decisions to make.

"Why Not Let Me Have One of Your Computers?"

I can't send you any of my old computers because I would have to evict the family of raccoons living inside them.

"Where Can I Buy a Computer Really Cheap?"

All over. But, do you *want* cheap? How about getting service and support instead? You need that more than you need to save a few bucks off the purchase price.

"Which Brands Do You Recommend?"

None. Brands are irrelevant to buying a computer. Another important thing to note is that brand names, as well as computer part numbers, change all the time. Looking at a brand name for a computer should be the *last* thing you do when you buy one. This book explains why, though, if you feel better buying a major brand-name computer, by all means, go ahead.

"Which Brands Do You Recommend Staying Away From?"

Specifically, those companies that would take me to court for mentioning their names right here! Seriously, brand names are irrelevant. Some do have ugly reputations. Ask around; read reviews; or check the paper to find some companies that produce crap, if that's what you're trying to avoid.

What I cannot print in this book, I can freely tell you on my Web page. Feel free to visit www.wambooli.com and check out my forums or my blog (both linked from the main page), and you can readily read my up-to-date brand-name opinions. Even so, brands still remain a wee, if not insignificant, part of the computer-buying decision.

"How Much Will My Computer Cost?"

Anywhere from $200 up to several thousand dollars, depending on which options you need or the size of your credit limit. Obviously, if you're spending someone else's money, you want to pay more for your computer.

"Shouldn't 1 Just Buy the Most Expensive Computer 1 Can Afford?"

No. Why pay for something you don't use? Expensive computers tend to fall into a category known as "file server." These beefed-up monsters are designed to run full computer networks for small- to medium-size businesses. You probably don't need one.

"Then Shouldn't 1 Buy the Fastest Computer 1 Can Afford?"

Yes, but speed is only a small part of the overall computer equation. You also have to consider storage, compatibility, and other options, plus all the software you need to get your work done. This question of speed doesn't need to be answered until just before you're ready to buy. The advertisements boast of a computer's speed, but you need to ignore that for now.

"How about a Laptop?"

Laptops are portable computers, lightweight and battery powered so that they can go anywhere. They have feature comparable to desktop systems, and they're ideal for many situations, such as taking your computer on the road, to college, to conventions, to a computer café, and the list goes on and on.

I once said that laptops are not good for first-time computer buyers, mostly because laptops have lots of issues not found in desktop systems. I'm changing that view with this edition of this book. Laptops make excellent first-time computers, though you pay more for the laptop than the desktop version of the same system. This book covers all the details.

"Should I Get a Used Computer?"

I don't recommend getting a used computer as a first computer purchase.

"What about 'Refab' Computers?"

They're okay, as long as they come with a warranty and proper service and support.

"Will the Computer Store Offer Me Deals? How Much Should I Expect to Pay Below the 'Sticker Price'?"

The days of wheeling and dealing computers are long over — unless you're buying several dozen computers at a time. Most often, the advertised price is the price you pay, though if you can find a competitor who offers a lower price, some dealers give you a discount. But, you really shouldn't be shopping price. This book tells you why.

"Where Can I Get More Information Beyond What's Covered in This Book?"

Many places. First, ask your friends or coworkers who are into computers. Second, look in your paper for local computer user group meetings. These meetings are geared toward beginners and not technical people (which is what you would expect). Third, pick up a good magazine to find what's new and gather some how-tos. A good magazine to try is *SmartComputing*. Try to avoid the techy magazines for now, and the large magazines that are all ads don't help you until you're ready to buy. Finally, check out the Internet. Even if you don't have a computer, you can get online at any public library.

"Does This Book Offer a Buyer's Guide?"

Nope.

"Can You Recommend Any Buyer's Guides?"

Not really. Buyer's guides are for the old hands at buying a computer — folks who really care about part numbers and bolt sizes. Unless you know of a buyer's guide that says "Hey! I'm perfect for you" after one of the entries, you don't really need one.

"Isn't There an Easy Way to Do This? Can't I Just Go Buy a Computer?"

Sure, why not? But, you got this book because you want to buy the best personal computer for you — not just an off-the-shelf unit that may not meet your needs or (worse) a computer packed with stuff you pay for and never use.

Chapter 1

Buying a Computer (Step-by-Step)

In This Chapter

▶ The five steps to buying a computer

▶ Step 1: Decide what you want the computer to do

▶ Step 2: Find software to get that job done

▶ Step 3: Find hardware to make the software go

▶ Step 4: Shop for service and support

▶ Step 5: Buy that computer!

*W*hether you're just walking through the door of the computer age, returning after getting one of those "free" Internet PCs of the late 1990s, or perhaps boldly returning to the store to purchase your sixth system this year, there are definitely good ways and bad ways to buy computers. This chapter shows you the good ways.

Relax — You Have Nothing to Fear

It's easy to understand why buying a computer can be a scary thing. It's a big investment. Not only that, but lots of scary terms and frightening technology are involved. Are you getting the right thing? Is the salesperson baffling you with bs?

Most people don't have the same natural fear of technology that they have of snakes, spiders, fire, and old fat guys with short pants and black socks. You have no need to worry about slipping into *The Twilight Zone;* no need to confirm that you're in a Fellini movie. As with buying anything, the more you know about what you're buying, the better you can make your decision.

A well-informed shopper is a smart shopper. The key to becoming a smart computer shopper is to follow the five easy steps outlined in this chapter.

✔ I should tell you upfront that the biggest mistake people make in buying a computer is shopping for price rather than service. Although lots of places can sell you the cheapest computer in the galaxy, don't expect them to offer much after-sale support.

✔ Yes, you need support.

✔ The second-biggest mistake is shopping for hardware before shopping for software, including shopping for brand-name computers. Just because the TV has trained you to think that such-and-such a company makes computers doesn't mean that you have to buy one of them.

✔ I explain the difference between hardware and software in Chapter 4. That's where I also inform you why software is more important.

✔ Although you can use this book to help you find a nice used computer, I don't recommend buying one as your first computer. Why? No support (see Chapter 21).

✔ You can also build your own computer, although I don't recommend this route for your first-time foray into the world of high tech. Why? Same reason: no support.

The Five Steps to Buying a Computer

If you want to buy the perfect computer, the one Santa would have given you had you been good all year, you should follow these five simple steps:

1. **Decide what you want the computer to do.**

   When you know what you want to do with the computer, the rest of the steps fall neatly into place. That's because the computer is a device that can do many, many things; you have more reasons to buy a computer than could possibly be listed by a computer! Getting a good idea of what you need the computer for — e-mail, digital photography, music, video, writing, education, or entertainment, for example — is that vital first step.

2. **Find the software that can get you the result you want.**

   It's the software that does the work.

3. **Find the hardware to run your software.**

   Most people confuse this step with Step 2, finding software. Despite all the advertising out there, software is really more important; the hardware merely obeys the software. To put it another way, you don't buy a home gym to own all that fancy metal and those pulleys and cushions. No, you buy a home gym to get into shape. You buy an oboe to play oboe music, not because it makes a unique vase. Likewise, you buy a computer to run software. Therefore, the software is more important, and you should look for it first. (I tell you more on this topic in Chapter 4.)

4. **Shop for service and support.**

   This step is the most important one — more important than knowing whether to push or pull the computer store's front door. Too many shoppers overlook service and support and regret it later. I rant about this subject at length later in this chapter.

5. **Buy that computer!**

   Although this statement seems obvious, I know lots of folks who put off the purchase and hold out for a better deal or newer technology that's just "moments away." Bah! When you're ready to buy, buy. 'Nuff said.

I use these steps myself and have touted them for years. They work. Especially when you're buying something high-ticket, like a computer, you don't want to make a simple mistake.

- ✔ If you haven't already decided what a computer can do for you, flip through Chapter 16 to see what the little beasties are capable of.

- ✔ The *software* gets the work done. You buy hardware to support the software you have chosen.

- ✔ *Service* means getting the computer fixed. *Support* means getting H-E-L-P when you need it. *Everyone* needs service and support with a new computer. Everyone.

Step 1: Figure out what you want to do with your computer

Believe it or not, knowing what you want to do with the computer before you buy it is really helpful. Even if your only reason for buying one is that it would match the décor of your high-tech office, that's a good enough reason. Other folks, though, usually have some inkling in mind about why the Emperor of All Gadgets would be useful to them.

The first step toward buying your own computer is to decide what you want to do with it. As with other handy devices you own — a telephone, a car, a refrigerator, and that lava lamp — you need a reason to have a computer. Well? What do you see yourself doing on a computer?

✔ The number-one reason to buy a computer now is "to do the Internet." With your computer, you can exchange e-mail, browse the Web, view news and sports, entertain yourself, chat, shop, trade stocks, mind your finances, or just plain goof off. Hey! That's a *great* reason to own a computer! If that's you, bravo!

✔ Some people know instantly what they want a computer to do. I want a computer to help me write. My son is into film, and he wants a digital video studio. My younger kids want to play games and send e-mail.

✔ If you ever work with lists, numbers, 3-x-5 cards, home finances, stocks, bonds, or Swiss bank accounts, or if you trade in plutonium from former communist republics, you need a computer.

✔ If you're buying a computer to complement the one at your office, you probably need something similar at home.

✔ If you're buying a computer for your kids in school, ask their teachers what types of computers best run the software the school uses. Buy something similar for home.

✔ A survey was taken a while back to find out why some people don't yet own a computer. The number-one reason? (Can you guess?) No, it wasn't that computers are too expensive. The number-one reason that people don't buy computers is that they haven't yet figured out what to do with one!

✔ If you're really stuck, it helps to picture yourself in the future, working on a computer. What are you doing (besides swearing at it)?

Step 2: Look for software

After you know what you want the computer to do, you go out and look for software to get the job done. *Software* refers to the computer programs that make computers behave in a certain way. The programs are also called *applications* in that they apply the computer's power to help you accomplish some task.

You need to visit some software stores to hunt down the software to make your computer do what you need it to do. Or, if you already have a computer, you can browse the software selection on the Internet and visit online software stores as well as the developers who make the software. Finally, you can ask around and see what kinds of software your friends use or what your accountant recommends or what that brilliant 14-year-old Chess Club genius down the block thinks you need. Advice is good!

When you have found the software you need, take notes. Each software package has its hardware requirements listed right on the box — like the nutritional contents on a box of cereal. Write that information down, by using a form similar to the one shown in Figure 1-1.

Software Worksheet

Product name: _____

Developer: _____

Price: _____

Category:
Office	Word processing	Spreadsheet	Presentation
Utility	Database	Graphics	Education
Internet	Networking	Programming	Financial
Multimedia	Entertainment	Reference	Other

Type of support: Vanilla   Chocolate   Carob   Fudge

Operating systems: Windows   2000 / NT   XP Home / Pro
Macintosh OS X
Linux: _____
Other: _____

Microprocessor: Pentium: _____
G4   G5   Other Mac: _____
Alpha
Speed: _____ MHz

Memory (RAM) needed: _____ megabytes

Hard disk storage: _____ gigabytes

Media: CD-ROM   DVD   Other: _____

Graphics: Memory: _____ megabytes   GPU   3D
PCI   AGP
ATI   NVIDIA

Printer: _____

Other: _____

Notes : _____

Figure 1-1:
The
software
worksheet.

Chapter 17 shows you how to fill out the form. That's your ticket for the next
step: Buy hardware to run your software.

➤ You should try software before you buy it. The better computer stores
let you try it: Sit down at the computer and play with the software you
plan to buy. See how much you like it. See whether it works the way you
expect it to. Does it make sense? If not, try something else.

✔ If you have high-speed Internet access, many developers let you download demo versions of their software. Note that these files can be quite large.

✔ No, you're not buying anything in this step. You're just looking at various software packages that you may purchase later and jotting down their hardware appetite. That information — the stuff on the side of the box — helps you assemble your perfect computer system.

✔ Any questions you have regarding the software worksheet, such as the line "Type of support," are answered elsewhere in this book.

✔ Software-store people don't mind if you're "just looking."

✔ After you find something you like, you fill in the software worksheet. Fill in one worksheet for each program you plan to buy.

Step 3: Find hardware

After reviewing your software lineup, your next step is to match the software's requirements with a suitable computer. The idea is to find the hardware that can run your software. The software knows what it needs (it's on the side of the box), and you have collected all that information on the software worksheet, so this next step is simple: Fill the order.

Figure 1-2 shows a sample of this book's hardware worksheet. The information you find there may look intimidating now, but after you do your software research, filling in the worksheet is a snap.

Thanks to the worksheet, you know exactly what type of computer hardware you need. You're never steered to the wrong machine.

Don't buy anything yet!

✔ Most people make the mistake of shopping for hardware first and software second. After all, what you're buying is a *computer*. But, now you know that what the computer *does* with software is more important.

✔ By matching your software needs to your computer hardware, you avoid a perilous fate: You *do not* become one of the sorry people who have to return to the computer store weeks later to upgrade their memory or hard drive or something else they should have had in the first place.

Hardware Worksheet

Operating system Windows: _____

Macintosh: _____

Linux: _____

Microprocessor: Pentium   G4/G5   Other:
Speed: _____ MHz

Memory (RAM): _____ megabytes

Hard drive storage: _____ gigabytes   Second hard drive   GB

Removable media: Floppy / No floppy
Digital media: _____
Other: _____

Optical media: CD-ROM   CD-R   CD-RW
DVD   DVD-R   DVD-RW   plus / minus
Combination drive   Other:

Graphics adapter: _____ megabytes   GPU   3D
PCI / AGP   ATI / NVIDIA
Other: _____

Monitor: Size: _____ inches   CRT / LCD
Other: _____

Modem: Internal   External
Dial-up   DSL   Cable   Satellite
Speed: _____ (Kbps)

Mouse/pointing device: Standard   Optical   Wireless   Wheel
Trackball   Other: _____

Ports: COM   Printer (LPT1)
USB   IEEE (FireWire)   Ethernet (RJ45)
Other: _____

Printer: Brand: _____
Laser   Ink   Impact
Color   Photo   All-in-one
Options: _____

Figure 1-2:
The
hardware
worksheet.

Step 4: Shop for service and support

Crazy Omar and Discount Dave may have deals on computers, and you can pick up a computer at the massive warehouse or membership store along with a six-month supply of pop and a vat of peanut butter — but, what kind of support do those places offer? Especially if you're a first-time buyer, there's no substitute for after-sale support. The support consideration far outweighs getting a deal or finding the cheapest computer in the land.

- ✔ You can easily forget service and support because they're not mentioned prominently in most ads. Instead, you see prices and deals and sales. Ignore them!

- ✔ *Service* is the ability to fix your computer if something goes wrong with it. The best service is on-site, where someone comes to you and fixes your little electronic friend right where it lives. The worst service is when you have to pack up your computer and ship it to some overseas factory.

- ✔ *Support* is help. It can be in the form of classes, phone support, or training.

- ✔ The trade-off for a cheap computer is little service and no support.

- ✔ Chapter 21 goes into more detail about shopping for service and support. That chapter is very important! Read it! I'm not being funny!

Step 5: Buy your computer

When you're ready to buy your computer, buy it. You know what you need the computer for, you know what software to buy, you know what hardware to buy, and you have found a proper dealer with service and support. So, *buy it!*

The buying process is covered in Part III of this book.

Have a little class

I don't steer any of my friends to a local computer store unless it has a classroom attached. It's wonderful to know that a store is so dedicated to happy users that it devotes floor space to a classroom.

Some people take classes *before* they buy their computers. I recommend buying the computer first and taking the classes afterward. That way, you have something to go home and practice on. Also, with the computer in your possession, you know specifically which questions to ask. (If you have already attended this type of class, you know that new computer owners ask more detailed and useful questions.)

Buyer beware!

I would like to tell you that lousy computer dealers don't exist, but they do. Even big businesses and longtime computer gurus get snagged into computer-buying tricks and traps. Here are my best tips and advice to avoid common computer-buying scams:

✔ **Check the ad for a street location.** Most fly-by-night operations work from P.O. boxes or rental mailboxes. Legitimate businesses have real street locations that you can drive by and see.

✔ **Never put money down on a computer.** That's typically the earmark of a rob-Peter-to-pay-Paul scheme. Pay the full price. You may have to wait while the system is being assembled, but that's not the same thing as making a down payment.

✔ **Run like the devil if the dealer insists that you pay only cash.**

✔ **Also consider running if the dealer doesn't accept credit cards.**

✔ **Always pay by credit card — never with cash or a check.** Many consumer protection laws are available to credit card users that are not available to people who pay with cash or by check.

✔ **Always make sure that you get what you pay for.** Check the invoice, and if you're suspicious, hire a third-party repair place to check your computer innards to be certain that you got what you want and what you paid for.

Don't Sit Around Waiting to Buy!

It's only natural to hesitate a bit before buying a new computer. In fact, Step 5 (buying your computer) is the hardest of all the steps.

Money isn't the main thing that keeps people from finally buying a new computer. No, it's the rapid advancement of technology that instills hesitation. Computer technology speeds forward like a rocket sled on a frozen lake. A computer you buy today is guaranteed to be obsolete in three years, a dinosaur in five years, and nearly useless in ten. People see this situation as a warning: Don't buy today's computer; wait for the next generation!

Oh, pish. . . .

Although it's true that the next generation of computers will be better, faster, and probably less expensive, it's also true that waiting . . . gets you nowhere. It's like not catching a bus, because you assume that the next bus will have fewer people on it or be cleaner. That may be the case, but while you're waiting, you're going nowhere.

The bottom line is, when you're ready to buy, buy.

Chapter 2

Basic Computer Identification

· ·

In This Chapter

▶ The console

▶ The monitor

▶ The keyboard

▶ The mouse

▶ The speakers

▶ The modem

▶ The printer

▶ The scanner or digital camera

▶ Other peripherals and options

· ·

*T*here really is no such thing as a typical computer. Even back in the bad old days, there were computer models that literally broke the mold. Today, computers come in all sorts of shapes, sizes, colors, and what have you. In fact, hobbyists love to create computers out of old radio sets or lunch boxes. But, out of all that, each computer still has basic parts, the necessary things required in order to let you and the computer interact.

This chapter is about basic computer hardware identification. Before you even think about trotting down to the computer store, first familiarize yourself with these computer terms and identify the most basic elements of a computer system. Consider this a vocabulary-building exercise.

Basic Parts

The three most basic parts of all computers are

- ✔ The console
- ✔ The monitor
- ✔ The keyboard

This section helps familiarize you with each item. The idea is to get you to the point where you can easily identify these things on site, or at least know the difference between them and other common items, such as a necktie, blender, or ukulele.

Console

The main part of any computer system is its *console*. It's a box that contains the computer's innards — all the electronics that make the computer go. Figure 2-1 illustrates a type of console.

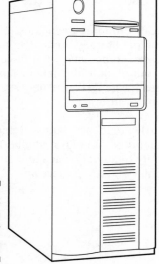

Figure 2-1:
A typical
computer
console.

Some consoles are mere boxes, usually with slots for inserting disks plus a host of buttons. Other consoles, such as those used in computer laptops, may contain *everything*. Whatever. The name for the box is console.

✔ That's "CON-sole," not "con-SOLE," which means to comfort someone who's expressing sorrow.

✔ The console is where the computer *really* is. My aunt thinks that the computer is in the monitor (covered next). But, that's just where you look. The real computer is in the console. Everything else is an add-on.

✔ Some computers, such as the iMac, combine the console and the monitor. Your typical laptop or notebook computer combines the monitor and the keyboard into the console.

✔ A *palmtop* computer is basically its own console. Ditto for game machines, which are merely computer consoles that you plug into a TV set.

Monitor

To see a computer's output, you need a monitor. In the old days, and it's still true for some game machines, a TV set was used rather than a monitor. But, as computer graphics grew more and more sophisticated, people preferred separate computer monitors (see Figure 2-2).

Figure 2-2:
A typical computer monitor.

The monitor displays information on the *screen,* which is the glassy part of the monitor. (The monitor itself is the entire box.) The screen shows you information generated by the computer, usually telling you what the computer is up to or giving you some other form of entertaining (or frustrating) feedback.

- ✔ Chapter 8 discusses monitors in depth, even flat-screen monitors.

- ✔ Because laptop and palmtop computers don't have a separate monitor box, the monitor on those systems is often referred to as just "the screen."

- ✔ Game consoles produce sophisticated graphics, yet don't display as much text as a desktop computer does. Therefore, although a TV set is okay for a game console's monitor, for a full-on computer, a TV set has too low a resolution to make it practical.

- ✔ Future digital televisions will most likely be fully compatible with your computer, and allow you to use your TV as an alternative form of computer monitor.

Keyboard

Computers lack ears. You would never know this fact by the way people continually yell at computers. Even so, that's not the main way you communicate with a computer. For most of us, typing is the key. For that, you need a keyboard, such as the one shown in Figure 2-3.

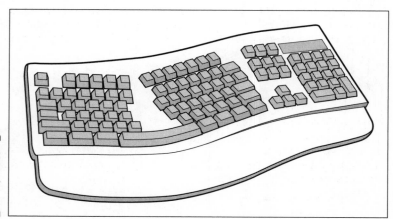

Figure 2-3:
A fancy type
of computer
keyboard.

The type of keyboard a computer has depends on the computer's purpose. Most computers have a full, typewriter-size keyboard connected to the console with a curly cable. Some computers, laptops, and handhelds have a built-in keyboard. Some computers, such as palmtops and game consoles, lack keyboards altogether.

- ✔ If a computer lacks a keyboard, you generally communicate with the computer in some other way. For palmtops, you use a pen (or your finger) to enter information, by either punching buttons or touching the screen directly. For game consoles, you use a gamepad or high-tech joystick for input.

- ✔ Despite most keyboards' similar look, a variety of them are available. Chapter 9 has more information on keyboards.

Beyond the Basic Parts

The console, monitor, and keyboard comprise a computer's basic parts — the big things you notice right away. They're also the traditional components, which date back to computers and terminals from the 1970s. So, if you go time traveling, you can truly take advantage of your computer-buying prowess in the previous century.

Beyond the basic parts lie what are called *peripherals*. These include any optional pieces of hardware — gizmos and such — that may enhance the standard computer system or make things more useful. Some of these items, such as the mouse and printer, aren't really considered optional any more, but they still fall under the category of peripherals. This section helps you identify these sometimes optional, often necessary, computer components.

Mouse

The keyboard's pal is the mouse.

No, not that kind of mouse. It's a computer mouse (see Figure 2-4), used with most computers to help you mess with graphical information. (Everything is graphics these days.)

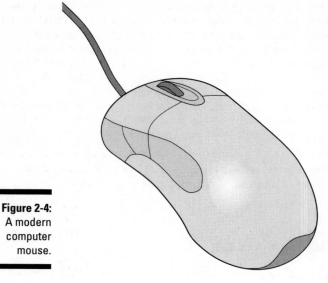

All computers sold now come with their own mouse. Even so, you can opt to toss that mouse out and buy yourself a better one — or you can order a better mouse with your computer when you make your buying decision.

- ✔ Chapter 9 explains more about your computer mice choices.

- ✔ It's called a mouse because it kind of looks like a mouse — well, a fat, plastic mouse, anyway. (At least they didn't call it the "bar of soap.")

- ✔ The mouse is officially known as a *pointing device*. That's because not every pointing device is a mouse. For example, most laptops use what's called a *touchpad*.

- ✔ Palmtop and game consoles don't need computer mice.

Speakers

All computers make noise. They hum. They chirp. They warble. But, the real sounds a computer makes are possible only through speakers. Sometimes, these speakers are nestled inside the console; at other times, you may find them on the monitor; or they can be separate speaker boxes, left and right, just like on a stereo.

Fortunately, unlike visiting the stereo store, you don't need to bone up that much on computer speakers. Generally, speakers are options for only some types of computers. Even then, your options are Basic, Very Good, and Overpriced. If you're into audio in any way, you probably care enough to know the proper terms, so this part of the computer isn't an issue to you. Otherwise, Chapter 11 goes into all the detail you should care to know.

- ✔ Most computers come with a set of cheapie speakers, though you often have the choice of upgrading to something swankier.

- ✔ Some laptops have external speaker options, but most laptop computers have tiny built-in speakers, designed merely to scare your seatmates when you play a DVD movie too loudly on an airplane. (Laptops also sport a headphone jack, to help keep you from annoying your seatmates.)

- ✔ Smaller, handheld, and palmtop computers lack true speakers, though they do have the ability to beep and bleep and may, in some cases, be able to play music. (The point is that you don't buy that type of computer specifically to hear opera.)

- ✔ Game consoles usually have left and right sound outputs, which you can either plug into a TV or directly into your home stereo.

Modem

Once an option on most computers, modems are now pretty much standard. What they do is allow your computer to use phone lines to communicate with other computers or the Internet. How computers do this is covered briefly in Chapter 11, but that's not important. The issue is that modems are necessary if you want to use your computer to cruise the Internet.

- ✔ Chapter 11 covers everything you need to know about choosing a modem.

- ✔ The type of modem that comes with a computer is the standard dial-up modem. If you plan to use DSL, cable, or satellite access to the Internet, you must buy a separate modem for that service. In that case, your PC doesn't need a dial-up modem (unless you want to use it as a backup).

- ✔ Dial-up modems are also used to send and receive faxes.

- ✔ Modems are generally included in laptop computers, though some of the less-expensive models may not have them. You should always ask.

Printer

Every computer needs a printer, though the printer itself isn't really thought of as part of the core computer system. That's because, unlike the other gizmos mentioned in this chapter, the printer is an extra purchase. Even so, that doesn't make it any less necessary.

A printer is used to put information on paper, to create a "hard copy" of the stuff you see on the screen, as shown in Figure 2-5. That copy is the final result of your computing efforts.

Ink cartridges (under cover)

Paper feed

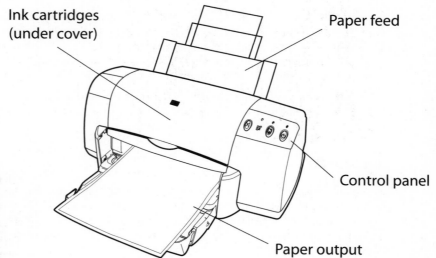

Control panel

Paper output

Figure 2-5:
A type of computer printer.

Computer printers come in a variety of styles, sizes, and abilities, all of which are covered in Chapter 24.

- ✔ Most computers need a printer, but keep in mind that printers don't come with computers. You must purchase printers separately.

- ✔ You can share one printer among several computers. You have a number of ways to do this, which are all covered in Chapter 24.

- ✔ You can use a printer with a laptop computer, as long as the laptop computer has a printer connection (a printer *port*).

- ✔ Printers aren't required for handheld computers or game machines.

Scanner and digital camera

Another once-optional item that's becoming more and more common is the *scanner* (see Figure 2-6). This device works like a photocopier, although, rather than make a duplicate, the scanner creates a graphical image of whatever you scan and saves that information inside the computer. That's how you can send out all those baby pictures via e-mail.

Figure 2-6: A type of computer scanner.

Along with the scanner comes the digital camera, another whiz-bang device that most computer folks can't live without. In one way, the digital camera is merely a portable version of the scanner, one that allows you to take pictures of the real world, like the scanner lets you duplicate flat images.

Scanners and digital cameras aren't required parts of the computer system, though they're popular and cheap enough that most people toss one or both in as part of their first-time computer purchase.

✔ If you're serious about digital imaging, you probably want to get a nice, expensive, feature-laden scanner. Otherwise, any cheap old scanner will do.

✔ It's possible to get a computer printer that doubles as a scanner — which is a great solution for many people. See Chapter 24 for information on all-in-one printers.

✔ More information on selecting a scanner or digital camera (or both) is in Chapter 13.

Peripherals and other expansion alternatives, various and sundry

The list of devices you can add to your computer system is endless. You're likely to pick up most of these items after you buy a computer, but you may want to have some of them installed at the time of purchase, especially if they're necessary to run your software.

Anything beyond the basic computer unit (console, monitor, keyboard, and mouse) is considered a *peripheral*. These devices expand or enhance your computer and what it can do.

For example, a printer is really a peripheral device. Another common peripheral is a scanner or digital camera.

Beyond peripherals, *expansion* options are added to the inside of a computer. For example, you can add a special TV card that lets you view TV or edit videotape on your computer. The possibilities are limitless.

- ✔ Just about anything hanging off a computer's main box is a peripheral. You can use the term *peripheral* to impress the people at the computer store.

- ✔ Peripherals are usually found in the domain of desktop computers. Laptops and smaller systems lack the expansion options of their larger cousins, mostly because laptops are all about portability, and having a lot of cables and external options doesn't properly fit into that equation.

Chapter 3

Computers from A to Z

· ·

In This Chapter

▶ Traditional PC computers

▶ The Macintosh

▶ Laptops

▶ Tablet PCs

▶ Palmtop and handheld computers

▶ WebTV

▶ Game machines

▶ Workstations, servers, and mainframes

▶ The so-called "free" computers

· ·

You think nothing now of having a telephone that looks like Elvis Presley, Mickey Mouse, or the starship *Enterprise*. Fifty years ago? No way! Phones back then were black, heavy desktop models. Some were mounted on the wall, but all phones were basically alike. Choices were few. Heck, folks back then would probably fear a phone that looked like a Coke-drinking polar bear.

Computers don't all look alike any more, either. There are different makes and models, from the ancient, boxy dinocomputers that weigh several tons apiece to the slender BlackBerry handheld that weighs only a few ounces. This chapter provides a swift introduction to the various makes, models, and styles of computers, from A to Z.

Chapter 2 has information on what the various computer components are.

What Is a Computer?

I suppose that in the book *Brain Transplants For Dummies* (Wiley Publishing, Inc.), one of the first chapters is titled "What Is a Brain?" Or, if I were writing the book, the chapter would be called "Brain and Brain! What Is Brain?" — an obscure *Star Trek* quote. But, anyway, the idea is that not everyone attempting to buy a computer (or a brain) is really all that comfortable with the concept. That's why *For Dummies* books are written: to remove the fear and put some fun into understanding difficult concepts!

The yin and yang of hardware and software

A computer is an electronic device. It consists of two parts: hardware and software. Say that out loud:

Hardware and software.

The *hardware* is the physical part of the computer: the console plus all the electronics inside and outside the console. In fact, everything described in Chapter 2 is hardware. It's the more familiar part of the computer, but that doesn't make it more important than software.

The *software* is more important than hardware because it's the brains of the operation. Software consists of special instructions (programs) that tell the hardware exactly what to do. Unlike hardware, software is tough to describe. Sure, it comes in boxes and lives on shiny discs, but the software is actually the instructions on those discs and not the discs themselves.

When you buy a computer, you're buying both hardware and software. Even though the emphasis is usually on the hardware (Dell-this, Toshiba-that), the software is more important.

I discuss hardware and software in more detail in Chapter 4 and in Part II. For now, however, know that computers or any number of similar computing devices consist of hardware and software. You need both to have a computer.

The traditional desktop computer

The original IBM PC (see Figure 3-1) is the prototype for all *desktop* computers. The main box, the *console,* sits flat and square on the desktop. The monitor perches on top of the console, and the keyboard sits in front. Despite this historical tradition, few of today's PCs resemble the IBM desktop original.

The most popular computer configuration now is the minitower model, which is like a desktop model turned on its side (see Figure 3-2). The minitower is more versatile than the old desktop style; you can set the console right next to the keyboard and monitor (as shown in Figure 3-2), or you can set the minitower on the floor and out of view.

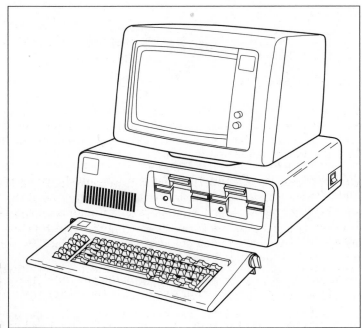

Figure 3-1:
The original
IBM PC.

Figure 3-2:
A present-
day mini-
tower
computer.

✔ *PC* is an acronym for *personal computer*. This name comes from the first IBM model, the IBM PC (International Business Machines Personal Computer).

✔ Before the IBM PC, personal computers were called *microcomputers*. It was a disparaging term because other computers of the day were much larger. They were called minicomputers and mainframes. Powerful things. Well, at the time.

✔ The term microcomputer wasn't based on the computer's small, desktop size but rather on the computer's main chip, the *microprocessor*.

✔ The minitower is named that way because the original on-its-side PC was dubbed the *tower* model. Minitowers are more compact than full-size towers and lack much of the internal expansion room in larger models.

✔ Smaller desktop models are still available. They're usually called *small-footprint* computers. The footprint in this case is the amount of space the computer occupies on your desk.

✔ Small-footprint computers lack expandability options. For example, if you want AGP graphics, you may not find that expansion option in a small-footprint computer case.

✔ Some new-model PCs have both the console and the monitor in the same box. These systems don't yet have an official nickname.

The Macintosh personal computer

A *Macintosh* is a personal computer made by Apple, and it has an enthusiastic following. Even though the Mac (as it's called) is still a personal computer, its owners don't like referring to it as a "PC." That's because PC more traditionally means the IBM type of computer system, as discussed in the preceding section.

The Macintosh computer stands apart from the rest of the personal computer flock on purpose. The Mac is known to be the irreverent computer, usually adored by creative types or people just wanting to be different.

The most popular Macintosh model sold now is the iMac (see Figure 3-3), where the *i* may stand for Internet or Intelligent or any of a number of Interesting things. The iMac is an all-in-one package — monitor and console — and it comes with everything you need to get started computing or using the Internet. It's the top-selling individual computer model.

Figure 3-3:
The iMac.

A more powerful and expandable alternative to the iMac is the Power Mac G5, which is more on par with a high-end minitower PC. The Power Mac model is much more expandable than the iMac, which makes it well suited to power users — folks who are into software that requires extra processor power, memory, and storage options.

- ✔ Truly, the Macintosh is the easiest computer to set up and use.

- ✔ The Mac mini is the most affordable Macintosh — and perhaps the best bargain for a personal computer. The unit itself is about the size of a portable CD player, but it doesn't come with a monitor, keyboard or mouse — stuff you need and which must be factored into the price.

- ✔ Generally speaking, the Mac excels at doing graphics and music. Most graphics production facilities prefer Macintoshes to PCs. In Hollywood, the Mac is the most popular computer model for just about everything.

- ✔ There's a myth that Macintosh computers are more expensive than your typical PCs. Although on a dollar-per-dollar basis, this statement is true, it's *not* true when you compare a Mac with a similarly equipped PC. In that case, the Mac is a bargain.

Laptops for every kind of lap

Portable computers aren't only for people on the go, but rather for anyone who wants a smaller computer than the traditional desktop model. For example, if you take your work home, it's just easier to have a laptop you can lug back and forth than to try to share information between home and office computers.

TIP

Be mindful of the case design!

Although some computer boxes look sleeker than others — that's a purchase decision — you have to make more practical decisions in choosing a case. For example, how noisy is the case?

Some case designs are quieter than others. Computers do make noise, mostly from their internal fans. Some manufacturers take care with their designs to make their computers quieter. For example, most Macintoshes make

hardly a sound, whereas some mom 'n' pop custom computers tend to be noisier than a room full of five-year-olds chasing a puppy.

Another consideration is those translucent cases and colorful computers. You pay a premium for buying those types of cases with your computer. However, many after-market dealers sell fancy computer case upgrades, similar to the after-sale market for car accessories.

Laptops have the same features as desktop computers, but are smaller. Figure 3-4 shows a typical PC laptop, which has everything a desktop computer has, all shoved into the space of a typical three-ring binder. Because of a laptop's smaller components, it usually runs more than twice the cost of a comparable desktop system.

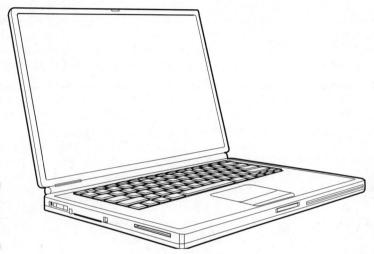

Figure 3-4:
A typical
PC laptop.

On the Macintosh side, two models are available, the iBook and PowerBook, which parallel the iMac and Power Mac lines for desktop systems. Unlike desktop Macintoshes, the laptop versions are price competitive with PC laptops.

- Laptop computers are also known as *notebooks*. (In the olden days, the term *notebook* implied a lightweight laptop, but all laptops are now light enough to be notebooks.)

- Also see Chapter 14, which covers the issues involved with buying a laptop.

The Tablet PC

The newest fad in computers is the Tablet PC, though you had better read this information quickly because the Tablet PC is turning out to be more of a flash in the pan than any other new computer type introduced in the past 20 years.

A *Tablet PC* is basically a laptop computer minus the keyboard, as shown in Figure 3-5. The Tablet PC is one large monitor on which you write directly using a special pen, or *stylus*. The stylus controls the graphical gizmos displayed on the screen, and the Tablet PC's software translates your chicken scratches into readable text.

Where does Linux fit in?

Linux is an operating system, or software. It's not a brand of computer. Like any other type of software, Linux requires hardware to make it go. Most often, the hardware Linux consumes is the standard hardware that makes up a PC or Windows computer. So Linux winds up installed on an old Windows computer, on a new PC, or, most often, on a custom-built PC.

Over the years, Linux enthusiasts have *hacked* various computer hardware to run Linux. Rumor has it that Linux can be found running on a Microsoft Xbox game console. Some handheld computers, as well as mainframe systems, also use Linux as their operating system. You can read more about this topic in Chapter 15, which discusses computer operating system software.

Figure 3-5:
A Tablet PC.

✔ Tablet PCs have an option to allow you to plug in an external keyboard, if you want.

✔ Some Tablet PCs are merely laptops where the flip-top screen can bend all the way around and the unit can be held like a clipboard.

Palmtop and handheld computers

A *palmtop,* or *handheld,* computer is a specialized, or custom, computer designed for data gathering and reporting. These systems generally lack the versatility, expandability, and processing power of their larger desktop and laptop brethren.

Another term for palmtop or handheld computer is PDA, or *p*ersonal *d*igital *a*ssistant. It primarily performs a limited range of tasks, such as scheduling, keeping track of addresses, managing to-do lists, and perhaps letting you play games or giving you limited Internet access (Web browsing and e-mail).

Physically, these systems are about the size of a pad of paper, with a large screen and a few handy buttons. Figure 3-6 illustrates the popular Palm computer, though it comes in a few other styles, including a combination digital camera/computer and cellphone computer.

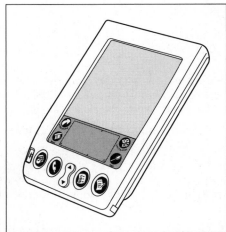

Figure 3-6:
The Palm
computer.

Because the Palm, as well as other handhelds, lacks a keyboard or mouse, you use a stylus to write directly on the computer's screen, which serves as both the display and the input device.

A popular alternative to the Palm handheld is the BlackBerry handheld computer. It's a PDA, like the Palm, but also contains wireless networking and cellphone abilities. It has a mini-keyboard for typing, as shown in Figure 3-7.

Figure 3-7:
The
BlackBerry.

✔ The first popular handheld computer was the Palm, which leads some folks to refer to this category as "Palm" computers, although many other handheld computer brands, makes, and models are available.

✔ The BlackBerry is now the most popular handheld computer.

✔ Unlike other, earlier small computers, the modern handheld system is revolutionary because it doesn't pretend to be a smaller version of a full-on computer. It serves as a notepad, address book, and scheduler, and it has lots of unique software. The handheld system does specialized tasks and does them well.

✔ One thing you must factor into the cost of a handheld computer is the cost of cellphone or Internet access. That's a monthly fee you have to pay, which can add up quickly — even if the handheld unit isn't that expensive.

✔ Some handheld computers can work with both Macintosh and PC computers, which makes them an ideal supplement to a desktop system.

What about Internet appliances?

A new category of computing device is the *Internet appliance*. The main feature of this type of gizmo is that it communicates with the Internet or uses the Internet to display or relay information.

A simple example of an Internet appliance is a desktop device specifically designed to read e-mail or browse the Web. That's all the device would be capable of doing; it would lack the expandability and programmability of a typical computer.

On the more strange and unusual side, Internet appliances may one day include things such as refrigerators that communicate directly with

dairies to reorder milk for customers automatically. Microsoft founder Bill Gates claims that one day even special refrigerator magnets will be used to display news or streaming stock quotes — another example of an Internet appliance. And, eventually, cars will have an Internet display, used to get directions or display information about nearby eating establishments.

These Internet appliances now exist mostly as "Wouldn't that be neat?" ideas in science magazines. Most of them have yet to leap off the drawing board. In the future, however, an Internet-enabled device may be just as common as an LCD clock display.

WebTV (MSN TV)

Some folks claim that the computer itself will eventually go away and be replaced by customized devices, such as the Internet appliance (see the nearby sidebar, "What about Internet appliances?"). I don't see things that way, but one clear sign that such a division may be coming is WebTV, which is now called MSN TV.

An *MSN TV* device isn't a computer. Instead, it's a device that gives you access to the Internet and e-mail by using your TV set and a small, set-top device.

On the plus side, MSN TV and similar gadgets don't carry the cost or learning curve that a traditional computer does. If all you need to do is access e-mail and browse the Web, the MSN TV setup may be all you need.

On the minus side, the MSN TV system lacks the expandability and power of a true computer. Many Web pages aren't properly displayed on a TV set. And, if you ever decide to expand your high-tech universe — for example, to include digital photography — you still need to buy a computer system.

Gaming consoles

Another example of a specific computer device is the gaming console. Just as MSN TV is a customized, set-top device designed specifically for e-mail and the Web, a *gaming console* is a computer specifically designed to play computer games, often with much better and more sophisticated graphics and sound technology than can be found in a typical desktop computer.

Several manufacturers make game consoles — for example, the Sony PlayStation 2 (see Figure 3-8), Nintendo Gamecube, and Microsoft Xbox. Each of these consoles has lots of technology built into it. It may not crunch numbers or process words, but it does one thing and does it well: plays games.

✔ As with buying any computer, the key here is *software*. Your choice of one of the game consoles most likely depends on which games you want to play — not on the technical "specs" of the console itself. (This lesson is an obvious one for game consoles, but one that people buying PCs and Macintoshes need to learn.)

✔ Some game consoles have graphics and computing technology that blow away anything you find in a desktop computer.

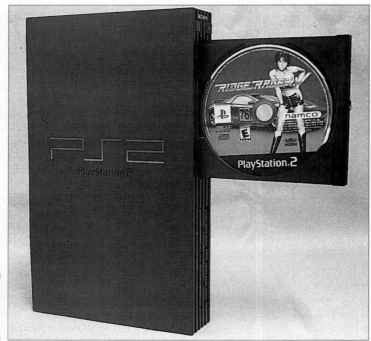

Figure 3-8:
A game
console.

Workstations and servers

The term *workstation* is loosely defined when it comes to computers. In one point of view, a workstation is any high-powered computer with a fast microprocessor, lots of memory, tons of hard disk storage, and a huge price tag.

Hey! That sounds like what I just bought!

Workstations can be targeted to specific tasks that require lots of computing power. For example, you could configure a standard PC with lots of memory and graphics horsepower and stir in the proper software, and you would have a graphics workstation capable of doing Hollywood-style video effects.

On the other end of the spectrum, workstations can also be dumb old computers. For example, a PC slaved to a network where some minion enters orders is a type of workstation. (The term is vague, but don't blame me!)

Then there's the server. A *server* is *another* high-end computer that works as the center of a computer network. For example, most large offices (and many small ones) have a central computer called the *server* (or *file server*). It contains the programs and information used by all other computers on the network. Again, this computer is a high-end, technology-packed PC or Macintosh that merely runs the network.

- ✔ Most readers of this book aren't buying themselves servers. These systems are installed by networking consultants or professionals configuring an entire office with computers. (The information in this book does apply to servers and to regular computers.)

- ✔ See Chapter 5 for more information on microprocessors.

The lure of those high-end microprocessors

Workstations and servers often use special high-end microprocessors not sold to the general public. Though these microprocessors are very fast, and some computer owners seethe with lust over them, the cold fact is that without the proper software to use those high-end microprocessors, the power is wasted.

For example, once upon a time, some computer gamers looked at the statistics regarding the high-end Itanium and Xeon microprocessors.

On paper, those chips beat the pants off the typical Pentium microprocessors found in most humble computers. But, there was a problem: The game software never took advantage of any of the advanced chip's faster and better features. In the end, gamers ended up spending a lot of money on high-tech computers (hardware) that couldn't do what they wanted (run game software).

Mainframes

The final computer category I describe is the most ancient, but not gone or forgotten: the mainframe, or "big iron," that used to do all the computing work before personal computers became popular in the late 1970s — and again at the turn of the 21st century. Though mainframe computers were once thought to be doomed relics of the past, they're now in high demand and selling better than some home-model computers.

Of course, as with high-end workstations and file servers, you probably won't purchase a mainframe to help you send e-mail or balance your checkbook. But, it's a category of computer, so I had to list it here. Consider the term fodder for your next cocktail party.

- ✔ It would be kind of cool to have a mainframe, although I don't know anyone on my street whom I could impress with the thing.

- ✔ Supercomputer is another classification of computer, although it's like a mainframe. A *supercomputer* is designed to do many tasks quickly.

"How Much Will This Cost?"

You're probably curious about how much this machine costs. Honestly, price isn't important right now. (Refer to the five steps in Chapter 1.) Still, you're probably curious, so why not toss out some numbers?

These numbers have no value until you're ready to buy a computer. (You understand why at the end of Part III.) If you want a state-of-the-art computer capable of handling most software, plan to spend about $1,000, and maybe a few hundred more or less. Some computers — such as workstations, high-end PCs and Macintoshes — cost more. You can pay, for example, $2,000 or more for the latest computer model with the fastest microprocessor and all that techy stuff. Laptops hover between $1,000 and $3,000, depending on their features, weight, battery life, and other laptoppy issues. See Chapter 14.

Then there's the cost of software, which is rarely added into the purchase price. Most people spend as much — if not more — on software than they do on their computer hardware.

There. Now you know. But, what does it all mean?

- ✔ The iMac is about the most affordable computer, considering the technology you get for the price. Ditto the iBook Macintosh laptop.

- ✔ Most laptops cost two to three times as much as their desktop counterparts. The reason? Miniaturization. That huge miniaturizing computer in Utah costs a lot to rent.

- Most game consoles run about $150.

- Handheld computers and palmtops run from less than $100 for the day-book models to around $700 for the recent stuff. Handheld computers integrated with cellphone technology cost more.

- Cost should *not* be the most important factor in buying a computer. Keep in mind the five steps in Chapter 1! Software availability, especially service and support, can affect price beyond what's printed in the newspaper.

The "free" computer

It was the rage in the late 1990s to sell computers with *no* cost. Yup, they were free. Of course, the computers weren't really given away. You had to pay for them, but you typically got back that much money (if not more) in the form of instant rebate coupons. So, the price ended up being nothing.

Nothing is free, of course. Although millions walked away with free computer hardware, they soon discovered that they had signed up for years of not-so-free Internet service. For example, a $700 computer was "given away," but the buyer had to pay for Internet service for *four years* at $20 a month. (That's $960.) Despite the long-term contract, people still walked away with "free" computers for months. But, consider this: If the computer broke or exploded or was lost or stolen, those suckers still had to pay $20 a month for the Internet. Even if they replaced their damaged or lost computers, they still had to pay.

Pay! Pay! Pay!

These scams are rare. Occasionally, you get a deal. But, beware of anything "free." Always check the fine print whenever you sign up for a service. For any price, being stuck with something you don't need is hardly being free.

Chapter 4

Introduction to Hardware and Software

Some scientists strive to find out what is the stuff the universe is made of. According to the old Disneyland attraction Adventures Through Inner Space, I knew at age 9 that the universe was composed of molecules, which are made up of atoms. At the center of the atom is the scary nucleus — and beyond that? *No! I dare not go on! I must return to the realm of the molecule before I go on shrinking . . . forever!* Yet some scientists push onward, smaller and smaller.

The scientists who work with computers are pretty sure that the entire computer universe can be divided into two parts: hardware and software. *No! I dare not go on!* In fact, when you know that the two biggest pieces of the computer universe are hardware and software, you're pretty much done; the ride is over. Collect all your belongings, exit your car on the right, and please buy some Disney merchandise.

This chapter covers the basics of all computer systems: hardware and software. You gotta know which is which because one is much more important than the other. It's when you don't know which is more important that you end up buying a computer that may not be right for you.

Hardware: The Hard Stuff

Computer hardware is easy to identify: It's anything you can touch. The monitor, computer box (console), keyboard, printer, modem, and doodads inside the box — it's all hardware.

✔ If you can touch it, it's hardware.

✔ If you drop it on your foot and you say "ouch," it's probably hardware.

✔ Here's one that baffles most people: CDs and DVDs are hardware. Even though they store software, the discs themselves are hardware. The software — like music on a cassette tape — is not the hardware on which it's stored.

✔ The most important piece of hardware is the computer's microprocessor, which I discuss later in this chapter. Oh! Never mind. Here it is.

The microprocessor (the main piece of hardware)

All hardware in any computer is geared to work best with a single chip. That chip is the computer's *microprocessor*.

The entire computer, no matter how big it is or who makes it, is designed around a single type of microprocessor. The microprocessor determines the design and potential of the rest of the computer.

All the details of the microprocessor are presented in Chapter 5. At this point, all you need to know is that the microprocessor is the most important piece of hardware in a computer.

✔ The microprocessor isn't the computer's brain; the brain part (if it has any) is the software, which is covered in the latter part of this chapter.

✔ The microprocessor is also called the CPU, or *c*entral *p*rocessing *u*nit.

✔ Some folks call the microprocessor just *processor*, for short. They're probably the same folks who call McDonald's Mickey Dee's, even though they're not saving any syllables.

The motherboard

The microprocessor isn't the computer. Though the type of microprocessor used in a computer tells you a great deal about the computer and the rest of the hardware, the microprocessor is merely the center of attention.

Supporting the microprocessor are many other items inside and outside the computer's box or console.

Directly supporting the microprocessor inside the console is a host of electronics, wires, diodes, and doodads. These devices all live on a single piece of circuitry called the *motherboard*, and worship the microprocessor like suppliants to their pagan god. Here's the short list:

✔ **Chipset:** The collective circuitry inside the computer comprises the computer's personality. This includes chips referred to as the BIOS ("BYE-oss"), which provide the Basic Input and Output System (BIOS) for the computer and all its devices. But now, because all the chips are sold prepackaged on the motherboard, the whole caboodle is referred to as the *chipset*. Sometimes, it's called *firmware*.

✔ **Memory:** By itself, the microprocessor doesn't remember much. It's like an absentminded professor: smart and quick but forgetful. To help the microprocessor store information to manipulate, Random Access Memory, or RAM, is used. Chapter 6 discusses memory.

✔ **Bus:** Not one of those big yellow vehicles that took you to school, the computer's *bus* is a line of communications between the microprocessor and everything else in the computer. Like the microprocessor, the bus operates at a specific speed. You pay more for a faster bus, but you get your money back in improved performance.

✔ **Expansion:** To keep the computer system flexible, various slots and connectors on the motherboard allow the computer system to be expanded in various internal and external ways.

Two other items inside the computer's case, but not necessarily a part of the motherboard, are the power supply and disk drives:

✔ **Power supply:** This gizmo is basically a sealed box that converts AC electricity into DC electricity, which is what a computer uses internally. In a laptop or handheld computer, the power supply is also tightly integrated into the system's battery for on-the-go power.

✔ **Storage devices:** Because computer memory is temporary, storage devices in the form of disk drives exist to give you long-term storage for your computer's software as well as the data you store or create.

This basic hardware (microprocessor, chipset, memory, bus, and storage devices) lives inside the console, for the most part. Other basic hardware surrounds the computer, like tentacles on an electronic octopus:

✔ The monitor

✔ The keyboard

✔ The mouse or pointing device

✔ The printer

- ✔ The modem (which is sometimes inside the console)
- ✔ The scanner
- ✔ Other gizmos

All this stuff is hardware, and all of it works with the microprocessor to create the hardware side of your computer system. By itself, hardware is unimportant. Only with the proper software driving everything do you get the most from your hardware.

- ✔ About half the computer hardware lives inside the computer box, officially known as the *console*. The other half sits outside, connected to the box with cables or, often, without cables, by using wireless technology.
- ✔ Even with wireless technology, cables remain a very big and ugly part of any computer — something they don't show you in the ads.
- ✔ Some external devices are called *peripherals*. For example, the printer is a peripheral. Although the keyboard and monitor can be considered peripherals, they're too important to the computer's basic operation to be called that. (It's a subject for semanticists and college professors to debate.)

- ✔ Notice that all computer hardware either produces input (sends information to the microprocessor) or generates output (receives or displays information from the microprocessor). Some devices, such as a modem, do both. This process is all part of something called I/O, or input/output, which is the basic function of all computers. It's nerdy stuff.

Software: The Other Hard Stuff

In a computer system, it's the *software* that is the brains of the operation. Some people claim that the microprocessor is the computer's brain. No. No. No. No. No. The microprocessor is just a big, flat, expensive piece of technology — like a Keebler fudge cake with metal legs. You need software to make the microprocessor seem like it has any sort of intelligence.

The operating system

The main piece of software controlling your computer is the *operating system*. The operating system — not the microprocessor — tells the whole computer what to do. All hardware, including the microprocessor, must obey the operating system. And, all software must work with the operating system.

The operating system has three important jobs: control the hardware, control the software, and give you (the human) a way to ultimately control everything.

Control that hardware! The operating system tells the computer what to do and how to do it. Although the microprocessor inside the computer may be doing the work, the operating system is giving the orders.

Closely linked to the operating system is the chipset (see the section "The motherboard," earlier in this chapter). The operating system gives instructions, in the course of its duties, to *both* the microprocessor and the chipset.

Supervise that software! All the software you use (everything — all the applications, programs, utilities, and games) must work with the operating system. In fact, software is written for the operating system, not for the computer or microprocessor. (Only a few games are written directly to the computer's hardware. Just about every other program is designed for a specific operating system.)

The key to a successful operating system is a large software base, which means lots of computer programs that work under that operating system. That base is what makes the traditional operating systems so successful. Even though everyone hated DOS, it could run millions of programs. That's what made it so popular (albeit infamously so).

Work with humans! Finally, the operating system has to present you, the person ultimately in charge of the computer, with a reasonable method of controlling things. Most operating systems use a graphical interface that shows you pictures and images to represent computer concepts.

The operating system has to show you ways to run programs and ways to control the computer's hardware. Chapter 15 discusses various operating system types in detail and shows you why some operating systems do this final job better than others.

  ✔ The operating system and the microprocessor must work together to give you the best possible computer. When they work together, they're said to be *compatible*.

  ✔ You're likely to use only one operating system. Some computers can have more than one, but that adds a layer of complexity to using the computer that I think you would rather avoid.

  ✔ Even handheld computers and game consoles have operating systems. They may not be as complex as a desktop computer's operating system, but the operating system is there nonetheless.

Applications and other software

Like a general without an army, an operating system by itself merely looks impressive. The operating system's army in this case consists of all the programs you have on your computer, which is how you get work done. (Operating systems merely control things; they don't do any real work for you.)

In the Big Picture, the application programs are the reasons that you buy your computer. You find yourself a nice and tidy word processor, which runs under a specific operating system, which requires a certain amount of hardware to help it do your stuff. That's the true chain of command.

Putting It All Together

Everything in your computer must work together if you ever expect to get anything from it. Operating systems are written toward specific microprocessors, chipsets, and other hardware. Programs are written toward specific operating systems as well as toward specific hardware. It all works together.

When hardware doesn't work with software, you have an incompatibility. (That's bad.) For example, you cannot run the Macintosh operating system on a PC. Why? Because the Macintosh uses a different type of microprocessor and has an utterly different chipset. Different hardware and software just don't work together.

The hardware must obey the software. The software must work under the operating system. And, everything has to work well with you. Then, everything — hardware, software, and you — can live happily ever after.

✔ Remember that *you* are in charge. You pick the software, which then tells you which hardware to get. That's the best way to buy a computer.

✔ All the pieces must fit together well for you to end up buying the best computer you can.

✔ What's the most important piece (besides you)? The software. That's why Step 2 in the buying process (refer to Chapter 1) is looking for software. When you find it, the rest of the pieces fall naturally into place.

Part II

Hardware and Software Overview

It's another cow box mutilation, Sheriff. Look how cleanly the case has been severed. And if my hunch is right, you won't find the motherboard within a thousand miles of here.

In this part . . .

*I*n the computer world, it's software that controls the hardware, which should have been drilled into your skull by now if you've read through Part I of this book. Yet, to understand the buying process, you must first know about some computer hardware. After all, if you buy software that says it works best with an ATI Radeon, for example, it helps to know just what the heck an ATI Radeon is.

The chapters in this part of the book cover computer hardware and software. This part has three purposes. The first is to familiarize you with various different types of computer hardware — specifically, those items you see in a computer ad. The second is to let you know how to buy those items, in case you want to upgrade your hardware and software in the future. The third is to familiarize you with the software and applications that the hardware supports. Read this stuff lightly first, and then get into the dirty details later, when the urge strikes you.

Chapter 5

All about Mr. Microprocessor

At the center of your new computer's hardware universe lives the microprocessor. All the hardware gizmos in your computer system, from the fattest memory chip to the teensiest resistor, are designed to work harmoniously with the microprocessor, and the microprocessor dutifully returns the favor.

Knowing about the microprocessor is central to understanding computer hardware in general. The microprocessor itself is a proper gauge of your computer's potential. You want to ensure that your new computer system sports a microprocessor that is good, fast, and ready for whatever software you plan to throw its way.

The Microprocessor Rules

As your computer's main chip, the microprocessor rules over all other hardware in the computer system. Truly, it's the center of the hardware universe: All hardware is geared to perform well with the microprocessor, and all software is written to be understood by the microprocessor.

Knowing how the microprocessor works isn't crucial. Supposedly, computers design modern microprocessors, so no human being alive truly understands exactly how they work. But, that doesn't matter!

Physically, a microprocessor is simply a computer chip, albeit a rather large computer chip when compared to other chips (such as RAM chips). Figure 5-1 illustrates the popular Pentium 4 CPU. Physically, the chip is about 2 inches square.

Figure 5-1:
A typical
Pentium 4
micro-
processor.

More important than knowing how a microprocessor works or what it looks like is being able to compare microprocessors to ensure that you get the best one you can afford in your new computer. To do that, you need to know three things about a microprocessor:

✔ Name
✔ Power
✔ Speed

True, there's more to a microprocessor than its name, power, and speed. And, recently, the microprocessor manufacturers have been trying to deemphasize speed — but, who are they kidding? This section discusses the basics of microprocessor names and speeds. Other sections in this chapter cover the more esoteric microprocessor details.

The name game

Microprocessors are known by names and numbers, much like the sad people who live in the futuristic totalitarian societies of science fiction.

For example, Plonk 238 could be another miserable cog in the Ministry of Paper Shuffling, or it could be the next greatest microprocessor that every high-tech nerd lusts for. Go figure.

In the name game, the microprocessor's name comes first. It's a family name that tells you which company made the chip or perhaps which generation of chips the microprocessor belongs to. Table 5-1 lists the currently popular microprocessor names.

Table 5-1	Microprocessor Names	
Name	**Manufacturer**	**Notes**
Pentium	Intel	Current best technology for the typical PC
Athlon	AMD	Pentium-compatible microprocessors from AMD
Celeron	Intel	Inexpensive Pentium III alternative from Intel
Sempron	AMD	Inexpensive Athlon alternative from AMD; replaced the older Duron
Opteron	AMD	Similar to the Intel Xeon
PowerPC	IBM/Motorola	Used primarily in the Macintosh
Xeon	Intel	High-end microprocessor found only in servers

Other microprocessors with other unique and oddball names exist. Indeed, hundreds of microprocessors are on the market, some of which are specific to running things other than computers (such as the microprocessor in your car). Table 5-1 lists only the major microprocessors likely to be found in a personal computer. That's because it's one of the few times you actually get to pick and choose which microprocessor your computer has. For other electronics — game consoles and handheld computers, for example — choosing a different microprocessor isn't an option.

✔ A letter or number, or sometimes both, often follows the name (refer to Table 5-1). That extra information tells you more about the microprocessor's history, compatibility, or other special options.

✔ Another term for microprocessor is CPU, or _central processing unit_. Many ads use CPU rather than microprocessor for space reasons.

✔ CPU is also improperly used to describe the computer box, or console. Beware of the double usage when you're shopping.

✔ The microprocessor can also be referred to as a *processor*.

✔ Two common microprocessors not mentioned in Table 5-1 are the DEC Alpha and Sun Microsystems' SPARC. Computer hobbyists are fond of the Alpha; the SPARC is found only in Sun's own proprietary workstations.

✔ As this book goes to press, a new line of Macintosh computers has been announced, which shifts the microprocessor from the IBM PowerPC to some as-yet-unnamed Intel microprocessor. Information regarding that switch will be provided in this book's 2007 edition, which will come out as those new Macintosh computers become available.

The measure of power

The power of a microprocessor is measured in *bits*. How many bits can the microprocessor swallow in one gulp? The more bits, the more information (data) the microprocessor is capable of bandying about and, therefore, the more powerful the microprocessor.

In a way, the number of bits can be compared to lanes on a freeway: If you have only two lanes, too many cars congest traffic, and things slow down. A six-lane freeway, however, has plenty of room for lots of cars, and traffic flows smoothly. With more bits, just as with more lanes on a freeway, the micro-processor can do more powerful things.

The current state of the art with microprocessors is 32 or 64 bits, and 64 is better. A few 128-bit microprocessors are even available. The problem with this is that it's difficult to divine the bit power of a microprocessor; that infor-mation isn't as readily available as the microprocessor's speed value. But, it's there if you know what you're looking for.

✔ Early microprocessors dealt with only 8 bits or 16 bits at a time.

✔ Most of the standard x86 microprocessors now handle information in 32-bit chunks or larger.

✔ Higher-end microprocessors can handle information in 64- and even 128-bit chunks. The drawback is that unless you have software that specifi-cally takes advantage of it, you gain no benefit. Therefore, 32-bit chunks are good enough for most mortals, such as you and me.

Vroom, vroom! (Microprocessor speed)

The only technical detail most folks pay attention to is a microprocessor's speed. How fast does it go?

Optional reading on the x86 family

The computer industry has given the family name *x86* to the type of microprocessor commonly found in a PC, or the typical Windows computer. The 86 refers to the last two digits of the original IBM PC microprocessor, the Intel 8086 (though the IBM PC used the 8086's sister chip, the 8088, for cost reasons).

Each new generation of Intel microprocessor that found its way into a PC's thorax was based on that original 8086 chip, and they were given similar numbers: 80286, 80386, 80486. Even non-Intel microprocessors, which were compatible with the Intel line, sported number-names that ended with or contained *86.*

Frustrated by the confusing numbers, and by the fact that you cannot trademark a number, Intel changed the name of its next generation of microprocessor from 80586 to *Pentium.* To avoid confusion with people who were used to numbers, Intel described the Pentium as the latest CPU in the x86 family.

Most of the PC microprocessors available now are part of the x86 family, which means that they're compatible with the original CPUs as well as with each other. As long as the description says *x86 family,* the name can be Athlon, Pentium, Celeron, or Sempron — it's all the same to the computer's software.

Honestly, speed is all relative. Comparing microprocessor speeds was important many years ago in buying a computer, but now, pretty much any computer you get is fast enough. Even so, the manufacturers still boast of their speed, and therefore, it's something you need to know.

Technically, microprocessor speed is measured in *hertz,* or cycles per second. That may satisfy the geeks, but to you and me, "cycles per second" means how many things the microprocessor can do in one second. For example, if you can hop on your left foot 100 times a second, you're moving at a pace of 100 hertz, or 100 Hz. The microprocessor, of course, is much faster.

How fast? Microprocessors are capable of doing *billions* of things in one second. Therefore, their speed is measured in gigahertz, abbreviated GHz.

A microprocessor that can do exactly 1 billion things per second is rated at 1.0 GHz.

A microprocessor that can do 3.66 billion things per second is rated at 3.66 GHz. This rate is much faster than 1.0 GHz.

Like driving your car on the freeway, the higher the speed value, the faster the chip. And, naturally, the faster the chip, the more expensive it is:

Fast microprocessor = Better ☺ = More expensive ☹

The premium you pay for the fastest microprocessor is amazing. For example, if I were to shop for the fastest Pentium I could buy today, I would pay about $300 for a 3.4 GHz chip. A 3.0 GHz chip, however, sells for $190. Is it worth a 57 percent premium in price to pay for a chip that's only 13 percent faster? And, that's only the raw speed — the actual difference in performance you see is probably negligible. Anyway: File that information away for future thought.

- ✔ Microprocessor speed is also referred to as *clock speed*. It's just another term for how fast the CPU goes.

- ✔ Avoid comparing speeds among different microprocessors; the true test lies in how fast the *software* runs. A graphical image may load faster on a Macintosh with a 2.0 GHz G5 than it does on a PC with a 3.2 GHz Pentium.

- ✔ Buy the fastest microprocessor you can afford!

- ✔ Eventually (or so they promise), the microprocessor industry plans to move away from boasting about CPU speed values. They have been saying this for a few years now, yet things won't change until the computer stores and salespeople stop referring to microprocessor speed as though it's important.

- ✔ Your brain has a speed rating of only about 2 MHz (not *you* individually — everyone in general). The human brain can do several million things at a time, whereas the microprocessor does only one thing at a time, which is one reason that humans consider themselves to be superior to computers.

Popular PC Processors

Here's the roundup of the types of microprocessors you find in the available batch of PCs now for sale:

Pentium 4: This one is the big daddy, the primary microprocessor used by most PCs made by computing pioneer Intel. There are several individual models of the Pentium 4, as covered later in this section.

Celeron: The Celeron is merely a low-end, less expensive version of the Pentium 4. It's not as fast, but where speed isn't necessary, and price is important, this is the next best thing to a Pentium.

Pentium HT: The HT stands for hyperthreading, or the ability of the microprocessor to do several things simultaneously. (See the section "What is 'hyperthreading'?" later in this chapter.)

Athlon XP: The Athlon XP was AMD's first attempt to take on the venerable Pentium 4. It's a fine alternative, not as expensive as the Pentium 4 and in many ways technologically superior.

Athlon 64: A full 64-bit microprocessor (the standard Pentium 4 is 32 bits), this CPU is favored by computer gamers because game software greatly benefits from the added speed and power the Athlon 64 offers.

Pentium D: The D stands for *d*ual-core; it's essentially two Pentium 4 chips in one. See the section "The core design," later in this chapter, for information on what a core is.

Pentium 4 Extreme Edition: This is Intel's answer to the Athlon 64, a custom Pentium 4 for games. It's a Pentium D with hyperthreading technology added.

Pentium M: A custom version of the Pentium 4 designed for low-power consumption and low-heat generation, specifically for use in laptop, or mobile, computers.

Mobile Athlon XP: A version of the Athlon XP specifically designed for use in laptop computers.

More information about the specifics on these microprocessors is found elsewhere in this chapter.

Beyond the Basic Microprocessor

Volumes of information have been published on the details of each and every microprocessor ever developed. The stuff can get really technical. For the typical computer-buying human, all the information you really need to know is contained in the first few sections of this chapter. The rest is trivial junk, but it does come up from time to time in advertisements and is handy for those willing to take on the task of building their own computers.

Out of the piles of technical microprocessor details, four items can be considered more interesting than the rest:

- ✔ Cache
- ✔ Front side bus
- ✔ Core
- ✔ Socket

These items are covered in this section in as painless a manner possible.

The cache

Another descriptive term for a microprocessor is cache. The most important thing to know here is that cache is pronounced "cash," not "ka-shay." For example, "Hand over all the cache!" or "I'm short on cache — will you accept an expansion card?"

A *cache* is a storage place. Pirates may have a cache of treasure. Terrorists may have a cache of weapons. And, microprocessors use a cache to help improve their speed and performance.

Two caches are in the typical microprocessor: the primary cache and the secondary cache.

The *primary* cache is a small area of memory storage right on the microprocessor chip itself.

The *secondary* cache is also known as the L2 cache, where L2 means Level 2, or second level, after the primary cache. It's typically larger and slower than the primary cache. Even so, having a larger L2 cache can greatly improve the microprocessor's speed and performance.

> ✔ The larger the cache, the better. A cache with a huge memory capacity can store lots of programming instructions and greatly improve the microprocessor's speed.

> ✔ The primary cache has two parts: an instruction cache and a data cache. That's a $600 answer on *Jeopardy!*, by the way.

> ✔ The L2 cache is often supplied on an external chip, in which case you should see "external L2 cache" in the microprocessor's description.

> ✔ Get as much Level 2 cache as possible. If you have a choice between two microprocessors and one has more L2 (Level 2) cache, get the one with more L2 cache.

The front side bus

It's not big and yellow, and the people don't go up and down as the tires go 'round and 'round. Inside a computer, a *bus* is a hardware connection between two devices where communication takes place.

The *front side bus (FSB)* is the main highway between the microprocessor and the two most important things inside the computer: the memory and the chipset.

Like the microprocessor, the front side bus operates at a certain speed, measured in megahertz or gigahertz. Unlike the microprocessor, however, the front side bus speed need not be the same as the microprocessor's speed. In fact, more often than not, the speeds are totally different.

It's not really important to know the front side bus speed, unless you're building your own computer or plan to speed it up by *overclocking* (covered later in this chapter), neither of which I recommend for beginners. Still, it's another bit of information to know when you're comparing microprocessors; a faster front side bus is better.

The core design

The main part of the microprocessor that actually does the work is known as the *core*. Though the microprocessor's name — Pentium or Athlon, for example — doesn't change over time, the technology used to make the core changes. In fact, custom cores are created for specific purposes, such as laptop computing or game consoles. To keep all those differences straight, each microprocessor line also has its internal list of core names.

Table 5-2 lists the core names found in the current lot of Pentium and Athlon CPUs. This information is for trivial purposes only; you see these names used in advertising. More important, if you plan to build your own PC, you need to ensure that the motherboard's chipset matches the proper CPU core design — techy stuff.

Table 5-2	x86 Family Core Names
Name	*CPU*
Barton	Athlon
Foster	Pentium
Gallatin	Pentium
Northwood	Pentium
Palomino	Athlon
Prescott	Pentium
Smithfield	Pentium
Thorton	Athlon
Thunderbird	Athlon
Willamette	Pentium

Socket to me

As a computer chip, the microprocessor plugs into the motherboard by means of a socket. This works similar to the way Legos connect together, though a typical Lego doesn't cost $250. As you might suspect, there is no one universal socket on which all computer microprocessors sit. In fact, each microprocessor may have several variations of sockets into which it plugs, depending on the microprocessor breed and purpose.

Do you need to know the microprocessor socket numbers? Of course not! But that information is often included with the CPU's description, and it's vital if you plan on building your own computer, as each motherboard comes with a different type of socket. Table 5-3 straightens things out.

Table 5-3	PC Microprocessor Sockets	
Socket	**Microprocessor**	**Notes**
370	Celeron	
423	Pentium 4	
462	Athlon, Duron, Athlon XP	Also known as Socket A
478	Celeron, Pentium 4	
479	Pentium M	M means "mobile," for laptops
563	Athlon M	Mobile Athlon XP
603	Xeon	
604	Xeon	
775	Pentium 4	Also known as LGA 775, as well as Socket T
754	Athlon 64	
939	Athlon 64	
940	Athlon 64, Opteron	

Some Microprocessor Q&A

The following common questions crop up when normal people attempt to understand computer microprocessors. The answers provided in this section educate you without converting you into a Jolt-cola-swilling, Doritos-munching computer geek.

"What does '[blank] or greater' mean when talking about a microprocessor?"

Computer hardware is always developed before computer software. As an example, consider that someone had to invent the bassoon before anyone could write music for it.

To deal with the lag time, software developers take advantage of the fact that older PC microprocessors are compatible with the recent stuff. Software that ran on an archaic IBM PC with an 8088 microprocessor could still run today on a Pentium. (It runs very fast.)

Because of this *backward compatibility,* and considering that the marketing folks like to ensure that their products are available to the widest possible audiences, software often advertises itself as requiring a "Pentium III or greater" microprocessor. That phrase means your computer needs at least a Pentium III CPU to run the software. Pentium 4, and anything else that came after the Pentium III or is compatible with those chips also applies. Pentium II or an older 486 CPU? No dice!

✔ The term "386 or greater" is often used, even though it has been years since you could buy a computer with a 386 microprocessor. Ditto for "486 or greater."

✔ My nerdy side just wants to blurt this out: Technologically speaking, a Pentium is really nothing more than a very fast 386. Design-wise, the chips operate identically; the latest Pentiums merely sport various speed-enhancing additions.

"Are all Pentium processors the same?"

Generally speaking, yes. However! If the software specifically requests a certain microprocessor, you *must* go with it. If the software says "Requires a Pentium 4 running at 1.4 GHz or better," you must get yourself that microprocessor *at a minimum*. I hope that you get something faster, such as a Pentium 4 running at 1.5 GHz or a higher speed.

Also note that if the software requires or can take advantage of a Pentium 4 with hyperthreading abilities, then getting such a CPU is worth your while.

TECHNICAL STUFF

"What happened to the math coprocessor?"

A *math coprocessor* is a special companion chip for the microprocessor, or FPU, for *floating-point unit*. This separate chip sat right next to the microprocessor and acted like the main CPU's pocket calculator. The math coprocessor's job was to do mathematical computations, and it was engineered to do them more swiftly than the microprocessor could do on its own.

All microprocessors now have built-in math coprocessors. If your software demands a math coprocessor, you're all set. Only if you buy a used computer do you otherwise have to question whether it has a math coprocessor.

"Should I buy an upgradeable microprocessor option?"

No. This was a fad for a while, but it never came to fruition. The problem is that newer microprocessors require newer chipsets, faster memory, and other upgrades that just make it cheaper to buy a whole new motherboard or a whole new computer as opposed to just a new microprocessor.

(See Chapter 25, about upgrading your equipment, for more ranting on this topic.)

"Is the Celeron a good Pentium compatible?"

The Celeron is made by Intel, so it's the closest thing you can get to a Pentium without the Pentium name. Essentially, a Celeron is a slower Pentium with either no L2 cache or a very small L2 cache. This "lack of cache" subtracts significantly from its speed, but reduces the price enough to make it an attractive processor for home systems.

I don't recommend getting a PC with a Celeron microprocessor unless it's all you can afford.

"Should I buy a non-Intel CPU if it saves me money?"

Absolutely. The days of flaky wannabe microprocessors are in the past. Any non-Intel microprocessor does the job and saves you some money. However, if buying an Intel microprocessor would make you sleep better at night, get one.

"Why not buy the biggest, baddest microprocessor on the block?"

Software! If the software you plan to run doesn't take advantage of a high-end Xeon microprocessor, you have just wasted a huge chunk of money.

"What's the 'heat sink'?"

Because the microprocessor runs so fast, it needs a way to help cool itself off. The computer console's fan just isn't up to the job, so scientists designed a *heat sink* to dissipate the heat generated by the CPU. The heat sink works like a fancy hat that sits atop the microprocessor chip, though without a sports-team logo.

Some CPUs have, rather than a heat sink, wee little fans attached to them to help dissipate the heat. The fan keeps the microprocessor cool.

When the microprocessor gets too hot, all hell breaks loose.

"What is 'hyperthreading'?"

Hyperthreading is a new technology on Pentium microprocessors, which are typically flagged as Pentium HT. As with all hardware, however, the hyperthreading technology is good only for software that takes advantage of it. If the software you need can get a boost from Pentium HT technology, pay the extra dollar. Otherwise, don't bother.

"What is 'overclocking'?"

Various tests are made in order to get a microprocessor rated at a specific clock speed. The tests ensure that the microprocessor is as fast as *or faster* than the rated speed. Computer hackers take advantage of that "or faster than" part to make their computers' microprocessors run at higher speeds than they're originally rated. This practice is called *overclocking* because the hacker adjusts the microprocessor's clock speed to a value over its stated rating.

Overclocking is easy to do, if you gather information about your computer and follow a few simple steps. In many cases, computer hackers have been able to squeeze much more speed from a low-rated CPU. In other cases, the act of overclocking literally fries the microprocessor and voids the computer's warranty.

I recommend against overclocking. Even if your enthusiastic computer pal claims that it doesn't harm a thing, *keep that geek away from your system!* If you want a faster computer, pay for one. Don't accept any shortcuts that may make you sorry later.

"Do computers with dual processors run faster than computers with single processors?"

Again, speed is relative. The advantage of a two- (or more) CPU computer is that the main *(master)* microprocessor can offload some duties to the companion *(slave)* microprocessors. That speeds things up, just as having several people working on your house at one time gets the job done faster.

Again, the real power is in the software. If yours takes advantage of multiple microprocessors, that's just great. I'm aware that Mac OS X runs on dual-processor G5 computers. Some versions of Windows, in addition to Linux and Unix, take advantage of dual-processor computers. Be certain that your software gets a boost from this type of situation before you make the hefty investment.

Note that having two microprocessors isn't the same as having a single microprocessor with dual-core technology. While dual-core technology is better than single core, it's not exactly the same thing as having two separate CPUs inside a single computer box.

Chapter 6

Memory Stuff (Temporary Storage)

· ·

In This Chapter

▶ Measuring computer memory

▶ Sizing up a memory chip

▶ Gauging memory speed

▶ Using DIMMs

▶ Understanding memory terms

▶ Knowing about main memory versus video memory

▶ Filling your memory banks

· ·

All computers require two types of storage: temporary storage and permanent storage. The temporary storage is RAM, or computer memory. Disk drives provide permanent storage.

Temporary and permanent storage shouldn't be strange to you — after all, human beings use both types. In your brain, you use memory as temporary storage. If you want to keep something long-term, you write it down — which is permanent storage. Similar things happen inside a computer, which is why two different forms of storage are needed.

This chapter is about the computer's temporary storage, also known as *memory,* or *RAM.* The more memory your computer has, the better it operates and the more information you can play with at one time. Knowing how much RAM is enough is something you figure out in Part III of this book. For now, this chapter offers an introduction to computer memory and its associated terms, jargon, and folderol.

Say Hello to Mr. Byte

All storage containers have a specific unit size. For example, paper is sold by the sheet; you don't buy a 1-inch-high stack of paper — you buy 500 sheets. The gas tank in your car stores fuel by the gallon. The storage unit for soda pop is the 12-ounce can. You don't buy 72 fluid ounces of Coke; you buy a 6-pack.

In a computer, the basic storage unit is a byte. The *byte* is used to measure storage, so it's important that you know a few byte-related terms.

Take a byte

What a byte is and how it works aren't important. What's important to know is what a byte stores:

One byte stores one character of information.

The word *byte,* for example, contains four letters, or four characters. A computer uses 4 bytes of storage to store that word.

The word *closet* requires 6 bytes of storage. The preceding sentence requires 44 bytes of storage, which includes all the letters, the spaces between the words, and the period at the end of the sentence.

Take a bigger byte

To make a large number of bytes easy to describe, modern scientists have stolen some ancient Greek words: *kilo, mega,* and *giga,* which sound like bad guys the Power Rangers fight, but are terms used to describe the size of something.

The kilobyte ("KILL-uh-bite") is approximately 1,000 bytes of information, or about a page of text. It's abbreviated K or KB.

The megabyte ("MEG-uh-bite") is approximately 1 million bytes of information. That's 1,000 pages of text, or about the size of a typical Stephen King novel before an editor gets hold of it. Megabyte is abbreviated M or MB.

The gigabyte ("GIG-uh-bite") is approximately 1 billion bytes of information, which is just about half the size of the U.S. Tax Code. It's abbreviated G or GB.

Finally, the terabyte ("TAYR-uh-bite") has approximately 1 trillion bytes — an awful number that's beyond human comprehension. It's abbreviated T or TB. Because it's a relatively new value in computerdom, you may see it referred to as 1,000GB for a while.

Table 6-1 puts these values in perspective.

Table 6-1		Measuring Computer Storage	
Unit	*Abbreviation*	*Approximate Number of Bytes*	*Exact Number of Bytes*
Byte	B	—	1
Kilobyte	KB	1,000 (thousand)	1,024
Megabyte	MB	1,000,000 (million)	1,048,576
Gigabyte	GB	1,000,000,000 (billion)	1,073,741,824
Terabyte	TB	1,000,000,000,000 (trillion)	1,099,511,627,776

✔ These terms — kilobyte, megabyte, and so on — are used to describe both temporary and permanent storage in a computer — how much room you have for the stuff you create.

✔ Gigabyte is pronounced "GIG-a-byte," not "JIG-a-byte" or "giggle-byte."

✔ Note that that there's a difference between approximate and exact storage — chump change, really. It accounts for the fact that the computer is counting in binary, or base 2, which doesn't always work out to the base 10 values we humans use. It's trivial, really.

Memory Madness

You may have heard the term RAM. And, you may have a brief understanding of computer memory. Although it's important to know memory quantities, as covered in the preceding section, the rest of the details regarding computer memory are truly boring. That's because they're technical.

For buying a computer, knowing how much memory your new computer needs is just about enough. Beyond that, you're faced with a slew of memory terms to boggle, baffle, and bewilder. Because there seems to be no getting around it, I've written this section to help describe these memory terms and jargon in happy, friendly language. That should help you sift through what's important and what's not when it comes to computer memory.

Behold the chip!

There must be a law somewhere that says "Chip is an inefficient term for describing anything." Look at your grocery store: The chip section is divided into regular potato chips, flavored chips, corn chips, tortilla chips, and even anti-chips, like those puffy cheese things and yummy pork rinds. Computer memory is similar.

Computer memory comes in the form of chips. But, because of some weird scientific mumbo jumbo, you need eight or nine chips for them to be useful in a computer. Those eight or nine chips create a *bank* of memory.

- ✔ There are no nacho-cheese-flavored memory chips.

- ✔ RAM chips are rarely sold singularly any more. Instead, they're soldered together in groups of eight or nine, which is covered in the section "Goodbye, Mr. Chips!" later in this chapter.

- ✔ Memory chips are RAM chips, though other annoying terms exist. See the section "A flock of technical memory terms," later in this chapter.

The size of the thing (capacity)

Though each memory chip is about the same physical size, what's important is the chip's *capacity*. How many bytes of RAM are in that single chip?

RAM chips come in several sizes, from tiny 1 kilobyte chips to chips that can store 512MB or more, all in one little package. Obviously, the higher the capacity, the more expensive the chip.

Which do you need? It depends on your computer and how it's set up, which is covered later in this chapter.

Fast memory and faster memory

In addition to its capacity, computer memory is gauged by its speed, similar to a microprocessor. With memory, the speed is measured in *nanoseconds* (abbreviated *ns*), or billionths of a second.

Here's one nanosecond: 0.000000001.

Whew! That's fast.

Or, if you have any deuterium pellets handy, plus a powerful laser, it takes one nanosecond to compress the pellet with the laser. Again, that's fast.

Back in the world of computers, you may see a RAM chip advertised as "6ns." That term means that the memory hums along at 6 nanoseconds.

- ✔ The speed describes how fast the memory can be accessed. This speed depends on your computer's configuration; adding faster RAM chips to a slow PC doesn't (unfortunately) perk things up.

- ✔ Memory speed isn't seriously important when you buy a computer. The dealer installs whichever memory works best in that system. Memory speed becomes an issue when you buy *more* memory for your computer. The speed of that additional memory should match the speed already used in your computer.

- ✔ Upgrading memory is covered in Chapter 27.

- ✔ Again, the faster the memory, the more you pay for it.

- ✔ Another aspect of RAM speed is how fast the computer's bus runs. You need to match the RAM speed to the PC's bus speed, or a multiple thereof — though this is a more technical aspect that's handled by the manufacturer or computer dealer than a choice you must make.

Goodbye, Mr. Chips!

To make handling the chips easier, memory manufacturers solder a whole bank of chips together on a single tiny strip of fiberglass about the size of a pocket comb. That strip is called a *DIMM,* as shown in Figure 6-1, and it does indeed make up one whole bank of memory. This is very handy.

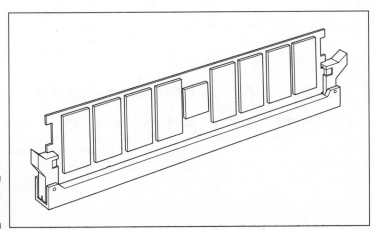

Figure 6-1:
A DIMM.

What is flash memory?

Flash memory is a special type of memory chip that retains its information even when the computer is turned off. Normally, memory (RAM) requires electricity in order to retain its information. Turn off the power, and the contents of RAM go bye-bye (which is why it's important to save information to disk, the computer's permanent storage area).

Flash memory doesn't require electricity in order to retain its information. It remembers things long after the power is off. For this reason, flash memory is used for special information that the computer must remember at all times.

It would be swell if all memory in a computer were flash memory so that you wouldn't have to worry about losing information during a power outage. Unfortunately, flash memory is more expensive and not as fast as regular memory. So, you typically find it used as digital camera storage, in special types of removable media or in other situations where speed isn't an object.

Like individual memory chips, DIMMs are described by their capacity (the amount of RAM they have) and their speed. A third measurement is the number of *pins*, or connections, the DIMM has.

DIMMs plug into a special slot inside the computer's case on the motherboard. Some slots have 72 connectors, some have 168, and some have other oddball numbers. These connectors are called *pins* even though they aren't really pins. If you ever upgrade memory, you need to ensure that you get the proper number of pins on a DIMM to match your computer's needs.

- ✔ DIMM stands for *dual in*-line *memory module*.

- ✔ A special type of DIMM is the SODIMM (or SO-DIMM), where the SO stands for Small-Outline. These supercompact memory modules are for use in laptop computers and other high-end PCs.

- ✔ Before the DIMM was the SIMM. You may still find one of these on an older computer. SIMM stands for Single Inline Memory Module.

A flock of technical memory terms

Memory isn't simply referred to as memory. Just when the computer industry reaches the point where memory can be just "memory," someone invents a new type of memory. So, along comes a new acronym or technical description to distinguish the New Memory from the Old Memory. Ugh.

Honestly, the only places you see these terms are in memory ads. In the real world, even engineers just call it RAM or memory. The rest is all scientific fluff that makes good (or bad) ad copy:

Bank: The slot into which a DIMM is inserted. Most computer motherboards come with two or four banks, numbered 0 and 1 or 0 through 3. Bank can also refer to a chunk of memory, such as a 64KB *bank* of RAM. See the section "Banks o' Memory (RAM)," later in this chapter.

DDR: Acronym for Double Data Rate, a type of SDRAM that's twice as fast as regular SDRAM.

DDR-*xxx*. The *xxx* here is a number that specifies the memory's speed with regard to the motherboard's data transfer rate — a technical thing, but if you plan to build your own computer, the *xxx* number on the RAM chips you buy must match the motherboard's *xxx* number.

DRAM: Another term for RAM. Pronounced "DEE-ram," it stands for Dynamic Random Access Memory. It's more impressive than RAM, I suppose, but not as impressive as SDRAM or EDO RAM. Whoa! No way!

ECC: An acronym for Error Checking and Correction, which can require extra circuits to ensure that memory is being properly written to and read from.

EDO RAM: An acronym for Extended Data Out, another fancy-schmancy type of memory and more powerful than mere SDRAM.

FPM: Acronym for Fast Page Mode, often used with RAM, as in FPM RAM. It's faster. Smarter. Better. Using it implies that the neighbor's dog is ugly.

Nonparity: Memory chips that don't use parity, as described next.

Parity: Another nerdy term; refers to a self-check that memory chips can perform on themselves every time the memory is accessed. Do you need parity? Maybe. A computer manufacturer decides whether it wants to put parity in its PCs. Other than that information, anything else I could say about parity would put you to sleep.

PC*xxx*: Refers to the speed of the computer's front side bus, where *xxx* is a numeric value (in megahertz). The SDRAM that's used should match the front side bus speed, though you can use slower memory on a faster bus (but I don't see why you would want to).

RDRAM: Special Rambus DRAM, which operates at superhigh speeds — but only on motherboards that use the Rambus chipset.

What about ROM?

ROM stands for Read-Only Memory. Like RAM, it's another type of memory in your computer. The microprocessor can read ROM just like RAM, but, unlike RAM, the contents of ROM cannot be changed. Hey! It's read-only.

When it comes to buying a computer, you have no need to worry about how much ROM is in a computer. All computers come with all the ROM they need.

SDRAM: *Synchronous* DRAM, also known as SDR SDRAM. Basically, it's just SDRAM or a common type of memory chip found in most computers (*see* DDR).

SRAM: An even faster type of RAM, especially when going downhill.

Generally speaking, these terms come and go. Some become obsolete (or worn out). Some new ones may crop up. Sometimes, a manufacturer may rename an older standard to make it sound newer in the ads. Whatever.

Main Memory versus Video Memory

Memory is used in computers in two places. First, there's main memory, where all the "action" takes place. Second, there's video memory, which is used to help the computer display graphics.

Both main and video memory values are often listed in computer ads. For example, you may see a new computer with 256MB of memory and also 64MB of video memory. That means that the computer has 256MB of memory in which you can work, and an additional 64MB for displaying fancy graphics.

Along with this different type of memory come two utterly confusing memory terms. Often, they're used in ads to describe the video memory in a computer:

SGRAM: A special type of video memory. It's just SDRAM (see the preceding section), but the *G* in this acronym stands for Graphics: Synchronous Graphics Random Access Memory.

VRAM: Video Random Access Memory, another form of video memory that's probably not as flashy as SGRAM because it has more letters in its acronym.

Again, this is advertisement-only information. Whenever you see VRAM or SGRAM or any other type of video-RAM-whatever, know that it's memory used by the computer for displaying graphics.

✔ Your computer needs both main and video memory.

✔ Some computers boast *shareable* memory, in which the main RAM is used to supplement video memory. This type is often a cheap alternative to stuffing a computer with both types of RAM. Yes, it works. No, I do not recommend this type of system — unless graphics or games are *not* one of the reasons you're getting a computer.

Banks o' Memory (RAM)

Science fiction TV shows typically feature computers with *banks* of memory. Although that term is accurate, it's also vague.

The computer you buy will indeed have banks of memory. The DIMM cards plug into these slots inside the computer. Each slot is known as a *bank*. What's important is how those banks are filled. Ideally, you want them filled in a manner that wastes no memory, in case you ever decide to upgrade.

When you order your computer, try to get the manufacturer to install all your computer's memory into as few banks as possible. For example, Figure 6-2 shows a setup with four banks of memory. A 128MB DIMM is plugged into each bank, which gives that computer a total of 512MB of RAM — a goodly amount for now, but what about future expansion?

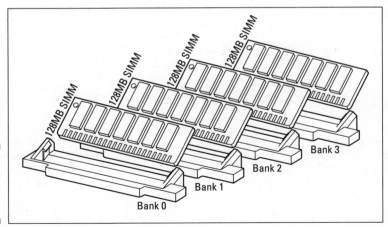

Figure 6-2:
Memory banks in a computer.

Memory is cheap, cheap, cheap!

It has been a while since I've bought memory for a computer, so I was utterly shocked when I saw how ridiculously *cheap* computer memory really is. Memory is cheaper now because so much of it is available on a single chip. Back in 1985, it took eight or nine 4-kilobit memory chips to make one 4KB bank. That may have cost you $40. I remember paying $150 for a 64KB bank of memory.

You can now get a bank of 256MB of memory and pay about $70 — 8,000 times cheaper than memory was 20 years ago. And, the prices are still going down.

Suppose that someday you want to add another 512MB of memory to the same computer. It sounds good, but because this system has only four banks and each one is full, you have only one option: Toss out all your memory (for which you paid dearly), and replace it with 1024MB of new memory. Yes, it's a waste.

A better situation is shown in Figure 6-3: All memory is plugged into one bank. Yes, this strategy is initially more expensive than configuring an identical system with four banks of lower-capacity DIMMs. But, when you upgrade, all you need is one other DIMM; nothing is thrown away! Plus, you still have more banks available for future upgrades.

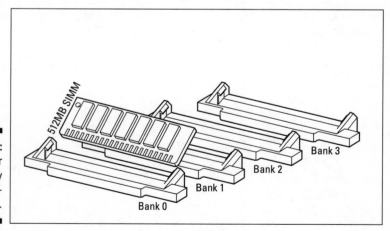

Figure 6-3:
A better memory bank configuration.

512MB SIMM

Bank 0

Bank 1

Bank 2

Bank 3

- Yes, one 512MB DIMM usually costs more than four 128MB DIMMs.

- Some computers insist that *all* memory banks have the same amount of memory. If you have three 265MB SIMMs in three banks and want to add a 128MB DIMM to the last bank, you can't do it. (Don't blame me! Beat up an engineer!) Also, some systems require you to install DIMMs in pairs, which requires additional thinking when you're buying additional memory.

How Much Memory Do You Need?

How much memory will your new computer need? The answer depends on your software. The bottom line is that you need memory (or RAM) in your computer. Memory in your computer is measured in *megabyte* units. The standard quantity for most new computers is 256MB of memory, or RAM. Some come with more memory — typically, 512MB. On a PC, Windows XP needs 128MB just to start, but it runs better with 256MB — best with 512MB.

Watch out for computers advertised with no memory or 0K or 0MB of RAM. This sales ploy makes a computer look cheaper than other models sold with memory. All computers need it, so you have to pay for it one way or another.

Chapter 7

Disks of Every Type (Permanent Storage)

A computer system needs to have only a microprocessor and some memory. That's enough to get the ball rolling for the simplest of computers, such as the computer in your car, the computer that runs the traffic lights, and the computer that eventually turns insane and starts another World War. But, that's just not enough for any personal computer you plan to buy.

The microprocessor has a modicum of storage for the fast things it does; otherwise, it relies on computer memory, or RAM, for storage. Sadly, both microprocessor and RAM storage are temporary; when the power is off, the contents of memory are gone. *Poof!* What you really need is a place to store your stuff long-term, a device that doesn't forget its contents after the power goes off. That's permanent storage.

After the microprocessor and computer memory, permanent storage is the next-most-important element in your new computer system. That permanent storage is usually offered in the form of disk drives. This chapter sifts through the spinning pile of disk information, to point out what's necessary and offer background information to help you read the various advertisements and make sense of them.

Why Permanent Storage?

Permanent storage is the second type of storage inside a computer. The first type is memory, or RAM. That's where the work takes place; the microprocessor busies itself there by running programs and storing all the wonderful stuff you create.

When you're done working, you need a more permanent place to store your stuff in the computer. The hardware to meet that requirement is the disk drive — specifically, the computer's *hard drive*. You direct the software that you're using to "save" your stuff on the hard drive, by making a permanent copy that you can use later.

- ✔ Not all computers need permanent storage. But, for computers that people use, permanent storage is a must.

- ✔ The most popular, inexpensive, and reliable form of permanent storage is the hard drive.

- ✔ Some computers even have several forms of disk storage: a hard drive, CD-ROM drive or DVD drive (or both), and maybe a floppy drive. Each of these has specific uses, as covered later in this chapter.

- ✔ Some handheld computers don't have physical disk drives. Instead, they contain special memory that isn't erased when the power is turned off.

- ✔ Game consoles use memory cards as permanent storage. Unlike regular RAM, the memory in the memory cards doesn't require power in order to remember its contents.

- ✔ Digital cameras also use memory cards for storage, what I call digital media cards. Several different formats can be used as storage "drives" on a personal computer as well.

- ✔ Some advertisements, and misinformed computer users, refer to permanent storage as "disk memory." Although that term is technically correct, the term is confusing. Please don't mistake disk memory for the memory inside your computer. Disk storage and RAM are two different places in a computer. Whenever you see the term disk memory, just think disk storage instead.

- ✔ For more information on microprocessors, see Chapter 5.

- ✔ Computer memory (RAM) is covered in Chapter 6.

What Is a Disk, and What Is a Drive?

Simply put, the *drive* is the thing that contains or eats the disk. So, although your computer has a hard disk, it's more proper to say "hard drive." Similarly, you may have a CD-ROM *drive*, floppy *drive*, DVD *drive,* and even digital media *drive*.

The *disk* is literally a disk. The computer writes information to the disk, where it's stored exactly like information is recorded on a cassette tape, only the disk media is flat and round — like a pancake.

The *drive* is the device that spins the disk, reading and writing information.

With some drives, the disk can be removed. This is true for CD-ROM, DVD, floppy, and other removable disks. With the hard drive, however, the disk cannot be removed. That's because the disk (or disks) inside the drive needs to be hermetically sealed to avoid contamination by rogue particles in the air.

Figure 7-1 illustrates a typical hard drive. The entire unit is the hard drive. Inside the unit are the hard disks, as shown in the figure.

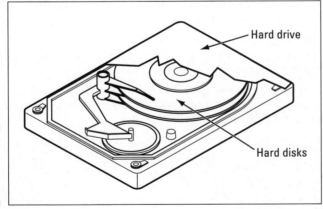

Figure 7-1:
A run-of-the-mill hard disk drive.

✔ Hard drives are available from which the disk can be removed. These special drives are expensive and not truly necessary; you have other, better ways to get information out of the computer than to fuss over the fact that you cannot remove hard disks from the drive.

✔ Sometimes, hard drives are referred to as *fixed disks*. This term doesn't mean that the disk was once broken. No, it means that the disk is "fixed," as in nonmovable.

Types of drives

Inside a typical computer, you find several types of permanent storage. Why not only one? Well, there are historical as well as technologically trivial reasons for each type of permanent storage. Rather than bore you with those details, just consider the following list of common permanent storage devices as an overview of what's available:

Hard drive: This standard, high-capacity, high-speed drive is found in all personal computers, desktops, and laptops. This drive is the primary form of permanent storage. Don't buy a computer without a hard drive!

CD-ROM: Nearly all computer software comes on CD, which makes the CD-ROM drive a must-have part of all standard desktop and laptop configurations. The standard CD-ROM drive, however, cannot be used to create your own CDs. For that you need a CD-R/RW drive.

DVD: Just as DVD is replacing videotape for the home theater market, DVD discs are slowly replacing CDs for computers. The transition from CD to DVD isn't taking place as quickly as videotape to CD, so not every new computer needs to come with a DVD drive. Even so, I recommend that you get one. Just as with creating your own CDs, if you want to create your own DVDs, you need to get a special type of DVD drive that creates discs. More on that later in this chapter.

Note that all DVD drives can read CDs. So, you don't really need separate CD and DVD drives on a computer. Special combo drives are even available (for a price) that can be used to create both CDs and DVDs.

Beyond the hard drive and a CD or DVD drive are several optional types of disk drives found on many PCs. Here's the list:

Floppy: Though traditionally the first type of disk drive found on a personal computer, floppy drive technology has not kept up with computer disk storage capacities. Many manufacturers still toss a floppy drive into the computer console, but relatively few computer users ever use it. Note that a floppy drive is often abbreviated FDD, for *f*loppy *d*isk *d*rive.

Zip: The Zip drive was introduced to replace the floppy drive, and it was very popular for many years. Now that most computers have the ability to create their own CDs, just like the floppy drive, the Zip drive is falling out of fashion.

Digital media cards: These nonspinning drives use solid-state memory that doesn't require power in order to retain its contents. Some of these drives, such as the USB Flash Drive or Jump Drive, are designed specifically for the desktop computer and prove to be an excellent way to transfer files between two computer systems. Other types of digital media cards are specifically designed for use in digital cameras. Having the digital media drive, or any gizmo that reads the digital memory cards, on the computer sure comes in handy.

You can find more information about each of these drive types later in this chapter.

Capacity

The first measure of all permanent storage is how much information can be stored. As with computer memory, the measuring rod of disk storage is the byte. (Refer to Chapter 6 for information on bytes and the capacities they measure.)

Table 7-1 lists the storage capacities of the common, popular types of permanent storage.

Table 7-1	Drive Storage Capacities
Drive Type	*Storage Capacity*
Floppy	1.4MB
Zip	100MB, 250MB, and 750MB
CD	Up to 720MB
Flash memory	Up to 8GB
DVD	Up to 8GB (16GB on two sides of the disk)
Hard drive	Up to 1,000GB (1TB — and higher)

The only figure you really need to pay attention to is for hard drive storage. Hard drives don't come in standard sizes. Instead, you find hard drives that store anywhere from 40GB of information up to a whopping 400GB and higher. You pay more for more storage or less for less. You want to ensure that you get more storage than you need so that you don't run out.

✔ Remember that a megabyte (MB) is 1 million bytes and a gigabyte (GB) is 1 billion bytes (or 1,000MB). Technology is rapidly approaching the terabyte (TB), or 1,000GB drive.

✔ How much storage capacity do you need? That depends on your software and how you use the computer. This book shows you how to calculate the exact amount and then add a bit more so that you don't run out of disk storage.

- ✔ If you're not satisfied with the preceding information tidbit, consider that I would have at least an 80GB hard drive in a new computer.

- ✔ Disk storage is relatively cheap. Buy more than you need, if you can afford it.

- ✔ Even if you do run out of disk storage, most computers have room to add a second hard drive internally, which gives you even more storage.

Hard drive speed

The faster the disk drive, the faster you can read information from that disk drive. Faster is definitely better. And, naturally, the faster it is, the more expensive the disk is. Speed doth have its price. . . .

Disk drive speed is measured in RPM, or *rotations per minute* — like old stereo records. Remember the 45 rpm and the 33 rpm? How about the old 78 rpm? Well, with disk drives, rpm is measured in the thousands.

If you can afford it, try to get a hard drive that spins at 7200 rpm. That type of drive performs better than one running at 5400 rpm.

Note that in the advertisements, these values may be listed as 7200 IDE and 5400 IDE. The IDE part refers to how the drives interface electronically with the motherboard — technical stuff.

Many technical values are associated with disk drives. Try not to get mired in the access time or transfer rate or anything else. Those values are trivial with respect to day-to-day operations; the differences among them are laughable (unless you're an engineer, of course, and you laugh only at ionization jokes).

CD-ROM drive speed

Unlike with hard drives, the speed of a CD-ROM drive is measured in terms of X. For example, you can have a 40X CD-ROM drive or a 52X CD-ROM drive.

The X is the number of times faster the drive is than the original computer CD-ROM drive. That drive, which is the same speed as a standard music CD player, was 1X. The next-generation drives could read data twice as fast and were dubbed 2X. And so on, and so on.

For example, if you see a 52X drive advertised, you now know in your computer-buying wisdom that the CD-ROM drive is a whopping 52 times faster than the piddly old original CD-ROM drive.

When a gigabyte is not a gigabyte

Hard drive capacity is measured in gigabytes, but the values that are used are deceptive. If you refer to Table 6-1, in Chapter 6, you see that a gigabyte is approximately 1 billion bytes of storage. Specifically, a gigabyte is 1,099,511,627,776 bytes. So, you would think that a 40GB hard drive would be 40 × 1,099,511,627,776 bytes — but it's not!

A 40GB hard drive is approximately 38,147MB. No, they're not cheating you. What the hard drive manufacturers do is take the literal value,

40 billion bytes, and not 40 × 1,099,511,627,776 bytes. So, a hard drive that can store 40 billion bytes has a capacity of just over 38GB.

Because all hard drive manufacturers pull the same type of calculation when stating their drives' capacities, no one is getting ripped off here. After you get your new computer home and notice that your 80GB hard drive doesn't really add up to 80 "true" gigabytes of storage, you'll know why.

CD-R drives have two X numbers, such as 52/32. The higher number, often listed first, is the speed at which data can be read. The lower number is the speed at which the drive can write information. To put this concept in practical terms, to record an hour's worth of music on a CD-R that can write at 32X takes just under two minutes. (That's 32 times faster than 1X, which takes one hour to write one hour's worth of music.)

CD-R/RW drives have a third X number, which is the speed at which the RW drives are written to. This number is different from the CD-R value because CD-RW discs are written to in a different manner from CD-R discs.

Cache or buffer memory

Another thing to look for in a hard drive is the cache memory.

The *cache* is a supplemental storage place on the drive, composed of a given amount of memory (special memory, not regular computer RAM). That memory is used to speed up the drive by storing often-read information in the cache memory. Reading the information from cache memory rather than from the disk itself can markedly increase the hard drive's performance.

The larger the cache memory on a disk drive, the better. A hard drive should have, at minimum, a 2MB cache. Top-of-the-line models may have as much as 16MB of cache memory. That's good.

Looking for a hard drive deal?

If you have money to throw, throw it at everything. Most of us aren't loaded, though, and have to face some tough buying decisions. Fortunately, I can relate a secret tip to you when it comes to getting a great deal on a hard drive.

The best value for a hard drive comes from the models two or three notches lower than the highest-capacity model. For example, rather than buy a top-of-the-line, high-capacity 300GB drive, consider a 100GB or 80GB drive as a better value. With the 300GB drive, you're paying more for leading-edge technology. On a dollar-per-megabyte scale, two 150GB drives may end up being a better deal.

> ✔ Cache is pronounced "cash."
>
> ✔ A hard drive cache may also be called buffer memory or just buffer.
>
> ✔ Other disk drives may also use cache memory. Again: More is better.

Bottom line: The higher the value for cache memory, the better.

The mystical drive controller

Nothing really plugs into anything else inside a computer. No, there are rules to be followed, protocols to be obeyed, and an interface to actually make the connection. The keyword for disk drives is *interface*, which is a $100 business word that means "to talk or exchange information." For example, "Larry cannot interface with the elevator" means that Larry doesn't know how to push the buttons.

With a disk drive, the interface is how the disk drive itself communicates with the rest of the computer. The interface is merely a clutch of electronics. The disk drive uses the interface to talk with the microprocessor, chipset, and other interesting parts of the computer.

Fortunately for you, hard drives now use the standard ATA interface or some variant of it. This means that you have nothing more to think about regarding how your hard drive connects to the computer. Whew! That's one less thing to know, but still know that this *disk drive controller* helps connect the disk drives to the computer's main circuitry, or motherboard.

Even more confusing disk drive terms!

Computer jargon is endless. Don't be surprised when the following disk drive terms visually assault you:

Form factor: This term is merely a description of the disk drive's physical dimensions. Each computer console has room for different-size drives. For example, you may have a spare half-height drive bay in your G5 Mac. You would need a half-height drive to fill that bay. That's the form factor in action. (This issue is obviously one you can refer to your dealer.)

IDE: This acronym, which stands for Integrated Drive Electronics, refers to the way the drive communicates with the chipset on the motherboard. Fortunately, pretty much all hard drives are now IDE types, so IDE is nothing to worry about it.

RAID: This acronym means, basically, a whole stack of hard drives — like a stack of pancakes.

Each hard drive mirrors information on the other drives, which means that information is rarely, if ever, lost. This type of hard drive setup is used only in mission-critical applications or for servers. Individual computer buyers need not concern themselves with RAID drives (they're too spendy, for one).

Head: In addition to being the froth at the top of a sloppily poured beer, a *head* on a disk drive is the device that reads and writes information. It's also called a floating head or flying head.

Serial ATA (SATA): This new disk drive interface standard has techy rules and such for determining how the drive talks to the rest of the computer. If possible, get this type of disk drive interface; wish the others only on your worst enemies.

Disk Driving Your Computer System

When you get your computer, you most likely get three disk drives in it:

- ✔ A hard drive
- ✔ A CD-ROM or DVD drive (or both)
- ✔ A floppy drive

That configuration should cover every possible disk drive need.

This section goes into more detail about each type of disk device and describes some additional decision-making thought processes and options.

DVD drives can read CD discs, so if your new computer has a DVD drive, you don't need a second CD drive — unless you want one (or a CD-R/RW drive) for the heck of it.

Things that fill up a hard drive

Your computer's operating system takes up room, as do your applications and, of course, the data you create. Generally speaking, such basic things occupy only a small slice of the hard drive pie. These items really consume disk storage:

Computer games: These programs take up lots of disk space, thanks to their 3D graphics and sounds.

Graphics: Individual graphics files aren't that big. A whole vacation's worth of pictures can take up anywhere from one to dozens of megabytes of disk space depending on the image's resolution. As you make the switch from old-fashioned

photography to digital, those megabytes add up quickly.

Music (MP3) files: If you're into storing music files on your computer, be prepared for them to take up lots of room. In fact, if this area is your thing, consider a PC with *two* hard drives, with one specifically dedicated to your music.

Video: Worse than music files, video files take up huge amounts of storage. If you're into video editing or just watching, you need lots of room. Again, consider a second hard drive specifically for your videos.

No, you don't really need a floppy drive, but you don't save any money by not having one included. A typical floppy drive may cost your dealer $10, which isn't much when you consider the entire cost of the computer.

Picking a hard drive

All personal computers must have at least one hard drive. You can compare speed and other trivia, but the real meat on the plate is the hard drive's capacity. You want to ensure that your new computer has enough hard drive storage for all your computer software as well as all the stuff you create and store there.

Part III of this book tells you how to determine the amount of hard drive storage you need. Generally speaking, you probably need anywhere from 10GB to 30GB of storage. Most computers are now typically sold with a hard drive well above that range, but be aware that you can order a computer with an even larger hard drive. Or, heck, order a computer with *two* hard drives. The manufacturers and dealers are flexible, as long as you have the moolah to pay for it.

✔ Your computer needs at least one hard drive.

✔ Beware! Some shifty dealers may advertise a computer without a hard drive! They do that to knock a few dollars off the purchase price and make their stuff appear competitively priced. Don't buy anything from those people!

- ✔ Some smaller systems, such as game machines and handhelds, don't require a hard drive. Instead, they use special memory to store information. In the case of game systems, storage sometimes takes the form of memory cartridges, which plug into the game's console.

- ✔ As with memory, you can always add more hard drives to your computer. The only limitation is the space inside *and* outside your computer.

- ✔ Laptop hard drives are very small and very expensive. Generally, you cannot add a second hard drive to a laptop internally, but you can add an external hard drive, a PCMCIA storage device, or a flash memory card to expand the laptop's storage capacity. My advice: Get a large hard drive in your laptop in the first place.

- ✔ Avoid buying any computer with less than a 20GB hard drive. Although those smaller sizes were popular a few years back, they're just not beefy enough to hold today's software.

- ✔ The first IBM PC was sold without a hard drive. The IBM PC/XT, introduced in 1983, came with a 10MB hard drive. Yes, that was considered oodles of storage space back then.

Your shiny, removable storage

The second most popular disk drive in your new computer is the read-only removable drive. In human terms: the CD-ROM or DVD drive. Either one is a must on any new system, with the emphasis on getting a DVD drive if you possibly can.

Why worry about hard drive size now when you can upgrade later?

Oops! Bad-Thinking Department: The whole idea behind this book is that you get the computer you want *when you buy it.* Sure, you can upgrade a computer later. That's one of the nifty things about the computer. Today's computers are easy and inexpensive to upgrade. But, if you make the right decision when you buy, you don't have to worry about upgrading later.

For the hard drive, the idea is to buy a nice, roomy hard drive when you get your computer — one that will store all your junk for years to come without your worrying about upgrading. Pay attention when you find out, later in this book, how to calculate disk storage. Don't let a dealer sell you short, either: Buy all the disk storage you need with the computer. Buy now, not later.

CD-ROM and DVD drives handle read-only media. That means that you can only read from the disks; you cannot store information there, like you can with a hard drive. That may sound like a gyp, but the truth is that lots of stuff you get for the computer is read-only. (If you need to write information, you can always use the hard drive.)

Another alternative is to get two drives: a CD-R/RW drive and a DVD drive. Or, better, get a combination CD-R/RW and DVD drive that can read DVD discs and both read and write CDs.

- ✔ Your computer should come with at least one CD-ROM drive. You need one.

- ✔ A great reason to get a DVD and CD-R/RW combo drive when you buy your computer is that the manufacturer sets up and configures everything. If you buy or upgrade after the sale, it's more of an ordeal to get the new hardware to work with your system.

- ✔ You cannot write information to a standard CD-ROM or DVD drive. It's read-only, which is the *RO* in CD-ROM: Compact Disc, Read-Only Memory. CD-R/RW and DVD-R drives can, however, create discs.

- ✔ You buy special discs to use a CD-R/RW or DVD-R drive. Furthermore, special software must be used to prepare a CD-R, CD-R/W, or DVD-RAM disc for writing. The software usually comes with the drive and can be used to create music or video discs.

- ✔ Oh, yes, you can play musical CDs on your computer (as long as your computer has speakers so that you can hear the music). A special program is required, although it should come with your computer or the operating system.

To floppy or not to floppy?

The floppy drive is no longer a requirement for all desktop computers. For years now, laptop computers haven't come with floppy drives. The computer maker Apple hasn't sold new computers with floppy drives for years.

Floppy drives are common on PCs, but are rapidly turning into the system's version of the human appendix. Like Apple, some PC manufacturers have gotten rid of the floppy drive as a standard feature; even so, they still offer the drive as an option. My advice: Why bother?

In only one instance do you need a floppy drive: if you're upgrading from a computer system that already has a floppy drive *and* you use and need that floppy drive. If so, get a floppy for your new PC. Otherwise, it's one less thing to pay for and worry about.

More DVD suffixes than you would care to know about

CD-ROM drives are simple. You want to write your own CD with a CD-R drive, where the R stands for *r*ecordable. You want a CD-R you can erase? Get a CD-RW drive, which is *r*ewritable. It's simple — even more so because CD-R/RW drives can do both operations at one time.

On the DVD side, however, things are a bit more confusing. Many formats are available for writing DVD discs, some of which are utterly incompatible with DVD players. Basically, it boils down to the plus or minus.

On the plus side are the DVD+R, DVD+RW, and DVD+R/RW formats. The minus side has the

DVD-R, DVD-RW, and DVD-R/RW formats. Rumor has it that the plus format is faster for a computer to read and write, but the minus format is more compatible with video DVD players.

At this point, the standards aren't anything to worry about. If you need to create DVD discs, just pick whichever standard your video software recommends. If compatibility concerns you, you can get one of the many drives that can read and write in a variety of standards. For example, a drive made by Sony — for a premium in price — reads and writes *all* DVD formats.

Digital media or flash memory drives

You should consider two types of digital media, or flash memory, drives for your PC system:

- ✔ A transportable drive, such as a USB flash drive or Jump disk
- ✔ A drive that can read your digital camera's media card

The transportable drive is a relatively new thing. About the size of a key chain, this solid-state drive plugs into the USB port that's found on most desktop and laptop computers. When the solid-state drive is plugged in, it gives your computer another 256MB to 8GB of removable storage. This type of drive provides a great way to move information between computers.

Digital media card readers are provided primarily for compatibility with a digital camera or PDA. For example, my digital camera uses the popular CompactFlash card. Using a special adapter, I can plug the CompactFlash card from my digital camera directly into my computer and access the pictures without the mess of tangly cables.

Similarly, the SecureDigital card can be used to share information between the Palm handheld computer and a desktop computer, as long as the desktop has a SecureDigital card reader.

Some devices, called *card readers,* accept a variety of flash memory media. These devices typically attach to a desktop or laptop computer by using the USB cable. They provide slots or connectors for a variety of flash media drives. Card readers make an excellent purchase along with your new computer system or as an after-purchase.

- ✔ Flash memory cards retain their contents even when they're unplugged. They don't require batteries or any other power source. When they're plugged in, they draw their power from the computer itself.

- ✔ Some USB flash memory drives require the USB 2.0 port (or better). Ensure that your new computer supports the proper USB standard for the flash memory you plan to use.

- ✔ See Chapter 10 for more information on USB ports.

Chapter 8

Monitor and Graphics Stuff

- -

- -

Computer monitors and graphics get far more attention than they deserve, probably because it's the monitor you see in the store. It's flashy. It's eye-catching. "Ooo! Look at the fish!" But this type of display can be misleading because there's much more to computer graphics than the monitor.

Fortunately, monitors are pretty basic, and choosing one isn't that tough. The other part of the computer graphics equation is the *graphics adapter* or *video card*, the hardware that controls the monitor. That topic can get a little technical, but not really tempestuous. This chapter helps erase any smudges from your graphical journey.

The Graphical System

All computers have two parts to their graphical systems: the monitor on the outside and the graphics adapter on the inside.

The monitor lives outside the computer. It's the part you see, the TV-set thing. Or, in the case of game consoles, it's a real TV. For most computers, laptops, and handheld computers, the monitor is what displays information.

The graphics adapter dwells inside the computer console. It's the circuitry that *drives* the monitor, by controlling how and where the information is displayed. See? The monitor is the dumb part because it requires another piece of hardware — the graphics adapter — to do the work, kind of like an actor requiring a writer, though very few computer monitors get to chat with Larry King.

- ✔ When you buy a computer, you need both a monitor and a graphics adapter.
- ✔ The graphics adapter is also called a video card.
- ✔ Laptops and handhelds come with the monitor built in.
- ✔ Most laptops let you connect an external monitor, either when using the laptop as a desktop system or when doing a presentation.

The Monitor Part

No personal computer is complete without a monitor. You need one. It's a choice you must make, though some computer models, such as the iMac and all laptops and handhelds, have the monitor included. Otherwise, the monitor is a thing you must select at the time of purchase.

All computer monitors sold now are color. All of them are technically similar with only a few variations (see the nearby sidebar "Mysterious monitor measurements"). The only decisions you need to make about a monitor are its size and whether to go with the traditional glass CRT monitor or one of the snazzy new flat-LCD displays.

- ✔ My best advice for judging a monitor is to look at it in the store. See whether you like the way it displays colors.
- ✔ Most stores have graphics or animation running on their demonstration monitors. Ask to view a document to better judge the image quality. Is the text crisp?
- ✔ You don't need to buy the same brand of monitor as your computer console. If you want, you can buy the monitor separately, in which case they knock a few dollars off the computer purchase price. Be aware, however, that buying the same brand of monitor is usually cheaper because of volume discounts offered by the manufacturer.

- ✔ Beware of computers advertised without a monitor. Because you need a monitor, you must add its cost to the computer purchase.
- ✔ What you see on the glassy part of the monitor is the *screen,* or *display.* The term *monitor* refers to the hardware itself.
- ✔ No, you cannot use your TV set as a monitor for your computer. Although TV sets are good for watching TV, their resolution isn't good enough for viewing computer information.

✔ A game console is geared for using a TV set as its monitor. The WebTV adapter also lets you use a TV as a monitor. These are the two exceptions to the preceding point.

✔ A few handheld computers have monochrome (noncolor) screens, which usually display several shades of gray. For most handheld computers, this is just fine. The color displays generally add a few dollars to the handheld's price.

CRT or LCD?

Nothing introduces you to the time-honored computer theme of using three-letter acronyms (TLAs) better than computer graphics. For the hardware, fortunately, only two TLAs are worth knowing: CRT and LCD. These terms describe the two basic types of monitors now available.

CRT stands for *cathode ray tube*, which is the glass part of any traditional TV set or computer monitor, as beautifully illustrated in Figure 8-1. The advantage of CRT monitors is that they're inexpensive. The disadvantages are that they take up a great deal of desk space and are bulkier, heavier, and not as energy efficient as LCD monitors. Still, that "cheap" aspect weighs in favor with most computer buyers, so they go with the traditional CRT monitor.

Figure 8-1:
A typical
CRT
monitor.

LCD stands for *liquid crystal display*, which is the new flat-screen monitor that's all the rage, as shown in Figure 8-2. These monitors are essentially the same types that appear on laptop computers, though they're designed for use with a desktop model. LCD monitors are thin, lightweight, and energy saving. Plus, they look very, very cool on your desk. The drawback? They cost more than comparable CRT monitors.

Mysterious monitor measurements

Oh, I could spend all day muttering over the various technical aspects of a computer monitor. Instead, I've jotted down some terms and descriptions that should help you if the need to know arises:

Bandwidth (frequency): The speed at which information is sent from a computer to a monitor, measured in megahertz (MHz). The higher this value, the better (less flickering).

Dot pitch: The distance between each dot (or *pixel*) on the graphics screen (measured from the center of each dot). The closer the dots, the better the image. A dot pitch of 0.28 millimeters is the minimum; smaller values are better.

Interlaced/non-interlaced: The method by which a monitor paints an image on a screen. An interlaced monitor paints the image twice, which tends to cause the image to flicker. What you want is a non-interlaced monitor, which doesn't flicker (as much).

Scan rate: The rate at which a monitor's electron gun paints an image on the screen, as measured in kilohertz (KHz). The higher the scan rate value, the better (again, less flickering).

Figure 8-2:
A typical
LCD
monitor.

- ✔ Both CRT and LCD monitors connect to the same type of graphics adapter plug on the back of your PC.

- ✔ Some high-end LCD monitors sport their own, unique digital graphics adapter. For example, the Apple LCD monitors connect to the digital port on the G5 Macintosh line of computers.

- ✔ Some LCD monitors rotate 90 degrees, which allows you to view them in portrait and landscape modes.

✔ The best way to judge an LCD monitor is to view only *text* on the screen. Don't be fooled at the store by fancy graphics displays, which always look stunning. The true test is viewing text, not graphics.

✔ Be sure to check the LCD in a variety of lighting situations. Some monitors cannot be seen in very bright lights. Some monitors cannot be seen from far right or left angles.

✔ Unlike LCD monitors, most CRTs let you display graphics in a variety of resolutions and color settings. LCDs, on the other hand, typically use only a few modes to display things.

✔ CRT monitors emit more radiation than their LCD counterparts, although it's not enough to create a 1950s-era horror movie creature.

✔ Be sure to compare LCD versus CRT at the larger aspect ratios. Some larger LCDs tend to lose their color saturation, whereas larger CRTs don't. Only the Apple Cinema displays seem to hold their color punch at higher resolutions.

✔ Don't confuse LCD with *flat-screen* monitors. All LCDs are flat screen. But a few CRTs have flat picture tubes and are advertised as being flat screen. It's not the same as having an LCD monitor, though the flat-screen CRTs display a nicer image than traditional curved-screen models.

✔ Don't get an LCD if you plan to play fast-action computer games! Generally speaking, LCDs are too slow to update for real-time game action. True gamers use only CRT monitors.

✔ Another area where CRT monitors are better than LCD is in high-end graphics. A CRT monitor can better render color images than an LCD, which has a more limited range of color reproduction.

LCD AWOL pixels

Unlike a CRT monitor, an LCD monitor creates its image by having millions of individual pixels on the screen — like tiny red, green, and blue lights. Although this technique produces a much sharper, less-flickering image than a CRT, the odds are really good that some pixels may arrive "dead" on your monitor.

A dead pixel on an LCD screen can be obvious or obscure. I have two on my 18-inch Mitsubishi monitor. They show up well only when the screen is blank; one pixel is green, and the other is red. Normally, however, I don't notice them.

Some of the better monitors don't have any dead pixels; I have yet to see a dead pixel on an Apple LCD display.

How many dead pixels are okay? It depends on the monitor manufacturer's warranty. For my Mitsubishi monitor, it's 12 pixels. Any more and I could get the monitor replaced. If you get an LCD monitor, first check the warranty to see how many dead pixels are considered okay. Then run a monitor diagnostics program to see whether the monitor has, in fact, any dead pixels. (The diagnostics program comes with the monitor.)

Judge me by my size, will you?

Monitors are measured like TV sets: diagonally in inches, as shown in Figure 8-3.

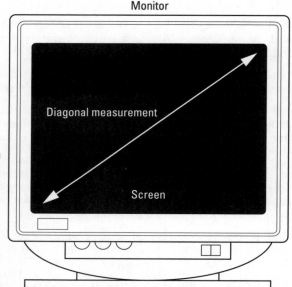

Figure 8-3: How the computer monitor diagonal measurement is made.

A typical monitor measures about 17 inches diagonally. Low-end models measure 15 and 14 inches diagonally. If you want to spoil yourself, consider a 19-inch or larger monitor. Those sizes are nice, but the bigger they are, the more they cost!

✔ Beware! A monitor's diagonal measurement may *not* be the same as its viewing area. On a CRT monitor, the screen size is a few inches smaller than the glass.

✔ LCD monitors have a diagonal measurement that's completely accurate; the screen size and image size are the same. Therefore, a typical 15-inch LCD monitor has roughly the same display area as a 17-inch CRT monitor.

✔ Large monitors are *very nice.* I bought one on a whim and now have *three* of them!

✔ If you're vision impaired, a 21-inch monitor is the answer to your prayers! It shows text nice and big.

I'll take two, please

Both the Macintosh and PC have the ability to support more than one monitor at a time. It sounds crazy, but by adding a second monitor, you greatly increase the amount of screen real estate available for your programs. Graphics mavens and folks into video editing love this type of setup.

- ✔ If you plan to use a second monitor, consider adding it later as an upgrade. Even so, a few dealers offer computer systems with two or more monitors out of the box.

- ✔ Although you can plug a second monitor into the iMac, doing so doesn't let you use both monitors at one time. Because of that, the iMac is an exception to the two-monitor rule. Other Macs, however, can have multiple monitors installed.

- ✔ A second monitor on a PC requires a second graphics adapter (hardware) as well as a version of Windows that supports the second monitor (software). When you select a graphics adapter, ensure that it's dual-monitor-capable. Also ensure that the version of Windows you get supports two monitors.

- ✔ Each monitor requires its own graphics adapter; however, some dual-monitor adapters run two monitors from a single adapter.

- ✔ Better than two monitors, consider getting just a single large-screen monitor. For example, two 17-inch monitors display just as much information as a 23-inch monitor, and the larger monitor may be cheaper than buying the two-monitor setup.

The Graphics Adapter Part

The graphics adapter (or *card*) is the part of your graphics system that lives inside the console. The card controls the image that's displayed on the monitor's screen. This type of device, though buried in your computer's bosom, is rendered in Figure 8-4 for entertainment purposes only.

Several yardsticks measure graphics cards. The most important is whether the graphics adapter is a separate card or piece of circuitry, or whether the graphics circuitry is simply part of the chipset on the motherboard. Either way, the two values by which the graphics adapter is judged is how much video RAM it can access and whether it has any high-end functions, such as 3D ability or its own graphics processing unit (GPU).

For graphics adapter cards (not part of the motherboard), another aspect to judge is the interface — whether the card plugs into a PCI or AGP slot. More on this in a few pages.

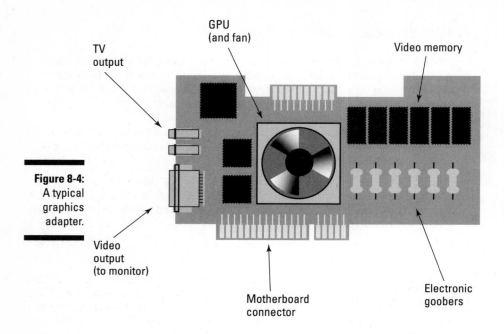

Figure 8-4:
A typical
graphics
adapter.

Video RAM

Video memory is special memory (RAM) used to help your PC's graphics controller display lots of colors and high-resolution graphics. The more video memory the graphics adapter has, the better — and more expensive — your graphics card.

✔ The minimum quantity of video RAM is 32MB. Avoid anything lower unless you're just utterly not interested in graphics.

✔ More video RAM is better — and more expensive. I've seen graphics cards with up to 640MB of graphics memory. Golly!

✔ The best way to find out how much video RAM you need? Check with your software! Fussy graphics and game software tells you *right there on the box* how much video RAM you need.

✔ Video RAM is called *VRAM*. Refer to Chapter 6 for more memory information.

✔ If graphics is your thing — if, for example, you're planning on playing games or working with graphics (not just viewing them) — avoid a computer advertised with "shared graphics memory." Although that's an okay option for typical computer use (browsing the Web or word processing), it's not acceptable for anything beyond.

How it plugs in

A hot graphics adapter may be the most prized part of your computer purchase, but make sure that it can plug into your new computer! The third thing you need to look for in a graphics adapter is its interface. Two types are available:

 ✔ **AGP:** This type of graphics adapter is the one you crave. It's meat on the bone! AGP stands for Accelerated Graphics Port, the fastest video interface available. Your computer's motherboard must have an AGP connector to use this type of card.

 ✔ **PCI:** If your computer lacks an AGP, you plug the graphics adapter into a PCI slot inside the computer case. PCI stands for Peripheral Component Interconnect (try saying that while chewing cauliflower). It's still a worthwhile way to connect a graphics adapter to your computer, but just not as good as AGP.

Some computers have built-in graphics adapters. In those cases, you can disable the internal components and add an AGP or PCI graphics adapter (if that type of slot is available inside the box). That's an easy way to upgrade your system without having to use a screwdriver or blowtorch.

 ✔ Not all computers come with an AGP connector on the motherboard.

 ✔ Special, proprietary connectors are also available, such as the digital display connector on Apple G5 computers. Some proprietary connectors may be sold with the monitor.

 ✔ For more information on AGP and PCI, see Chapter 10.

The GPU

For the longest time, graphics adapters would rely on the computer's microprocessor to do most of the dirty work. Then, along came 3D graphics, which required special chips on the graphics adapter. Then, finally, the graphics card makers gave up and decided to create a microprocessor just for graphics. The result is the GPU, or graphics *p*rocessing *u*nit.

 ✔ Only the truly high-end graphics cards sport a GPU. You pay extra for it, but if graphics are your thing, you will be pleased.

 ✔ Obviously, getting a graphics adapter with a GPU and only a paltry amount of memory would be silly. If you're going to splurge on the GPU, get the 512MB or 640MB graphics adapter. Be a sport!

Graphics cards for real video

You can't walk into a movie any more without wondering how much of it is computer generated and how much is real. Computer graphics (CG) are pretty common in Hollywood. And, on your computer? Real graphics are getting more and more common too.

It's entirely possible to hook your computer up to a videocamera, VCR, or television to record, edit, play, and save your own videos. If that's what you're after, you should consider another few goodies for your new computer.

First, remember that all your hardware requirements are dictated by your software. Following this book's five steps, you need to first look for your video-editing software. After you find that, the box lists recommended hardware. If any special graphics adapter is required, it's listed.

Second, mostly what you need in order to work with real-life video on a computer is some way to get the video *out* of the computer and into the real world. To make this possible, many video adapters come with video decoding ability and *video out* connectors (also called RCA jacks). If video editing is a path you're considering, you should add this type of connector to your wish list for a graphics adapter.

Life on the high end

After the dust settles, only two standards exist for graphics adapters:

- ✔ Radeon (from ATI)
- ✔ GeForce (from NVIDIA)

Both these graphics adapter standards sport high-powered GPUs, lots of memory, 3D technology, and supercomputer speed.

I cannot recommend one over the other, though your software will certainly tell you which it likes better. If games are your thing, chalk up which games enjoy which graphics adapter best, and then go with that model.

When You're Reading an Advertisement, Beware the Blech!

Sometimes, the way a PC graphics card is described in a computer ad can drive you nuts. You may find Voodoo and Rage and other, often strange monikers. Hey! Relax. It's all marketing mustard, a tangy bit of spice spread over the dull circuitry to give the kids something to boast about during recess.

Outside of games, high-end video production, or serious graphics editing, the main thing you need to pay attention to is the amount of video memory the card has. Avoid anything less than 32MB of video RAM. Try to avoid "shared" video memory systems.

A few graphics acronyms are also used to describe the abilities of the graphics adapters. These acronyms were important standards in the early days of the personal computer, but now they're merely marketing mustard; feel free to ignore them.

Use any other technical mumbo jumbo for comparison only. When in doubt, refer to your software. It informs you of any special graphics needs.

It isn't really a problem when the graphics adapter is part of the motherboard. Remember that you can always upgrade later.

Chapter 9

Keyboard, Mouse, and Gamepad

I call them input devices. They're the gizmos you use to "speak" with the computer. Although it would be great to just talk to the computer the same way that Mr. Spock did on *Star Trek*, computer systems just aren't there yet. To make up for their lack of years, a slew of input devices are offered to help you express your desires to the computer.

The main input device for a computer is the keyboard. Closely following the keyboard, and especially necessary for today's graphical computing environments, is the computer mouse. There's also the gamepad or joystick, which helps with that all-important activity of playing games on the computer.

I admit that most people don't give a second thought to the keyboard or mouse included with a computer, but you really do have a choice. Many fancier dealers and manufacturers offer several brands. And, you can always buy a better keyboard or mouse after your purchase. This chapter takes you on the tour, complete with pictures.

✔ The only time you're truly limited in your keyboard or mouse choices is with laptop or handheld computers. With those, you take what they give you.

✔ Some handheld computers use a *stylus* — essentially, a plastic stick — as their only input device.

Clackity-Clack-Clack Goes the Keyboard

Keyboards allow you to "talk" to your computer. They're a necessary part of any computer system, and as such, the keyboard usually comes in the same box as the computer console. Despite this pairing, you still have a choice when it comes to keyboards.

Most computer manufacturers and dealers give you the option of choosing your own kind of keyboard. You can opt for the traditional keyboard, the standard 105-key keyboard. Or, you can select from among a number of options and a variety of different keyboard types.

Over in Chapter 2, you can see the fancy Microsoft Natural keyboard, designed to be easier on your wrists than standard computer keyboards. Keyboards like this one are available for both PC and Macintosh computers.

Another keyboard option you may consider is going wireless. The new wireless keyboards have the advantage of not being tethered to the computer by a too-short cable. With a wireless keyboard, you can sit back in your chair with the keyboard on your lap and type at your leisure (assuming that you can still see the screen).

✔ Keyboard selection is a personal thing. You may want to wait until after your computer purchase to get a fancy keyboard. Unlike other computer hardware, keyboards can be easily replaced at any time.

✔ Macintosh and PC keyboards are different. If you're going to buy a keyboard separately from your computer, make sure that it matches your computer choice.

✔ A USB keyboard works with any Macintosh or PC that has a USB port. See Chapter 10 for more information on USB ports.

✔ The iMac uses a USB keyboard. If you buy a replacement, make sure that it's a USB keyboard designed for the iMac.

✔ Handheld and palmtop computers have built-in keyboards or touch pads, which is part of their charm. Even so, if you need to "type" on this type of computer, you can get optional keyboards.

✔ Game consoles use gamepads or controllers rather than keyboards.

✔ If you're getting a wireless keyboard, consider also getting a wireless mouse. Sometimes, both are sold together in a package at considerable savings.

✔ Aside from ergonomic variations, some keyboards come with special features: built-in speakers, clocks, USB hubs, calculators, touch pads or built-in mouselike controllers, and biometric thumbprint ID pads.

✔ Some keyboards come with specialty buttons — for example, buttons to instantly connect you to the Internet or pick up your e-mail. Keep in mind that these buttons are *not* part of a standard computer setup and they require special software to perform their various functions.

✔ Before personal computers became popular, computer terminals had these incredible keyboards. They had the basic keyboard layout on a typewriter and a number of specific function keys. Some terminals even had keys that said Insert Line, Move Block, Close File, and Get Me Cola. These days, computer keyboards are a little more conservative.

Special keys to look for on laptop computer keyboards

Everything on a laptop is smaller than its desktop counterpart, and that includes the keyboard. Although the keyboard's main layout on a laptop is approximately the same size as a desktop computer's, a key's *travel* (up and down movement) is less. The keyboard may have an embedded numeric keypad, and some of the cursor-movement keys — such as Page Up, Page Down, Home, and End — may be found in unusual locations.

One special key that blesses the laptop's keyboard is the Fn, or function, key. It serves to activate secondary functions on certain keys. Usually, the Fn key and those special functions are color coded. For example, the Fn key and the special function icons may all be blue. That scheme means that you press the Fn key in combination with those special keys.

The types of special Fn keys that are available are important. As an all-in-one unit, those special

keys should perform the following functions, and the more, the better:

- ✔ Turn the volume control up or down, or mute it.

- ✔ Turn the screen brightness up or down or the contrast up or down.

- ✔ Activate Sleep mode.

- ✔ Eject the CD or DVD media.

- ✔ Activate the external monitor (for presentations).

- ✔ Enable or disable wireless networking.

- ✔ Activate the keyboard light.

You may see additional Fn features, depending on your laptop's make and model and its features.

Pointing Devices

Thanks to today's modern graphical operating systems, your computer also needs what's generically called a *pointing device*. It's a required form of input device; you just cannot use a computer without one.

Eeek!

The most common type of pointing device is the mouse. Chapter 2 illustrates the traditional, typical Microsoft mouse, which comes with most PC computers.

Nearly every desktop computer now sold comes with a mouse. As with the keyboard, you don't have to settle for the mouse that comes with your computer. Your computer dealer or manufacturer may have a selection for you, and you can always buy a replacement after the computer purchase.

- ✔ Computer mice scurry along your desktop, just as real mice scurry along the kitchen floor and frighten the bejeezus out of people.

- ✔ The standard PC mouse is the Microsoft mouse, though other manufacturers, especially Logitech, are more creative with their mice.

- ✔ As the computer mouse, or pointing device, is moved along the desktop, a mouse pointer or arrow moves in a similar manner on the computer screen.

- ✔ Some PC mice plug into a PC's mouse port. Otherwise, most mice use a USB port to connect to the computer, which means that they can be used by any desktop computer system — PC or Mac.

- ✔ You can always upgrade to a newer, better mouse after your computer purchase.

- ✔ The plural of *computer mouse* is *computer mice,* though you need only one mouse for your computer.

Optical mice versus mechanical mice

Two main types of computer mice exist: optical and mechanical. This description refers to how the mouse determines when it's being moved.

The optical mouse is better because it uses an electronic eye to detect movement. This mouse can be used on any nonreflective surface, and it's much easier to clean and maintain than a mechanical mouse. Alas, it's also more expensive.

Mechanical mice are cheaper than optical mice. This type of mouse detects movement by using a rolling ball. It requires a special type of surface for the ball to get a proper grip, which is why I recommend getting and using a mousepad with a mechanical mouse.

- ✔ Optical mice require less desktop space than mechanical mice do.

- ✔ If you're into games, I recommend testing the optical mouse for reliability before you commit to using it for game control. Although the mouse works, its optical sensor may have a tendency to make the mouse pointer "jump" at times, which isn't helpful when your little man is in a firefight with mutant members of the Space Marines.

✔ A *mouse pad* is a small piece of fabric, roughly the size of a 14-inch computer monitor, but flat, like a rubber mat. The texture on top of the pad is ideal for rolling around a mechanical mouse.

Wireless mice versus wired mice

The latest trend in computing is wireless *everything!* Although that mostly applies to computer networking, wireless mice are also available. Two types of wireless mice are available: RF and infrared. *RF* stands for *radio frequency*; that type of mouse uses a low-powered radio signal to communicate with a base station, or hub, connected (by wire) to the computer. The *infrared* mouse uses infrared light to communicate with the base station, similar to the infrared light a remote uses to control a TV, VCR, or DVD player.

Between RF and infrared, I recommend the RF type of wireless mouse. Because the infrared mouse may require a line of site to its base station, a cluttered desk or something large, like a book, in front of the base station may interfere with the mouse's signal. That's not a problem with the RF type of mouse.

✔ Note that both types of wireless mouse require batteries. Standard flashlight batteries work well, but ensure that you have a steady supply. (Costco and Sam's Club usually have the best deals on AA batteries.)

✔ If you're into Bluetooth at all, definitely consider getting and using a Bluetooth-happy wireless mouse. Note that the computer must be Bluetooth compatible for Bluetooth wireless devices to work.

✔ A rechargeable wireless mouse is highly recommended — especially if the recharging unit also serves as a "cradle" for the mouse when you're not using it.

✔ The cradle also helps you find the mouse in a hurry when you need it; cordless mice do tend to wander.

The mouse wears buttons

The computer mouse isn't truly useful unless it has one or more buttons on its back. The button is how you *click* the mouse to select an object on the screen or perform a number of other useful graphical duties.

The minimum number of buttons on a computer mouse is one; the Macintosh's mouse has only one button. (However, computer guru Ted Nelson claims that the Mac's mouse has *four* buttons, three of which are on the keyboard.)

The standard PC mouse has two buttons: a right and left.

The new mouse craze is the Microsoft IntelliMouse. It has a third button, or *wheel,* between the standard left and right buttons. As with all hardware, however, to make the best use of it, you need software that works with it.

Some mice have even more buttons, including buttons for navigating the Internet or other special duties.

Nonmousy pointing devices

The variety of computer mice is seemingly endless. You can choose among trackballs or upside-down mice, mice that work when you hold them in the air, pen mice, tablet mice, and a host of other mice. See how they run? *Ahem!*

The most common alternative, or specialty, computer mouse is the trackball mouse. Often called the upside-down mouse, a *trackball* has a large, easily manipulated ball on top; it doesn't roll around on your desktop. Artists and graphical types love this type of mouse because it offers more control over the mouse pointer on the screen than traditional, handheld mice.

Then again, graphical artist types also love the electric pen and tablet, which is more like traditional painting than using any type of computer mouse. This mouse setup is ideal, especially if your graphics software can detect "pen pressure" when you paint with the mouse pen.

Finally, the oddest mouse I've ever seen is one that works as you hold it in the air. It works more like a laser pointer: You manipulate the mouse arrow on-screen by pointing the mouse at the arrow and moving it. Very strange.

Gamepads (Joysticks)

They look at you funny these days when you call it a joystick. That term just implies too much fun for the serious-minded computer gamer. No, they're *gamepads* now, or *game controllers*. Even the early IBM PC documentation referred to the joystick connection on the back of the computer as an "analog-to-digital port." How stuffy.

The variety of gamepads available these days is almost endless. There are traditional joysticks; gamepad controllers, such as you would find on a game console; special "gravity" controllers that detect 3D movement in the air; and custom gamepads designed to look like car steering wheels, complete with foot pedals or yokes for use with flight simulator games. (It's amazing what you can find when you visit a game software store.)

The traditional joystick — no longer does it resemble the simple X-Y digital joystick of decades past. Joysticks now look like they belong in a fighter jet rather than on your desktop. They have buttons, "hat" switches, swivels, locks, and all sorts of amazing doodads to flip, pull, and throw (see Figure 9-1).

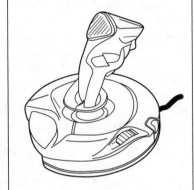

Figure 9-1:
A typical, rather tame type of joystick.

Of course, the big question is "Which gamepad do I need?" To pick the perfect gamepad, merely look at the back of the game software box. Sophisticated games sport a list of recommended gamepads or joysticks. Buy one of those listed. If you have more than one game that could use a joystick, choose whichever controller is compatible with (or recommended by) both games.

✔ A gamepad is *not* part of the traditional computer purchase. Generally, you buy it later.

✔ Though your computer may have a joystick port specifically designed to connect the joystick, most gamers now prefer the USB brand of gamepad over the old joystick-port type.

✔ Never rush out and buy a gamepad because it's "cool." Confirm that your software works well with the joystick before buying.

✔ Not all computer games require a gamepad. Many games, in fact, play better with the mouse or a combination of the mouse and keyboard. Quite a few game players become adept at using the keyboard all by itself.

Weird gamepad things to look for

Many computer users are serious about games. I know computer gamesters who rush out to buy and configure a single PC to play a specific game. They're nuts! But, the results are worth it. Plus, they have the inside scoop; so many games have a recommended list of graphics cards, RAM needs, audio specs, and joysticks that it makes putting this type of system together a cinch.

Here are some of the more interesting joystick features you can look for:

Analog versus digital: Serious gamers prefer an analog gamepad, which offers more real-world response than a digital one. Digital joysticks are gauged in absolute measurements. For example, an old digital joystick may register only eight directions, like the standard eight compass directions. But an analog joystick on a gamepad can point in any direction easily.

The base: Some players like to hold the gamepad in their hands. In fact, that's the reason the gamepad succeeded over the traditional joystick: You hold it. Other players prefer the kind of joystick that sits stable on the desktop. If you want that type of joystick, ensure that the base is either heavy enough to do so or that it has suction cups or some other method of keeping the joystick secure while you play.

Force feedback: Some gamepads are designed to provide the realistic sensation of resistance as you pilot your spaceship or zoom around the Indianapolis Motor Speedway. For example, the gamepad "pushes" against you if you try to take a turn too tightly. Or, if you hit a wall, you "feel" that sensation through the gamepad.

HAT switch: I'm sure that HAT is a military term and stands for something. Either that, or it's that the HAT switch is typically mounted on top of a joystick, like a hat. HAT switches are used like a joystick on top of a joystick. In many 3D games, the HAT switch lets you "slide" left and right or up and down. Or, you can use it to position a firing reticule on the screen without changing the player's orientation. Whatever the purpose, having the HAT switch is nice. (Note that some gamepads come with two joysticks, one of which serves the HAT function.)

Programmable buttons: Some gamepads come with extra buttons (I've seen more than 16) that you can assign to specific functions in the game. These buttons come in handy because you can play the game without having to type keyboard commands. Or, by having programmable buttons, you may be able to change the function of many buttons on the gamepad and give yourself control in a way you're more accustomed to.

Chapter 10

Expansion Options

· ·

· ·

One benefit of the personal computer is that it's extremely expandable. That means that you can add new hardware to your computer, both internally and externally, to expand the things your computer can do or allow it to do certain things faster or better. That expandability has been the key to the personal computer's success for more than three decades now. Indeed, computer history is littered with heaps of long-dead computers that lacked expansion options.

This chapter covers computer expansion. It's not a glamorous thing, not flashy like the monitor or high-tech like the microprocessor. Yet, knowing about and having expansion options in your personal computer is the key to whether you can continue using and enjoying your computer in the years to come.

Expanding Your High-Tech Universe by Using Ports

The word *port* may conjure up images of exotic sea ports: dark and damp, reeking of the salty ocean, with huge ships creaking up and down in the water, burdened with cargo mysterious and forbidden. Or, you may think of *port* as in the dessert wine, which can really cap off a fine meal, particularly when someone else is paying. On a computer, however, a port is simply a hole.

A port isn't only the hole; it's the *type* of hole. It's the connector that plugs into the hole. It's the software that controls the hole. And, it's the world of hardware that plugs into the hole.

As with a seaport, having a port in your computer opens up a whole world of communications and connections to devices necessary and exotic. A well-fitted computer must come with a host of ports, able to access the wonderful variety of devices those ports can host.

Here's the list of the most common types of ports on a computer:

- ✔ USB
- ✔ FireWire, or IEEE 1394
- ✔ RJ-45, or Ethernet
- ✔ Printer, or parallel
- ✔ Serial
- ✔ Monitor
- ✔ Keyboard and mouse
- ✔ RJ-11, or modem

This section describes each type of port, whether you need it, and why you would want it.

- ✔ Not every computer needs every type of port. Just a few will do.

- ✔ In fact, in the future, computers may just come with one or two types of ports. One of them will most likely be the USB port, which is proving to be quite popular and versatile.

- ✔ Laptop and handheld computers have their own special ports. See Chapter 14 for more information on laptops.

The USB port

 The most popular and versatile port you can have on a computer is the USB port. *USB,* which stands for Universal Serial Bus, offers a quick and easy method of adding external devices to your computer — plug-in simple, in fact.

The number of USB devices you can add to your computer is almost unlimited. The types of devices are nearly as varied: digital cameras, scanners, gamepads, keyboards, mice, modems, external disk drives, and the list goes on and on.

✔ Get a computer with at least two USB ports.

✔ The current standard for the USB port is known as USB 2.0, or High Speed USB. Ensure that your computer comes with this type of USB port because it's the best way to add and access high-speed USB devices, such as external disk drives and digital video.

✔ Note that some PCs have extra USB ports on the front of their consoles. Sometimes, these ports are hidden by little doors. Their purpose? Game controller connections!

✔ You can add more USB ports to any computer. A USB *hub* can be purchased to add more ports, or, often, some USB devices come with extra ports on them.

✔ Actually, there's a limit on the number of USB devices you can connect to a single computer: 127. But, hey, that's almost unlimited!

✔ On the Mac, you use the USB port to connect your keyboard, mouse, printer, scanner, and any other external devices you may buy; the Mac lacks the specific printer, mouse, and keyboard ports that the PC has.

The FireWire, or IEEE, port

This port has many names. Apple calls it FireWire, and I prefer that name. But, on the PC, you may see it called an IEEE, 1394, High Performance Serial Bus (HPSB), or even I-Link bus. It's all the same name for the same type of hole in your computer.

The *FireWire* port works much like the USB port: You can use it to connect one device after another, expand your system with FireWire hubs, and even plug and unplug FireWire devices without having to turn your computer off and on.

Recently, FireWire has been best put to use for adding external high-speed devices to the Macintosh, primarily external disk drives, plus digital video-cameras and scanners. On the PC, the USB connection can be used for these devices because most PCs don't come with FireWire, nor is it necessary to add FireWire to a PC.

The Ethernet port

Networking is covered in Chapter 12; for now, know that the hole through which the network communicates is a *port,* which deems it worthy enough to be mentioned here.

To network your computer, by connecting it to another computer, to a central hub, or even to a DSL, cable, or satellite modem, you need the same type of port: An *Ethernet port*, or RJ-45 jack. Physically, it looks like a large phone jack, the hole into which you plug a phone cord.

Ethernet ports are more or less standard on all desktop and laptop computers sold now. Even so, I would confirm that your new computer has this type of port. If not, you may have to add an Ethernet (or wireless networking) expansion card to your computer. See Chapter 12 for more information.

The printer port

Shockingly enough, a *printer port* is the hole in the back of your computer where you plug in your printer. That's easy.

- ✔ All PCs have at least one printer port. It's part of the computer console.

- ✔ Macintoshes use the USB port for printing.

- ✔ Eventually, PCs will drop the printer port in favor of a USB port, just like the Macintosh.

- ✔ Handheld computers and game consoles don't need printers. Note that handheld computers that use the Bluetooth wireless standard can print, as long as a Bluetooth connection to a printer is available.

- ✔ The printer port may also be known as a parallel port, EPP/ECP port, or Centronics port. Officially, it's LPT1, which is the old IBM PC designation (and is still used in some remote parts of Windows).

The serial port

The serial port was the original "versatile" computer port. Used primarily with early computer modems, the serial port could also connect a mouse, scanner, printer, or a number of other interesting devices to a computer.

The *serial port* is now generally used to connect an external dial-up modem to a computer. (See Chapter 11 for more information on modems.) The serial port may also be used to connect two computers for file-exchange purposes. And, some PCs still use it to connect a serial computer mouse.

Beyond the simple options I mention, the serial port has really fallen out of favor recently. In fact, in a few years it may vanish from the computer's rear end, replaced by the more efficient USB port.

- ✔ A serial port is no longer required for most PCs. Even so, some desktop model PCs sport two serial ports.

✔ A serial port has two different types of connectors: the smaller 9-pin D-shell connector and the larger 25-pin D-shell connector. Most PCs now use only the smaller 9-pin connectors. If your computer has a larger 25-pin connector, be careful not to confuse that port with the printer port, which also has 25 pins.

✔ The Mac doesn't have a serial port and instead uses the USB port to attach devices.

✔ Serial ports have a variety of different names used to describe them: modem port, COM1 (the old IBM PC name), AUX, mouse port, and RS-232C port.

The monitor port

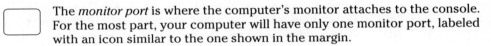

The *monitor port* is where the computer's monitor attaches to the console. For the most part, your computer will have only one monitor port, labeled with an icon similar to the one shown in the margin.

Computers with advanced graphics, however, may sport two monitor ports. One may be clustered with the rest of the computer's ports (USB or printer, for example), and a second may be located in the expansion card area of the computer. If so, use that second monitor port to connect your computer's monitor. That port is more likely the better of the two, powered by a special video graphics adapter and not the video circuitry on the motherboard.

✔ Unlike other ports on the computer, only the monitor plugs into the monitor port.

✔ Digital monitors have special connectors that plug only into digital monitor ports. Don't try to force a digital monitor connector into a standard monitor port.

✔ Special adapters are made to allow standard PC monitors to be used on Macintosh computers. These adapters allow the PC monitor to be plugged into the Mac's monitor port.

✔ Refer to Chapter 8 for more information on computer monitors.

Mouse and keyboard ports

The mouse and keyboard ports are used to — can you guess? — connect a mouse or keyboard to a PC. A computer has one port for each device, and though the ports look the same, they really are different. Obey the labels! The mouse port is for the mouse, and the keyboard port is for the keyboard.

✔ Beyond the keyboard and mouse, nothing else plugs into the keyboard and mouse ports on a PC.

TECHNICAL STUFF

Optional information on infrared ports

Another type of port, found mostly on laptop and other portable computers, is the *infrared (IR)* port. It allows other computers with infrared ports to connect and share data, though it may also be used to connect a computer wirelessly to some device. For this reason, this port isn't considered a standard on most desktop computers. About the only place it's standard is on various handhelds, where the IR port can be used to quickly "beam" information between two systems.

✔ Future PCs will, I hope, abandon the mouse and keyboard ports in favor of the USB port. In fact, if you have a USB mouse and USB keyboard for your PC, you can plug them into USB ports and not even use the specialty mouse and keyboard ports.

Modem port

The *modem port* is where the phone cord plugs into your computer, to allow the modem to communicate with other computers and the Internet. The nerds call it the RJ-11 jack, but you can say "modem port" without shame.

Some modems may have two ports. One is for the line that goes to the wall. That port is marked with the text Line or an icon of a phone jack. The other port is for a telephone you can connect to the modem for making voice calls. That port is marked with the text Phone or the icon of a telephone.

A Full House of Cards

The key to any computer's hardware success is expandability. The old Apple computer triumphed over its peers in the late 1970s because the Apple II could be expanded; inside the computer's case was a row of *expansion slots.* Into those slots, users could plug *expansion cards,* which greatly increased the computer's abilities.

The first IBM PC also had expansion slots, which helped ensure its success. And, though the early Macs lacked expansion slots, pressure from users eventually won Apple over, and the top-of-the-line Mac models sport expansion slots for power users who want them. (The iMac doesn't have expansion slots.)

Why you may need expansion slots

Expansion slots allow you to add new options or features to those that come with a standard computer. The slots aren't as necessary as they were in the past; early IBM PCs lacked such luxurious features as video adapters, serial ports, and even extra memory. You could add all that by plugging in the proper expansion cards.

Computers now often come with everything you need. For example, the iMac has an internal modem and a network adapter and room for more memory. Any further expansion can be added via the USB or FireWire ports. Some power users may want more than that, though, so other computers come with expansion slots.

- ✔ Expansion slots simply increase the flexibility of your computer system.

- ✔ Some low-end home computers or all-in-one systems, like the iMac, are designed for people who need basic computers and, therefore, probably don't need expansion slots. If you need expansion slots, however, steer clear of those systems.

- ✔ For example, if you want to add a network card, a second monitor or video adapter, a satellite modem, a FireWire adapter, a port, an improved sound card, or any of a number of options, your computer needs expansion slots.

- ✔ Expansion cards usually ensure that you can upgrade and improve your system in the years to come.

Types of expansion slots

As with everything else, a computer can't have just one typical expansion slot. After all, technology has vastly improved since the days of Tinker Toys.

For historical and evolutionary reasons, most computers have several different types of expansion slots inside their boxes. Sure, some are better than others. Still, a mixture of several types is generally preferred. Here are the popular ones:

- ✔ **PCI:** This type of expansion slot is the most popular one on both the G5 Macintosh and the PC. The PCI expansion slot connects directly to the computer's microprocessor, which makes it very fast. It stands for Peripheral Component Interconnect, just in case that question comes up on *Jeopardy!*

- ✔ **AGP:** A special slot designed specifically for video adapters (refer to Chapter 8) is the Accelerated Graphics Port, or AGP, slot. Although PCI video adapters are available, if your computer has an AGP port, you're better off buying and using an AGP video adapter.

✔ **ISA:** The original slot found on the first IBM PC is still around, mostly because ISA expansion cards are still with us. In fact, ISA isn't really an acronym for anything; it stands for Industry Standard Architecture, which is just a TLA (three-letter acronym) for "what everyone uses."

Which type of expansion slots should you have? Well, supposing that you want a computer with plenty of expansion slots, I recommend three to five (or more) PCI slots. PCs (not Macs) may also have one or two ISA slots for backward compatibility (though they're optional). And, having an AGP slot is nice if you want to use the latest, greatest video adapters (on the PC).

✔ Computer memory once plugged into expansion cards. Computers are now designed so that their memory chips plug directly into the computer's main circuitry (refer to Chapter 6, the section about RAM).

✔ Some PCI expansion cards can even be used in either a PC or a Mac. (I've purchased both a network card and a USB expansion card that can work with either the Mac or the PC.) Be aware that some PCI cards are Mac- or PC-only.

✔ Computer scientist types refer to the expansion slots as the *bus*, so they use the term PCI bus rather than PCI slot. Same difference.

AGP assortment

All AGP slots look alike, and you can plug any AGP video card into any AGP slot, but that's just not proper enough for graphics mavens. No, it turns out that various AGP standards are out there, again abusing the letter *x* to specify the difference between the standards.

The AGP array now goes like this: AGP 1x, AGP 2x, AGP 4x, AGP 8x, AGP Pro, and 64-bit AGP. Generally speaking, an AGP slot can handle an AGP card of equal or lesser value, though you

probably want to match your AGP slot with a graphics card powerful enough to take advantage of the slot's advanced graphical goodness. If your computer's motherboard sports an AGP 8x slot, get an AGP 8x graphics card.

Also note that some AGP graphics cards require their own power. If so, ensure that the motherboard has an extra power dongle to connect to the graphics adapter. This step may seem silly, but to a graphics nut, it's important!

Chapter 11

Modems and Sound

· ·

· ·

The desktop computer is just about 25 years old. And, like most young people, it wants its own phone. Actually, the phone isn't the issue. What the computer wants is to *communicate*. To meet that end, you can plug in or add on a variety of devices to a computer to make it more communicative. This includes not only modems to talk with other computers but also a speaker so that the computer can make sound for everyone in the room to share!

This chapter covers two oddball components that would be too lonely to put in chapters by themselves: the modem and the computer's sound abilities. Although the sound portion may not be as big of a deal as it once was, choosing a modem is definitely something you should put high on your chart of high-tech hardware desires. This chapter shows you what's important, what's merely flash, and what to avoid.

Say Hello to Mr. Modem

A *modem* is a device that lets your computer communicate with other computers. A variety of types, models, and speeds of modems is available, which all depends on how you eventually connect your computer to the Internet.

✔ Traditionally, modems were used to connect one computer to another over phone lines. Modems can now use special wires, the same cable as your cable TV, or even no wires.

✔ Mostly, modems are used to connect your computer to the Internet.

✔ Modems also serve to turn your computer into a fax machine.

✔ Modem is a contraction of *modulator-demodulator*. The original modems converted digital signals from the computer (ones and zeroes) into tones that could travel over phone lines. That's *modulation*. The receiving modem then converted the tones from the phone line back into digital signals for the computer. That's *demodulation*.

Modems are measured by their speed

Regardless of the type of modem, the main modem measurement is speed. How fast does it go?

Modem speed is measured in *kilobits per second,* or Kbps. The higher the value, the better.

The typical dial-up modem (see the next section) is known as the 56 Kbps modem. That term means that it communicates at speeds as fast as 56 Kbps, (though often not that fast).

DSL, cable, and other, faster modems are capable of speeds of 128 Kbps and upward. Some cable-modem connections can even achieve speeds of 6,000 Kbps (or faster), which is about the fastest form of online communications you can get with a computer. (To go faster requires special — and expensive — telephone company connections.)

✔ Obviously, you want the fastest modem you can afford.

✔ You may hear the term *baud rate* used to describe a modem's speed. This term is arcane — and you can even tell the joker that he's being arcane to use a silly term like *baud rate*. The more accurate term is *bps;* baud rate is used to describe signal changes in Teletype equipment, which used to apply to computer modems in the 1970s, but now is no longer the case.

Your typical, everyday dial-up modem

The most common computer modem is known as the *dial-up modem*. That's because it uses standard phone lines to connect to the Internet and has to dial the phone just like you do. These are the slowest modems, but they're also the most common and least expensive. Only if you really need online speed do you want anything more powerful.

TECHNICAL STUFF

Silly modem nonsense you don't have to read

Way back in the 1970s, when the first personal computer modems appeared for the Apple II computers, the phone system was *analog*. Your voice was never compressed or digitized or otherwise electronically coerced as it was sent over the phone lines.

Modems were required for computer-to-computer communication because of the phone system's analog nature. The computer is a digital device. The modem's job was to translate all that digital information into tones that could be sent over the analog phone system.

When two computers communicated, four different types of sounds were traveling over the analog phone system: The calling computer sent data at a certain pitch along with a carrier wave at a certain pitch. At two different pitches, the answering computer sent its own data as well as a carrier wave. These four different pitches comprise the warbling sounds you may hear when one modem connects with another.

Sometime in the 1990s, the phone system switched from analog to digital. This digital nature is one reason that you can access the Internet with DSL by using a regular phone line. But, if you use a modem, it converts the digital signal from the computer to analog for the phone company, which then converts it back to digital. On the other end, the phone company converts the digital signal back to analog, which the modem then converts to digital for the computer. My hope is that someday this illogical situation will be fixed, but it doesn't seem like it's going to happen any time soon!

Most computers come with an internal modem preinstalled. The brand name and other features are selected by the computer dealer or manufacturer, which makes this decision a no-brainer.

- ✔ The modem connects the computer to a phone line by using a standard phone cable. You can also plug a telephone into the modem so that you can use the telephone when the computer isn't *online,* or connected to the Internet.

- ✔ Dial-up modems can also be external. My advice: Get the internal modem when you buy your computer. That way, it's all installed, configured, set up, and running. You have nothing else to mess with.

- ✔ External dial-up modems are nice in that you can turn them off. But, they're also more expensive and pretty much an oddity now.

- ✔ Dial-up modems don't raise your phone bill. Using a modem is like using a telephone. The only difference is that your computer is doing the talking (it's more like horribly screeching) into the phone. Your phone company charges you the same whether you or your computer make the call, and long-distance charges still apply. And, of course, you have to pay for Internet access, but that's an access fee and not a charge for using the modem.

✔ Dial-up modems also double as fax modems. Using special software, you can let your computer send or receive faxes. This feature is one not offered with other types of modems.

✔ If you're going to use a dial-up modem, my advice is to have a second phone line — one dedicated to the computer — installed in your home or office.

Faster modems: broadband

Beyond the dial-up modem is the high-end modem, for the fastest Internet connection. This category of modem is referred to as *broadband*, which is merely a term meaning "very fast communications." (The Go-Go's were my favorite broad band of the 1980s.)

Unlike the internal dial-up modem, a broadband modem is *not* purchased with a computer. Instead, you pick it up separately, after you find out what type of broadband service you have (cable or DSL), or the broadband company may lease the modem to you or sell it themselves. This all depends on the broadband company and the type of service you sign up for.

To run your broadband modem, your computer needs a *network card*, also known as a *NIC*. This hardware is required in order to connect your computer to the cable, DSL, or satellite modem — even if you don't plan on putting your computer on a local-area network. So, even though you may not be able to buy a modem when you get a computer, plan on getting the network card. (Check with your Internet provider, to be sure.)

Three types of broadband modems are available: cable, DSL, and satellite, as covered in the following subsections.

✔ Most DSL and cable modems are external. I've seen satellite modems that are internal, but I know that external models are also available. Even so, installation of an internal model would have to take place after you buy the computer and bring it home.

✔ I also strongly recommend that you get a router if you plan on using a broadband modem. Ensure that the router comes with a firewall for protection from the hostile environs of the Internet. More information on routers and firewalls is in Chapter 12.

✔ Even though you have a fast modem, consider keeping a dial-up modem in your computer. You can use the modem as a backup, and it's always good for sending and receiving faxes.

Cable modems

These modems are available anywhere cable service is available (though not all cable providers offer Internet service). It's the cheapest and fastest Internet connection you can buy.

- Cable modems can go up to 6,000 Kbps or faster. Note that the speed here is typically the downstream speed, or the speed of information sent from the Internet to your computer. The upstream speed, or the speed of information you send to the Internet, is usually much slower.

- The only true drawback to the cable modem is that the more people there are online, the slower the connection. (The speed isn't guaranteed.)

- Another drawback is that cable modem service isn't available everywhere.

- For playing online games, cable modems are the best, hands down!

DSL modems

These fast modems are available in limited areas, usually within a few miles of the phone company's main office. If you're within that area (and your Internet provider lets you know), you can use this service.

- DSL stands for Digital Subscriber Line.

- DSL modem speeds range speed from 128 Kbps through 1,500 Kbps. The speed depends on the modem, but also on your location and distance from the phone company's office.

- DSL modems have two speeds: sending and receiving. The speeds don't need to be the same. For example, you could have a DSL modem that receives information at 512 Kbps, and sends at only 128 Kbps. That would be cheaper than getting a "symmetrical" 512 Kbps modem, also written as a 512/512 Kbps DSL modem.

- Obviously, if you don't plan to send large quantities of information, getting a DSL modem with a slower sending speed saves you money.

Satellite modems

The satellite modem is a great option for areas where neither cable nor DSL is available. This technology has come a long way in recent years; its speed has gone up, and its price has gone down. However, the setup cost remains high because you need the satellite modem *and* a satellite dish.

Some satellite modems are receive-only. You dial out using a traditional dial-up modem, and information is sent to you via the satellite. Other satellite systems are both send and receive.

Do you really need a modem?

Modems are optional now. Honestly, if you don't plan to connect your computer to the Internet or if you already have a broadband connection in mind, you can save yourself $10 to $30 on your computer purchase by forgoing the modem.

- ✔ A few years ago, manufacturers would balk if you ordered a computer without a modem. Now, it's far more common.

- ✔ Some modems are part of the motherboard's circuitry. Therefore, you cannot order the computer without the modem, although you can use the computer's hardware setup program to disable the modem.

Sound Off!

If you're after peace and quiet, consider that the computer has a mute button — but that's software! On the hardware side, computers now sold are designed to beep, bleep, squeak, squawk, play music, make music, sing, and chant. In some cases, you just can't get the computer to be quiet!

The bleeping circuitry

All computers come with built-in sound circuitry. They're all capable of producing just about any sound, from synthesized music to CD-quality sound to human-voice imitations. Many computer demos you see in the store have top-notch sound playing, although management turns down the volume, to keep the employees sane.

- ✔ All computers contain the basic circuitry required in order to play computer games. Specialty sound hardware can be purchased as an upgrade. In fact, if you're into audio production or running your own digital music studio, you no doubt want better sound circuitry than what comes with the typical PC.

- ✔ The sound circuitry also includes a music synthesizer, which allows the computer to play music synthesizer or MIDI ("MIH-dee") files. You can also create your own music, if you have MIDI-creation software.

- ✔ Special software is required in order to produce a human voice on a computer. All Macintosh computers come with this software as part of the operating system; Windows has speech synthesis as part of its suite of programs to assist the visually impaired.

- ✔ Though the computer can talk — or more accurately, read text displayed on the screen — it still can't hear what you scream at it. See the section "Talking to your computer," at the end of this chapter.

Tweeting and woofing (speakers)

In addition to having sound circuitry, all computers are sold with speakers. The number and quality of the speakers vary, of course.

Some computers have stereo speakers built into the console or monitor. I've seen speakers built into a keyboard. For the most part, a computer comes with two tiny speakers: one left and one right, for stereo sound reproduction.

Although it's nice that computers come with speakers, the better speakers are bought as upgrades or after-purchase specials. Usually, the speakers come with a subwoofer or are simply better designed than the el cheapo speakers that come with the computer. Expect to pay around $90 for a nice after-sale set of computer speakers, complete with subwoofer for that deep bass sound.

✔ Unless you're really into sound (music, games, video), don't worry about buying your computer new speakers. The speakers that come with your computer work fine.

✔ External speakers, or speakers that come as separate left–right units, work better than speakers built into the monitor or keyboard.

✔ Avoid battery-powered external speakers. If you're stuck with a pair, buy an AC adapter for them so that you don't have to mess with batteries. (Radio Shack sells AC adapters, and most office supply stores have them as well.)

✔ Speakers are measured in wattage; the larger the wattage value, the fuller the sound.

✔ Watch out for speakers rated with a combined sound wattage value. Each speaker should be rated individually.

✔ Be sure that you get and use speakers designed for computers. Those old stereo speakers may work, but they can also electronically interfere with the computer — specifically, the monitor.

✔ A *subwoofer* is a special bass booster, usually sitting on the floor beneath the computer desk. Try to get a subwoofer rated between 100 and 150 watts — or more, if you like that bass sound.

✔ If you would rather not scare the neighbors with your computer sounds, you can always plug in a pair of headphones.

✔ If you go with surround sound, ensure that you have the proper number of speakers for the surround sound specification. For Dolby 5.1, that's five speakers — left, center, right, left-surround, and right-surround — plus a subwoofer, or bass. Dolby 6.1 uses six speakers and a bass (a rear-center speaker is added). Dolby 7.1 uses seven speakers and a bass (three speakers in front and four in the back).

Adding a microphone

All computer sound circuitry comes with the ability for input, which is provided in the form of a microphone. This item allows you to record your own
voice or enjoy such diversions as Internet Phone.

Whether or not a microphone is included with a computer is anyone's guess.
Sometimes they come; sometimes they don't. When they do come with the
computer, the microphone is usually of marginal quality or built into the monitor or console somehow — not the best possible place for a microphone.

✔ If you're into computer recording, you can always add a nice, trusty mic
later. Computers use a standard mini-din connector (a teensy plug-in
thing) for mic input.

✔ If you plan to experiment with computer dictation, get a combination
headset microphone. Often, an inexpensive model is bundled with the
computer dictation software.

Talking to your computer

Yes, you can talk to your computer. To do so, you need the hardware, which
is merely a microphone plugged into the computer's microphone jack, and
software that helps the computer to make sense of what you say.

Go ahead and dash those dreams of your talking with the computer à la Mr.
Spock of *Star Trek*. All computer talking (if any) is now in the form of *dictation*;
special software translates your voice into text that's "typed" on the screen.
For slow typists, this type of software can be invaluable. For fast typists, the
keyboard beats the microphone, hands down.

✔ The best microphone setup to get for dictation is a headset microphone.
It allows you to keep the mic close to your mouth *and* keep your hands
free to use the keyboard when necessary.

✔ The best software for computer dictation is Dragon's Naturally Speaking.
Dictation software is also in the current version of Microsoft Office. IBM
has speech-recognition software named ViaVoice.

✔ Here's the part they never tell you about computer dictation: To get it
to work best, you have to train the computer to understand your voice.
This process requires many hours of your time, between 3 to 15 hours
of your sitting and reading aloud to the computer as it learns your voice.
That's a big investment in time, but the payoff is that the more time you
spend training the computer, the better it takes dictation.

Chapter 12

Networking Your Computer

. . . .

In This Chapter

▶ Understanding computer networking

▶ Getting a NIC for your computer

▶ Going wireless

▶ Connecting computers

▶ Using a hub, switch, or router

▶ Adding software to make the network work

. . . .

*A*t one time, networking was the holy grail of computing. The ability to get several computers in the office to easily share data, as well as resources such as hard drives and printers, was a dream to behold. Sadly, competing networking standards, confusing software installation, incompatibilities, and really bad-tasting coffee made the whole undertaking seem futile.

Computer networking isn't only common now, it's almost a necessity — specifically, for high-speed Internet connections. As an individual, you may have no thought about adding networking hardware to your computer. But, if you do plan to use a high-speed modem (DSL, cable, or satellite), or if you have more than one computer in your home or small office, I recommend that you look into networking hardware. This chapter explains the ropes.

Networking Overview

Like kindergarten, computer networking is about sharing. What's shared are *resources*. These include disk drives and the files and programs that live on them, printers, and modems. The networking hardware provides the connection between each computer. The networking software ensures that communication takes place and that no one shouts or pushes in line.

Networking makes sense for a large — or even small — office. The computers can be connected so that everyone in the office shares a single printer. Customer files and other important data can be shared between several computers. And, the process of maintaining and updating computers is easier when the computers have a line of communications between them. Yes, that all makes sense.

For an individual computer owner, surprisingly, networks can also make sense. Specifically, a network can help you when you have more than one computer in the house and you have a fast, or broadband, Internet connection. Networking in either or both situations is a handy way to tackle potential problems.

St. NIC (Networking Hardware)

If you decide to buy a computer and put it on a network, whether at home or in an office, you must ensure that it comes with the proper network hardware. That hardware is the *n*etwork *i*nterface *c*ard, or NIC ("nick"), also known as a network adapter.

Most desktop computers sold now, and nearly all laptops, come with a NIC included; typically, as part of the chipset on the motherboard. The NIC is featured prominently in the advertising, or you can easily confirm that the computer has a NIC by checking for the telltale RJ-45 port on its rump.

The computer doesn't come with a NIC, but you can easily add one. NIC expansion cards are cheap! On a laptop computer, you can get a USB NIC adapter or a NIC on a PCMCIA card — cheap!

Beyond the NIC itself are two other things to look for: whether you want wireless networking and the NIC's speed.

✔ My advice is to buy the NIC when you order the computer. That way, it's installed and properly configured for you.

✔ Generally speaking, networking hardware is the same for all desktop and laptop computers, whether they're Macs, PCs with Windows, or even PCs running Linux.

✔ Refer to Chapter 10 for more information on the RJ-45 port.

✔ The RJ-45 is merely the connector. The port itself is referred to as 10BaseT, 100BaseTX, or 1000BaseTX, depending on the NIC's speed. It's all nerdy stuff.

Going wireless

Everything is going wireless! It's a craze! At the center of the wireless dust storm is computer networking. By going wireless, you avoid having to attach *another* wire to your computer and having to snake cables through attics, elevators, and crawl spaces. Most folks figure anything that reduces the wire count by one must be a good thing.

A wireless NIC works just like a wired NIC, though it has no wire. Instead, it uses an antenna. The antenna connects to a base station. The base station acts as a wireless hub or router, and it can connect the wireless network to a broadband modem, a wire-based network, a shared printer, or even another wireless base station.

To keep all your wireless networking devices happy, they must support the same networking standard. The standard is known by a famous number: in this case, 802.11. That number is followed by a letter, either a little A, B, or G. If you go wireless, ensure that all your gizmos match the same standard, such as 802.11b or 802.11g. You can also pay more for wireless devices that match multiple standards, such as a wireless 802.11a/b/g NIC.

✔ The setup for wireless networks is much more involved than setting up a wired network. Wireless networks are also more expensive and not as secure.

✔ Apple is known to advertise its Macintosh computers as AirPort-ready, which means that they're capable of accessing the Apple AirPort network. Note that you still need to buy the AirPort card (or NIC) to make your Macintosh wireless.

✔ Ensure that your version of Linux supports whatever wireless networking standard you choose, which will most likely be 802.11b. Again, hardware is needed for this software dictating; you don't want to be stuck having to write your own Linux wireless networking drivers!

Networking speed

NICs are rated by their speed in *Mbps,* or megabits per second. Common speeds are 10 Mbps, 100 Mbps, and 1,000 Mbps, or 1 Gbps. Faster is better. Faster is more expensive — you know the drill if you're reading this book sequentially.

Most NICs support a variety of speeds. You see them advertised as 10/100 or even 10/100/1000. This label means that the NIC is capable of keeping up with speeds that fast. And, the network runs as fast as it can, unless a computer with a slower NIC or another networking gizmo runs at a slower speed, in which case connections to that NIC or gizmo run at the slower speed. Otherwise, things go as fast as they can on the network.

For wireless networking, the speed is measured in megabits per second *(Mbps)*, just like with wired NICs. The actual speed of the wireless network depends on many things, so consider the advertised speed as an ideal used for comparison only. Most wireless NICs talk at between 11 Mbps and upward of 50 Mbps.

- *Gb* means gigabit, or 1 billion bits. You may see it used when describing networking speed; 1,000 Mb = 1 Gb.
- Fast Ethernet is another term for a NIC that communicates at 100 Mbps, also known as 100BaseTX.

Other Networking Hardware

After computers have NICs, the next step is to connect them. This process requires more hardware, which can be purchased at a computer store or any office supply store. You do this after you buy the computer, though some dealers may offer network setup as part of your computer purchase agreement.

Networking cable

To connect the computers, you need special networking cable — unless everything is wireless, in which case you still need cable, but not as much.

Today's computer networks need CAT 5 cable, also known as "twisted pair," though four sets of twisted pairs are usually inside the cable, for a total of eight wires. (The network uses only two).

The length of cable you need depends on how far each computer is from a central location. That's the place where you find the hub, switch, or router, as described in the next section.

- The CAT 5 cable has an RJ-45 connector at both ends. You can connect either end to the computer; the cable isn't fussy about which way it's pointing.
- Unless you have been working with cables or wires most of your life, you'll probably underestimate the cable lengths you need by at least half.
- Special CAT 5 cable is required if you're running the cable through crawl spaces, attics, or heating ducts. It's called *plenum* cable.
- You can find standard-length, ready-made CAT 5 cables at any computer or office supply store. They come in lengths from 1 foot to 30 feet or more.

The hub, switch, or router

At the center of the network is the gizmo into which you plug all the network cables from all the computers. This gizmo is called a *hub, switch,* or *router,* depending on its powers and abilities, as well as how much you paid for it.

Hub: This is the cheapest way to connect computers on a network. It's basically a box with several ports on it, one for each computer on the network. The hub helps transfer information from one computer to the other over the networking cables.

Switch: A switch is basically a better, faster version of a hub. You pay a little more for a switch, but the cost is worth it.

Router: The best way to connect your computers, especially if you plan add a high-speed modem to the network, is with a router. The router not only connects the computers but also helps wisely manage them. It also helps put up a firewall between your computer network and the vicious environment of the Internet.

Note that the wireless hub, switch, or router may require a wire to connect it to the high-speed modem, as well as to other wire-based computers on the network.

- ✔ If you're connecting a computer to a high-speed modem, get a router. Especially look for a router with built-in firewall protection.

- ✔ Ensure that whatever hub, switch, or router you get matches the fastest speed of your network.

- ✔ Placement of the wireless hub or router is vital. Despite the manufacturer's boasts, wireless networking has an effective range of only several feet. The best way to set up a wireless network is with the hub or base station (router) in the same room as the wireless computers. Otherwise, something as innocent as a wall can effectively dampen the wireless signal to the point of being useless.

- ✔ The Apple AirPort wireless base station is a type of router.

- ✔ The AirPort can be used with both PCs and Macs, as long as the PCs have a compatible 802.11g NIC.

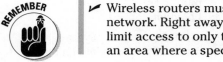

- ✔ Wireless routers must be configured immediately after you set up your network. Right away, you need to set a new password for the router and limit access to only those computers on your wireless network. This is an area where a specialist comes in handy.

What is Bluetooth?

Bluetooth is an odd yet memorable name for a wireless communications standard — specifically, one that connects a variety of smaller devices and gizmos. Each of the Bluetooth-enabled gadgets is able to easily communicate with another, as well as with a personal computer. The goal of Bluetooth is to utterly eliminate wires.

The best way to use Bluetooth with your computer is to first ensure that your PC or Mac has Bluetooth hardware. Then you can use Bluetooth-enabled devices on your computer after adding them, such as wireless keyboards, mice, printers, and MP3 music players. As long as the device is Bluetooth compatible, it should work well with your computer — and without wires!

Adding your high-speed modem

The final hardware goodie your network may need is a high-speed modem. This device is generally attached directly to the hub, switch, or router, as shown in Figure 12-1. In fact, most routers have a specially marked RJ-45 jack for the high-speed modem. The rest of the jacks are for plugging in other computers or shared resources, such as a networked printer (as shown in Figure 12-1).

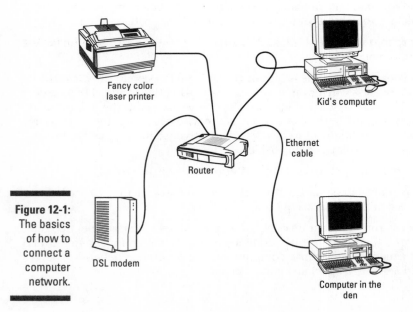

Fancy color
laser printer

Kid's computer

Ethernet
cable

Router

Figure 12-1:
The basics
of how to
connect a
computer
network.

DSL modem

Computer in the
den

A wireless setup works the same as the wire-based setup. The difference is that in Figure 12-1, no wires would be between the switch and the two computers and printer.

Though the router isn't visible in Figure 12-1, it has built-in firewall protection to insulate the two PCs from nasty things on the Internet. This item is very important! Without a router and firewall, those computers could be abused by various nasty things. A firewall helps protect your PCs, but you also need both antivirus software and anti-spyware software. (A software firewall isn't necessary if the router has a built-in firewall.)

Networking Software

Like everything else in a computer, networking has a software side in addition to a hardware side. Fortunately, modern operating systems already sport all the networking software you need. That's nice. On the other hand, *configuring* the networking software can be a royal pain in the butt. That's a subject best left for after the purchase.

- ✔ Windows XP comes with the smarts for doing both wireless and wire-based networking. A Windows XP system instantly recognizes other computers on the network, even resources such as shared hard drives and shared printers, which are instantly made available.

- ✔ Macintosh OS X also comes with smarts to instantly and effectively set up networking. I feel that the Mac's wireless abilities are far superior to Windows, especially if you go with the Apple AirPort technology.

- ✔ Linux and other Unix variations are well geared toward networking. Refer to the SAMBA program for information on integrating Windows computers into your Linux network.

Chapter 13

Scanners and Digital Cameras

Scanners were once considered rather exotic things. They were available as peripherals, but not really considered necessary for anyone except computer graphics professionals. Digital cameras began life as expensive toys that captured crummy low-resolution images, similar to the old Instamatic cameras of years gone by.

Thanks to advancing technology and dropping prices, having a scanner or digital camera as part of your computer now is considered as common as having a keyboard. Although the scanner or digital camera may not be part of your initial computer purchase, it's still something to consider for your computer's future. This chapter discusses the basic features to look for in both a scanner and a camera.

Scanning the Scanner Horizon

Scanners work like photocopiers, except that the material that's scanned in appears as a graphical image on your computer screen instead of being duplicated on a sheet of paper. You can then edit that image, save it to a file, send it via e-mail on the Internet, or do any number of things with it.

An archetypal scanner is shown over in Chapter 2, though most scanners are skinnier than that model.

Several things are worthy of consideration when you choose a scanner:

- ✓ Price
- ✓ Size
- ✓ Image sensor
- ✓ Resolution and color depth
- ✓ Interface
- ✓ Optional goodies
- ✓ Software

This section covers each of these items.

- ✓ It's not important to choose a scanner when you buy your computer. However, you may need to plan some things before your scanner purchase. For example, if you need a high-speed scanner, you may need a computer with a high-speed port, such as a FireWire/IEEE port. Or, the photo-editing software you plan to use may require a specific amount of memory. These things need to be noted before you purchase a computer.

- ✓ Scanners are well suited to capturing images, such as photographs, pictures from books or magazines, or anything flat.

- ✓ Yes, you can scan your face. Be sure to clean the scanner's glass after doing so.

- ✓ At this point, lawyers go ape over copyright laws. Remember that nearly every image (especially the good ones) are copyrighted and cannot be reproduced. For more information, visit a slimy lawyer near you.

Price scanning

You can pay anywhere from less than $50 to more than $1,000 for a scanner. Thanks to advancing technology, a good scanner can be had for about $200 to $300. The typical home scanner goes for less than $100.

The scanner's price is based on its features as well as on the software that's included. The more you pay, the more features the scanner offers, the better its scanning ability, and the more and better software is included.

- ✓ No, you don't need to use the software that comes with the scanner.

- ✓ All scanners can copy text. The text is saved as a graphical image, just as the scanner would scan and save an image of a puppy playing in a grassy field, utterly unaware of the nearby threshing machine. To read text into the computer, however, you need *optical character recognition,* or *OCR,* software. It may be bundled with the scanner or available as a separate software package.

Scanners big and scanners little

It amazes me how thin scanners are getting. My first scanner was almost as big as the computer's printer — or a photocopier. The next generation got a little thinner, and now you can find scanners that are about a ½-inch thick. Imagine losing a scanner in a stack of papers!

Surprisingly enough, a thin scanner isn't necessarily more expensive than a fatter model. In this case, its size depends more on the optional features that are available than on any premium you would pay for teensy technology.

✔ The scanner's size isn't really indicated by its physical dimensions, but rather by the size of the glassy area where the image is placed. For most scanners, the glassy area is the size of a sheet of paper or slightly larger. You pay more for a scanner that can read in a larger image — for example, legal size or larger.

✔ Only one scanner type is now available: the flatbed scanner, which looks like a squatty photocopier. A few years ago, some handheld scanners worked like tiny vacuum cleaners you swiped over an image.

✔ Okay, you can get another type of scanner: that all-in-one combination printer–copier–scanner office thing. In that case, the image is scanned from a sheet of paper that's fed into the scanner.

✔ Some specialty scanners exist. I have seen tiny business card scanners. Some special scanners scan only color slides. A highly portable hand-held scanner, more commonly known as a digital camera, is covered later in this chapter.

The image sensor

The *image sensor* is the doohickey inside the scanner that does the scanning. It reads the image pressed against the glass with the help of a bright light.

A scanner can have one of two types of image sensor: CCD or CIS.

CCD: The Charge-Coupled Device (CCD) image sensor is capable of higher resolution than the CIS type. However, the CCD requires more electronics to do its job, which means that a scanner with this type of image sensor is more expensive.

CIS: This type of image sensor is found mostly in smaller, lighter scanners. CIS stands for *contact image sensor*. It's also called a CMOS image sensor.

If you're serious about scanning, get a CCD scanner. If price is more important, you will probably end up with a CIS model.

Optical versus interpolated resolution

Be aware that some scanners have two resolution values: optical and interpolated.

The *optical* value, the more honest of the two, describes the actual amount of dpi the scanner's hardware is capable of beholding. Use the optical dpi value when you're comparing scanners.

The *interpolated* value, also known as MIR, or *m*aximum *i*nterpolated *r*esolution, is higher than the optical value, but it's not really a true resolution. By using software, the scanner can pretend that it's scanning at a high resolution. That's okay for some images, but in the case of film negatives or color slides, you want a true optical resolution value, not an interpolated one.

Resolution and image-quality issues

The main reason that one scanner is more or less expensive than another is the scanner's *resolution*. That's the measurement of how much information the scanner grabs from the image. The higher the resolution, the more detail and information the scanner can read.

The scanner's resolution is measured in dots per inch (dpi). Values range from 300 dpi to 2400 dpi or even higher. The *dpi value* tells you how many pieces of an image the scanner can read on a horizontal line. A value of 300 dpi is high enough for just about any image. The higher values are necessary when you plan to scan film negatives, color slides, or other transparencies.

Walking hand in hand with the scanner's resolution is the *color depth* value. This value, measured in bits, determines how many levels of color the scanner can capture. In a nutshell: The higher the bit value, the better the scanner can discern between two subtly different shades of the same color. That's a plus.

- ✔ For e-mail or the Web, images scanned at about 100 dpi are perfect. This resolution is possible with any type of scanner.

- ✔ For scanning film negatives, color slides, or other transparencies, I recommend a scanner with at least a 2400 dpi resolution.

- ✔ The minimum color depth on a typical scanner is 24 bits; 36-bit color depth is just peachy. With 48 bits and more, you're in heaven, baby!

- ✔ Another indicator of scanner quality is the scanner's optical density (OD), though few scanners seem to tout this value on their boxes any more. *OD* measures brightness values in an image; higher OD values are better than low values. Most scanners have an optical density of 2.8OD to 3.0OD. If you plan to scan color slides or film, you need a scanner with an optical density of at least 3.2OD or 3.4OD.

How does the scanner connect to the computer?

A scanner can chat with your computer in several ways: by using the USB port, the IEEE port, and other ports without popular acronyms. You need to ensure that whatever scanner you choose uses a port you already have on your computer. Better plan for it now.

A computer scanner uses one of two common interfaces:

- USB
- FireWire/IEEE

USB: USB is the most common interface for a computer scanner. Pretty much any scanner you buy now is a USB model. Note that some USB scanners are even USB powered: The USB cable is the only thing that plugs into the scanner. That can be a blessing, especially if you're angry about the number of cables in your life.

FireWire/IEEE: The FireWire interface is one of the fastest ways to connect a scanner to your computer. It's the best interface for anyone serious about scanning or when you're configuring your scanner with a sheet feeder to "read" stacks of documents. If your computer has a FireWire port and you need a high-powered scanner, get a scanner with the FireWire interface. Otherwise, the USB interface works just peachy.

Optional scanner goodies

Scanners come with a plethora of options, each of which adds to the price but also expands the scanner's abilities.

Those handy buttons on the front of a scanner — one for e-mail, another for printing, and others? They add no value to the scanner. They're merely shortcuts for operations you most likely perform by using the scanner's software. The buttons may seem to make scanning easy, but they really don't.

The most common option is a *transparency adapter,* which allows a film negative or color slide to be scanned. This gizmo is necessary because the scanner's light must *shine through* a transparency and not be reflected off it, as is the case with the glass part of the scanner. If you plan to scan slides or reproduce images from film negatives, you need a scanner with a transparency adapter.

I see, after the transparency adapters, quite a few scanners sold with a menu of push buttons on their snouts. These buttons are used to quickly scan common types of images or to activate specific software inside the computer. For example, an E-Mail button may direct the scanner to scan and size an image for sending via e-mail and then automatically open your e-mail program with the image attached. That's impressive.

Another scanner option is the automatic document feeder, used primarily with OCR software in business applications. The *document feeder* can store dozens of pages of text and automatically sift those pages through the scanner as the text is being read. These amazing devices are impressive to watch, though they add a considerable price tag to the scanner.

- ✔ Scanners sold with transparency adapters also have all the necessary technology to scan those transparencies at the proper resolutions.

- ✔ Avoid buying a scanner that has a transparency adapter "upgrade." If you need the transparency adapter, buy it with the scanner.

- ✔ Some transparency adapters are limited in size, and can scan only 35mm film. If you need to scan larger transparencies, you have to find a scanner that's capable of holding larger images.

- ✔ Transparency adapters may be called TPAs or TPUs. I have no idea what these acronyms stand for, though they're commonly used.

- ✔ Scanners with automatic document feeders also come with document-management software.

Scanner software

All scanners come with software. They have to. The scanner needs to come with, at minimum, special *driver* software, required so that the computer can recognize and control the scanner hardware.

Beyond basic driver software, most scanners come with a smattering of software. Sometimes it's really good stuff, and sometimes it's mediocre stuff; regardless, the software helps get you started and become familiar enough with computer graphics that you can upgrade to something better, if you want.

- ✔ The scanners come with some type of control program, which allows you to scan images, do basic editing, and save the images to disk.

- ✔ Most scanners come with some type of photo-editing software.

- ✔ The good stuff is Adobe Photoshop, the professional-level photo-editing program.

✔ Some scanners also come with OCR, or optical character recognition, software, which lets you turn your scanner into a page reader. This software is generally a limited version of more advanced and speedier software that does the same thing.

✔ Although scanner hardware works with either a PC or Macintosh, the software may not. If you have a Macintosh, ensure that the scanner comes with Mac software. You *need* it in order to control the scanner!

✔ Don't feel pressured to install all that software at one time! Use the scanner as you feel necessary, and refer to the manual or online tutorial as needed.

Getting a Digital Camera

On the nuts-and-bolts level, a *digital camera* is really nothing more than a handheld portable scanner. The technologies found in a flatbed scanner and a digital camera are, for the most part, identical. But, even as a portable scanner, the digital camera exists in a 3D world and is capable of every task done by a traditional film camera.

This section mulls over some important points worth considering when you're purchasing a digital camera.

✔ You can buy a digital camera before or after you buy the computer, though I recommend getting a digital camera later, so as not to overwhelm yourself with new technology.

✔ In 2005, more digital cameras were sold than traditional film cameras.

✔ Disposable digital cameras will soon replace the disposable film cameras you often see at vacation spots.

✔ Digital cameras aren't made in PC or Mac models. Any digital camera works with any desktop or laptop computer.

✔ Be mindful of the software that comes with the camera. Especially if you have a Macintosh, you want to ensure that the camera comes with Mac-compatible software.

What exactly is a digital camera?

A *digital camera* is a gizmo that takes digital pictures. It works exactly like its film-based cousin: It has a lens, a flash, and various controls and knobs, but the image is captured by an electronic eye and stored as a graphics file on special media, just as a graphics file is stored on a computer's hard drive.

One major difference between film and digital cameras is that digital cameras require special digital storage. It's usually in the form of a memory card, though some digital cameras have their own proprietary media, and some even use floppy disks.

Another major difference is that digital cameras require more power. A film camera uses a battery that may last for several years of regular use. But, a digital camera requires more power to get the job done, and it chews through batteries like a puppy chews through expensive shoes.

One other major difference is that digital cameras require no processing or developing. The images you take can be printed instantly, saved on a computer for long-term storage, e-mailed, or basically treated like any file in a computer. Over the long haul, therefore, outside of buying or recharging batteries, digital cameras are often an inexpensive and more efficient alternative to film cameras.

The information in this chapter applies specifically to digital still cameras. You can also get videocameras for the computer, which range from inexpensive and tiny cameras, also known as Webcams, to professional-level digital videocameras used in Hollywood. You have to look elsewhere for information on those types of cameras.

Things worth noting when you're choosing a digital camera

One basic similarity between film and digital cameras is the eternal question "How much do you want to spend?" The more money you spend, the better the camera. Don't pay for features you don't need and will never use.

The price of a digital camera has gone down to the point where the price is, feature by feature, comparable to that of an analog camera. You can pay as much as $200 for a reasonable consumer digital camera; between $200 and $600 for a semiprofessional, or "prosumer," camera; and more than $600 for the professional stuff. The price is based on features. Here's what to look for:

- ✔ Resolution (in megapixels)
- ✔ Camera features
- ✔ Digital storage medium
- ✔ Batteries

From this list, megapixels are the most important and generally get the most attention. Even so, try not to neglect the other features.

Megapixels: Technically, a *megapixel* is 1 million pixels; *mega* means million and *pixel* is a contraction of *pic*ture *el*ements.

One *pixel* is a single dot in a digital image. The more dots, the more detailed the image and the more closely it resembles a film camera image.

It helps to think of 1 megapixel as a huge grid of 1,024 x 1,024 pixels, or dots. That's a good enough level of quality for a 5-x-7-inch photograph. It's roughly equivalent to the same type of image you get when you scan a 5-x-7 photograph at 200 dpi.

A 3-megapixel camera can capture an image with about 3 million pixels, or dots. That's a grid of about 3,072 x 3,072 pixels — more than enough resolution to produce quality 8-x-10 photo enlargements.

Today's 5-megapixel (and higher) cameras capture details that rival those of film cameras.

Regardless of the camera's highest resolution setting, ensure that the camera offers controls for setting each image's resolution as you take pictures. For example, when you compose images for the Internet, you most likely want the lowest resolution — 640 x 480 pixels, for example. Anything higher is too big to see on the screen and too large to make sending it efficient.

Camera features: Beyond resolution, you should look for digital camera features similarly to how you would look for film camera features.

For example, a cheap camera has a fixed-focus lens. A moderately priced camera may have a self-focusing zoom lens. On the high consumer end, a digital camera should come with auto- and self-focusing options as well as ways to set the aperture and shutter speed.

Better cameras have exchangeable lenses, just like film cameras. The camera should have an LCD screen for previewing and editing images, with the option of turning the LCD screen off and using the viewfinder. (The LCD screen uses a lot of battery juice.)

Generally speaking, any digital camera feature that matches that of a standard film SLR (single lens reflex) camera is good.

On the low end, ensure that the camera has a flash and some method of changing the image's resolution.

Some digital cameras have an annoying "hang time" between when the shutter button is pressed and the picture is taken. Avoid them. To keep from being frustrated, get a camera that snaps its picture at the same time the button is pressed. It helps avert that urge to hurl the camera against a brick wall.

Digital storage medium: Most cameras use a digital media card to store their images. The two most popular types are Compact Flash and Secure Digital. Each comes in a variety of sizes, measured in megabytes (or gigabytes). Some digital cameras use memory sticks, floppy disks, or other proprietary media, though I recommend the standard Compact Flash and Secure Digital media.

You can always buy a secondary media card for your digital camera, which allows the total number of pictures the camera can store to be literally infinite — as long as you have new media cards.

The nifty thing about media cards is that you can erase pictures on them and start afresh. I typically copy my camera's images from its memory card to my desktop computer. You can also take them to a digital film printing kiosk and get your pics right away. Afterward, I erase the memory card and start over.

You can also use the camera's features to delete images from a memory card, especially pictures that don't turn out right or that make various body parts appear too large.

Batteries: Having rechargeable batteries is a good thing for a digital camera, but a better option is a camera that uses both rechargeable and standard flashlight batteries.

My digital camera has four rechargeable AA batteries, but I seldom use them; they take too long to recharge and don't last as long as store-bought batteries.

Try to get a camera that uses NiMH (*ni*ckel-*m*etal-*h*ydroxide) or lithium-ion rechargeable batteries. Avoid NiCad (*ni*ckel-*cad*mium) batteries, which are an older technology subject to problems such as "battery memory" and a decreasing charge over their life spans.

Avoid a digital camera that uses its own, unique battery system. Even if you want and use rechargeable batteries, get the type that can be replaced with standard flashlight batteries, if necessary.

Getting the image into the computer

If your computer doesn't come with a media card, or digital film reader, get one. It's the easiest way to get images from the digital camera into your computer. Otherwise, ensure that the camera comes with cables for connecting your PC to the camera for image exchange.

The camera may also come with cables for a TV video connection, to allow you to "play" the images inside the camera on a TV set.

Note that some cameras can connect directly to a photo printer, either via a cable or by plugging in their digital media. This step avoids using a computer, but those photo printers can be *very slow*. See Chapter 24 for more information on printers, particularly photo printers.

Chapter 14

Special Issues for Notebook and Laptop Computers

*L*aptop computers, officially known as *notebooks*, are piece-by-part identical to their desktop brethren. The big difference is, of course, that laptops are designed to be portable and to run off battery power in addition to the juice from the wall. Laptops are computers on the go, which makes them ideal in many work situations where you're away from the office or as a supplement to your standard desktop system.

Buying a laptop works just like buying any computer: The same five steps outlined in Chapter 1 still apply. Beyond that, you must pay special attention to those laptop features that differ from desktop features. This chapter outlines those issues, to allow you to select the best laptop hardware for your needs.

✔ Laptops make an ideal computer for anyone "on the go." Salespeople thrive on laptops.

✔ Laptops make an excellent second computer because they allow you to take work with you when you're away from your desktop.

✔ Laptops are ideal for students away at college, who may not have the room for a bulky desktop.

> ✓ Refer to my book *Laptops For Dummies* (Wiley Publishing, Inc.) for lots of good laptop information, including details on setup, security, wireless networking, and battery power.
>
> ✓ As an old fogey who has been around the computer business for quite a while, I prefer using the term laptop as opposed to notebook. When you shop, you often see either term or both terms. I use *laptop* because it was the first term used to describe this type of computer, back in the late 1980s.

Laptop Considerations

Desktop computers won their fame by being expandable. Laptop computers won their fame by sacrificing expandability for portability; you don't buy a laptop with the notion of "upgrading it later." You buy a laptop to have a computer anywhere you are: in a plane flying across the country, in a coffee shop, or in a bungalow over the lagoon in Bora Bora.

All technical descriptions of a desktop computer apply to laptops as well: microprocessor, RAM, and disk storage, for example. Beyond that, laptops have special considerations that desktop users would never dream of. Chief among these are

> ✓ Microprocessor
>
> ✓ Battery life
>
> ✓ Weight
>
> ✓ Pointing device
>
> ✓ Removable or swappable drives
>
> ✓ Communications

Each of these considerations is discussed in this section.

What about software?

There's nothing special about software on a computer laptop. If the program works on a desktop system, it also works on the laptop model. Some applications have special "minimum" installation options, so as not to use too much of the laptop's hard drive space. Plus, you may find some special laptop software that helps you use your portable system, such as a program to use the fax machine or wireless modem or to configure the system to play music on a portable MP3 player — but that software typically comes with the laptop itself.

Special (expensive) microprocessors

Laptops use special versions of the microprocessors used in desktop computers. These microprocessors are often physically smaller and use less power than their desktop brethren. They also contain the circuitry required to manage the laptop's battery. Because of that, they're also more expensive.

- ✔ The Intel Pentium M series is specifically designed for *mobile,* or laptop, computers. AMD microprocessors use the word *mobile* in their descriptions.

- ✔ The G4 microprocessor is used in Macintosh laptops. The G5 chip just cannot be manufactured to run cool enough for a Mac laptop, which is another reason for Apple switching to Intel microprocessors for the next generation of Macintoshes.

- ✔ The smaller nature of many of a laptop's components makes laptops more expensive than desktop computers.

- ✔ Other internal electronics, in addition to the microprocessor, are smaller and use less power, which again adds to the price of the laptop.

- ✔ Avoid laptops that use standard desktop microprocessors. Those chips use battery power quickly and also tend to get too hot for the laptops' tiny cases. If in doubt, ask: "Does this laptop have a special laptop microprocessor?"

Disk drives

Laptops come with very small hard drives, but don't let their size fool you. Often, a teensy laptop hard drive can store as much as its desktop counterpart. The difference in size is made up for by the price; tiny hard drives are expensive.

Forget about a floppy drive with your laptop. Instead, get — at minimum — a laptop with a CD-R/RW drive. That way, your laptop can read all CD discs and create its own CD-R or CD-RW discs.

Also consider the CD-R/RW and DVD-R/RW drives, such as the SuperDrive, which comes on Apple Macintosh laptops. These drives can read all the shiny media, both CDs and DVDs, and write to CD and DVD discs. Again, you pay a premium price to have it all.

Some laptops boast a swappable disk drive system, where you can plug in a DVD drive, hard drive, CD-ROM drive, floppy drive, or any other drive into a special hardware slot on the computer. Beware of them! Although this type of feature may give you lots of removable storage options, the key behind a laptop is *portability,* not expandability. Don't pay for expensive features you may never use.

Some hardware you may want to have in a PC laptop

The special Intel laptop technology is named *Centrino*. It's a marketing term for a combination of technologies that make the laptop computer wireless, lighter, and smaller, and with improved performance and battery management — and it tastes great on salads. (Just kidding.)

The Centrino technology includes a special Pentium M microprocessor, designed for top laptop performance. Plus, the Centrino laptop includes the latest wireless communications technology, which means that your laptop is ready to go to any of the new cybercafé or wireless computer locations in the country and immediately take advantage of that technology.

Obviously, buying a laptop with Centrino technology is a good thing. (Other, technical aspects of the Centrino technology also help laptop performance — stuff too geeky to mention here.)

A battery of issues

A laptop can use electricity from a wall outlet or its own, internal battery. The length of time the battery can power the laptop is, obviously, important. A fancy, high-end laptop may have impressive hardware statistics, but if you can use the thing for only an hour before having to plug it in, you may as well lug around a desktop.

A good laptop should have batteries that power it for at least two hours, though three is average. Any quotes for longer battery life are most likely exaggerated — or they're using two sets of batteries and swapping in a fresh one when the old one drains.

The best *type* of battery you can get is *lithium ion*. The second best is *nickel-metal hydride* (NiMH). Both are rechargeable and can be recharged without having to drain them fully.

Avoid NiCad batteries. Although they're rechargeable, they suffer from *the memory effect,* which means that if you run one on battery power, you have to fully drain its battery before it's recharged, or else the battery's life gets cut short.

✔ Battery-life tests are made under ideal conditions — not the same conditions under which you would use the laptop.

✔ You may notice an interesting trade-off between laptop features and battery life. High-performance features drain battery juice quickly. So, if using your laptop unplugged is important to you, cut back on the RAM and microprocessor speed.

✔ Some laptops can *hot swap* batteries. That is, you use one for two hours and it drains. Then, you can instantly replace that battery with another — without turning off the laptop. This process works only when the spare battery is fully charged.

✔ If possible, try to use your laptop without using its battery. Most laptop owners are adept at finding power sockets in airports, hotel lobbies, and restaurants. If you must, you can always rely on the batteries.

✔ Charge your laptop's battery the night before you leave on a trip. That way, the battery is always ready to go in the morning.

✔ Many handheld and palmtop computers use standard flashlight batteries. Because those computers don't consume lots of power, they can operate for hours — sometimes days — on a pair of AA or AAA batteries.

The skinny on laptop weight

The ideal laptop weighs in at about 4 pounds. Less is better, but also more expensive.

I've seen some laptop heifers weigh in at 10 pounds. Big screens add weight to a laptop like you wouldn't believe!

Now, you may scoff at the difference between a 4-pound and 10-pound laptop. Six pounds! Ha! But, wait until you lug a laptop across O'Hare Airport, in Chicago. You want to look light and carefree toting your laptop, not like you're trying to smuggle plutonium.

✔ All laptops weigh more than their advertising boasts. What the manufacturers fail to mention is the weight of their portable AC adapters, spare batteries, carrying cases, and other add-ons. Consider all that when you buy.

✔ If weight is a serious issue for you, consider getting a handheld or palmtop PC.

✔ Going along with weight is the issue of size. Laptop size can vary from the dimensions of a college dictionary to superthin, like a magazine.

The anti-mouse

The best way to use a laptop computer is with a standard desktop mouse. That's because the laptop's own pointing device is this silly thing called a *touchpad*. It wouldn't be so bad, but the touchpad lives in a spot below the keyboard where you may end up resting your wrists.

Despite the availability of a touchpad, ensure that your laptop has a mouse port or a USB port, into which you can plug a standard desktop mouse, and consider that mouse part of the laptop purchase price. Then, disable the touchpad.

IBM and Dell laptops have a special joystick-like mouse that looks like a pencil eraser jammed into the keyboard (between the G and H keys). This pointing device is much better than a touchpad, though it's still not as handy as a standard computer mouse.

Laptop communications

Get a laptop that comes with a standard dial-up modem as well as built-in networking through the standard Ethernet RJ-45 jack. Try to avoid any laptop that lacks either of these important options. (Note that laptops with wireless networking may lack the RJ-45 jack.)

Avoid getting a laptop with built-in wireless networking. Get a wireless networking PCMCIA card instead. That gives you two advantages over built-in wireless networking:

First, your laptop will have an external antenna, which is much better than an internal wire at picking up signals.

Second, when the wireless networking standard changes (again), it will be cheaper to replace a small PCMCIA networking card than it will be to buy a whole new laptop.

Refer to the section "The PCMCIA port," at the end of this chapter, for more information on PCMCIA cards.

Security issues

The same things that make laptops appealing to computer buyers also make them appealing to computer thieves: Laptops are easy to steal. To prevent this problem, get a laptop that lets you attach a security device.

- ✔ The security device can be as simple as inserting a locking cable through the laptop's case. You can purchase a locking cable anywhere.

- ✔ Forget software passwords and encryption. Although that may protect your laptop's data, it's not the files on the hard drive that the crooks are after — it's the unit itself! Hard drives are often erased before the laptop is resold. You can do that whether or not your files are encrypted or password protected.

✔ For more security issues, options, and solutions, refer to my book *Laptops For Dummies*, published by Wiley Publishing, Inc.

Laptop Expansion Options

Despite their teensy size, laptops have various options for expanding their worlds. For example, most laptops have room for you to add more memory. Some let you swap out a CD-ROM drive for a second hard drive or perhaps some specialty drive. Beyond these specifics, most laptops have common expansion features.

"I've seen these ports before!"

Like desktop computers, laptops come with ports for connecting external devices. For example, most laptops come with a connector to add on a mouse, a keyboard, or an external monitor. Laptops may also have a printer port, a USB port, or even a FireWire/IEEE port for even more diverse connectivity.

✔ Most newer laptops use the USB port to let you add an external keyboard or mouse.

✔ The monitor port not only lets you use a larger monitor with the laptop, but also works to support a second monitor or video projector when you're making a presentation: You connect the digital project to the laptop's monitor port and then use your software to set up that port as a second monitor.

✔ Some laptops lack ports and use instead a *docking station,* or *port replicator.* This device attaches to the laptop, and then you can use that device to attach standard PC peripherals.

✔ Note that Macintosh laptops use USB ports as their printer ports. PC laptops can do so as well!

The PCMCIA port

The PCMCIA port is the way most laptops deal with expansion. PCMCIA ports eat PCMCIA cards, popularly called PC Cards. A *PC Card* is a tiny slab of electronics about the size of a credit card but ¼-inch thick (or thicker).

You can use a PC Card to expand your laptop's abilities in a number of ways. Most commonly, the cards come with network adapters, though some cards contain extra memory, USB or FireWire/IEEE ports, hard drives, or other expansion options that increase a laptop's hardware universe.

✔ If your laptop already comes with everything you need, having a PCMCIA port may not be necessary.

✔ The current PCMCIA standard is known as Type II.

✔ PCMCIA stands for Personal Computer Memory Card International Association. So, now you know. But, it has been rumored that PCMCIA stands for People Can't Memorize Computer Industry Acronyms.

Chapter 15

Your Computer's Operating System

*A*ll computer hardware, from the slowest microprocessor to the fastest graphics system, is utterly worthless without the proper software to control it. I know, I know: Hardware is all the flash when you buy a computer. But, all the hardware covered in Chapters 5 through 14 means nothing unless you have the software to take advantage of it.

The number-one piece of software in any computer is the operating system. It's the first program that runs when you turn on your computer, the program other programs defer to, the head program in charge, the boss, the czar, *el queso grande,* the king o' everything. This chapter discusses your operating system options.

✔ Choosing an operating system is a decision you should make *before* you select computer hardware. (Hardware is covered first in this book because you need to know those terms before you can select the software.)

✔ Yes, you have a choice when it comes to operating systems. Much to Microsoft's chagrin, the entire world doesn't run on Windows; there's still that 7 percent that uses Linux or Mac OS X.

Understanding Operating Systems

An *operating system* is a program that controls your computer. It coordinates three things:

- ✔ Your computer's software
- ✔ Your computer's hardware
- ✔ You

Each of these items is important. All these items together comprise your computer system. So, as the grand coordinator, the operating system is an important element, by bringing it all together and keeping everything running smoothly.

- ✔ Of the three elements, you (obviously) are the most important. How the operating system interacts with you is your primary concern in choosing an operating system.
- ✔ Second most important is the *software base,* the number and variety of programs available to a specific operating system.
- ✔ Finally, the operating system is written to control specific hardware.

By itself, the operating system doesn't really *do* anything. It's not productivity software, like a word processor or graphics program. It's not a game or a utility or even remotely entertaining. The operating system is merely in charge. Something has to be.

Working with you

Software is more important than hardware, and the most important piece of software is the computer's operating system. Therefore, your choice of operating system must be a good one.

 Forget about the hardware! Shut out the junk around the screen, and merely concentrate on the information being presented by the operating system. Does it make sense? Is it easy? Does it give you the control you need? Can you figure things out? Are you familiar or comfortable with it? These questions are all important ones to ask, more important than "I wonder who made this nifty monitor?"

Operating systems can be either friendly or powerful. *Friendly* means that the operating systems are easy to learn and use. *Powerful* means that the operating system may not be friendly, but it offers you more direct control over the computer itself.

✔ Try out an operating system by running a program. See how it goes.

✔ Check out how the operating system displays information about files and folders. (Have someone in the store demonstrate. Have that person show you a file and a folder.)

✔ Make a note of which operating system appeals to you the most. Don't let any hardware prejudices unfairly influence you — not yet, at least.

✔ You can easily become bored or frustrated with an easy and friendly operating system, even if you like that type of operating system when you first start using a computer. Therefore, if you're at all technically minded, consider a more powerful operating system rather than a friendly one.

✔ On the friendliness scale, the Macintosh operating system is about as friendly as you can get. Windows tries, but it's still not as friendly as a Mac.

✔ Linux is the least friendly operating system. It can look as friendly as Windows or the Macintosh, but it requires much more training and has greater potential for letting you do dangerous things quite easily.

✔ Friendly operating systems generally sport friendly software. The programs on a Macintosh, for example, are intuitive after you know the feel of the operating system.

Controlling the software

The second gauge of an operating system's worthiness is its software base. A *software base* is merely the number and variety of programs available to a specific operating system. The more, the better.

The trap here is a technical one. Suppose that you find and love an operating system that works with you. The operating system is well designed, friendly where it's supposed to be, and powerful where you need it. Alas, it just doesn't have any software available. Maybe you can find a few programs, but some of the software you really need just isn't there or isn't as nice as you want. In that case, forget about using that operating system.

✔ One of the operating system's jobs is to control the software. As such, software is geared to work with a particular operating system, and the software reflects many characteristics of the operating system under which it works.

✔ A larger software base ensures an operating system's success, even if that operating system stinks.

✔ Of course, an overabundance of software shouldn't be the key to buying any computer. If the operating system you choose has exactly the software you need, you're set.

✔ Sometimes, a vast software base isn't the only way to judge an operating system. For example, most of the best graphics and design software is still available primarily for the Macintosh. Although Windows versions of these types of software exist, those programs are generally not as good as the Mac originals.

✔ If you're using proprietary software, such as an inventory system written specifically for your company, you need whichever operating system that software requires. This example is one of the rare instances in which the software base doesn't matter.

Controlling the hardware

The operating system's final task is to control the computer hardware, by telling it exactly what to do with itself. So, when you tell a program to print, the operating system is the one which ensures that the information is properly sent to the printer.

Each operating system is written to one or more hardware standard. For example, Windows is written to the PC hardware standard. The Macintosh operating system runs only on Macintosh computers.

Some operating systems are *multiplatform,* which means that they can run on a variety of hardware configurations. For example, Linux can run on a variety of computers. If you have a PC, therefore, you buy Linux for the PC; if you have some other type of computer, you buy Linux for it.

✔ An operating system carries with it a software base. For example, you can choose Windows as your operating system because it's friendly to you and has lots of software available.

✔ You generally purchase operating systems at the time you buy your computer, which means that the dealer sets everything up for you.

✔ The operating system controls the microprocessor. In fact, operating systems are written for specific microprocessors.

Operating System Survey

Believe it or not, you have a choice when it comes to selecting an operating system. Not every computer store carries all operating systems at one time, so you may have to shop around. But, options are out there and available — *if* you're willing to look.

This section highlights the various operating systems now available. Consider this section a mere survey; use your own, personal observations and judgments to select an operating system just for you.

Windows XP, Home and Professional

Windows is the most popular operating system available, sold with almost every PC. It's friendly and powerful (see Figure 15-1), with a large software base and plenty of games. Chances are that your new computer will have Windows XP installed.

Windows XP comes in two flavors: Home and Professional (Pro). Both are *very* similar, with only a few subtle differences between them. Even so, the only real reason to go with Home over Professional is if you plan to play computer games, especially older Windows games. Otherwise, Windows XP Professional is the way to go.

Figure 15-1:
Windows
XP looks
like this.

✔ If you want to play games or you consider yourself more of a "consumer" than a business user, get Windows XP Home Edition.

✔ Note that Windows XP Professional costs more than the Home version.

✔ Yes, Windows XP Professional can also play computer games, but they must be designed specifically for Windows XP.

✔ Only a few extra features are in Windows XP Pro that Windows XP Home lacks. Visually, the two operating systems are indistinguishable from each other.

✔ A special version of Windows is available for tablet computers.

Mac OS

The Macintosh operating system, or OS (see Figure 15-2), is synonymous with the Macintosh hardware: Buy a Mac; get an operating system. Although it would be nice to purchase the Mac OS (operating system) for the PC, you just can't. Alas.

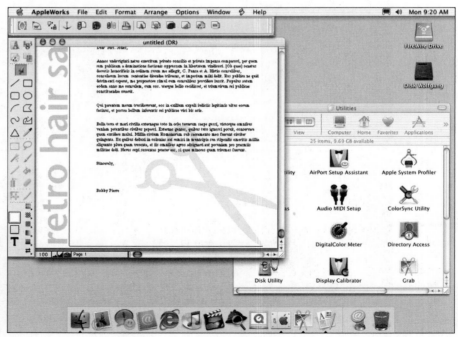

Figure 15-2:
The
Macintosh
OS looks
like this.

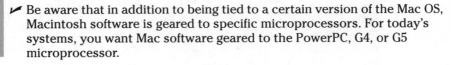

"How is the BIOS different from the operating system?"

If the operating system is the main software program in charge of the computer, what's the BIOS for?

The *BIOS* is software that's written and "saved" to a ROM chip inside the computer. The instructions there tell the computer how to do basic things and accomplish simple tasks. But, the software doesn't control the computer itself. Instead, the operating system takes over and uses the BIOS to help it control everything.

Even if you know that your plans include a PC with Windows, I urge you to find a computer store that sells the Apple Macintosh and then sit down and take a test drive. You find that the salespeople are enthusiastic and helpful and that it's a good thing to survey the variety before you consign yourself to Windows slavery.

- The Mac OS is the only true alternative to Windows.

- If you're planning to use your computer for graphics, you would be remiss not to survey what's available on the Mac.

- The Mac OS is tightly tied to Macintosh hardware.

- Be aware that in addition to being tied to a certain version of the Mac OS, Macintosh software is geared to specific microprocessors. For today's systems, you want Mac software geared to the PowerPC, G4, or G5 microprocessor.

Linux

Linux is a free operating system that runs on just about any computer hardware platform, and particularly on PCs.

Well, Linux isn't *exactly* free. You do pay for a release or *distribution* of Linux, but that also includes bells and whistles and programs that make installing Linux a snap. You can even add Linux to a computer that already runs Windows and "share" both operating systems.

Linux can be cryptic at times, but as long as you add a friendly *shell,* which adds a graphical user interface to the program, it can be easy to use. So, unless you're a programmer or Unix maven, look for a version of Linux with a shell program that helps you get used to the operating system. (This is the trade-off for Linux being as powerful as it is — even more powerful than Windows.) Figure 15-3 shows Linux being run with a shell.

- ✔ Linux is similar to the Unix operating system. If you like, you can get the Unix operating system for your computer as well. But, why bother when Linux can be had for next to nothing?

- ✔ Linux distributions go by product names such as Red Hat Linux, Mandrake Linux, and SuSE Linux.

- ✔ Linux fans like to use the word *distro* instead of distribution.

- ✔ Some versions of Linux are paid for by subscription. For example, you may pay $50 a year. For that price, you get new updates when they come out, plus support by e-mail or direct phone call.

- ✔ Although Linux can be run on Mac hardware, what's the point? The Mac OS X is a better version of Unix than what Linux offers, and it has better software.

- ✔ With continued modification, Linux may one day be a popular alternative to the Windows hegemony.

Figure 15-3:
Here is
Linux
running a
graphical
interface.

Here comes the Sun

On the high end, computers made by Sun Microsystems run the Solaris operating system, a version of Unix customized by Sun. At one time, you could buy versions of Solaris for PC hardware; although, by being free, Linux has pretty much taken the wind from Solaris' sails.

I don't really talk about Sun in this book, although its equipment is solid and reliable and many businesses run on Sun workstations. These machines aren't for individual or home users or even for small businesses, yet they remain a viable alternative for larger companies.

The antique, the immortal, and the dead

Even more operating systems are available. New ones are being developed all the time, though rarely do you see a stack of software boxes for them in the Software-o-Rama. These are the curiosities. The ugly cousins. The ancestors of today's computer operating systems.

DOS: Yeah, DOS is dead. IBM still makes a version of it, though, named PC-DOS. Lots of DOS programs are still out there, many of them available for free (because the developers don't stand a chance of making money any other way!). A free version of DOS, named Open DOS, is also available from the Internet. It's quite popular with the anti–Windows crowd.

OS/2: Before Windows, OS/2 was to be the successor to DOS. Ha! Never happened. IBM still makes OS/2 available, though. But, you can't get software for it, or at least nothing worth looking at. And, if it has no software, the thing really has no point to it, eh?

Unix: Unix is the oldest operating system available, originally developed for minicomputers but now available for just about every computer made. Various flavors of Unix are available, from the Solaris operating system for Sun workstations to FreeBSD and OpenBSD for most hardware platforms.

I could probably rattle off about a dozen other operating systems that have come and gone over the years. Each one had its time and place, but now they're consigned to the dustbin of history.

Chapter 16

Everything You Wanted to Know about Software (But Were Afraid to Ask)

*Y*our computer needs software like an orchestra needs a conductor, like a car needs a driver, like an actor needs a script — you get the idea. Whatever it is that a computer does, it does it because of software. And, you can choose from a great heaping hoard of software out there.

The information in this chapter properly describes the more popular categories of software and what each one does. Odds are good that you will pick one or more of these types of software, depending on your needs, likes, and whims.

Doing the Internet

The most popular thing to do with a computer now is communicate online by using the Internet. To do that, you need various pieces of software; the Internet itself isn't a specific program; rather, many programs *use* the Internet's communications abilities to send and receive information all over the galaxy.

The good news about the Internet is that most of the software you need comes with a computer. Even if the software isn't part of the operating system, the manufacturer tosses in sample Internet programs to help you get started. The two main programs are the Web browser and the e-mail program.

Browsing the Web

What most people call "the Internet" is really the World Wide Web. To surf its many pages, locations, and interesting places, you need a piece of software called a *Web browser*.

Windows comes with the Internet Explorer Web browser, which is considered by Microsoft to be a part of the Windows operating system.

The Macintosh uses Apple's own browser, named Safari.

Linux systems come with a host of browsers — usually, the Mozilla browser, Opera, Netscape, and many others.

The good news is that even more browsers are out there to choose from. Many are available for free on the Internet. If you don't like what you have, you can always pick up and try something new without spending a dime.

Getting your e-mail

Another basic program is an e-mail reader, which also comes included with each operating system. As with a Web browser, many free alternatives are available on the Internet, if you're not happy with what your operating system provides.

Some high-end e-mail programs come with various "office" types of applications. For example, with Microsoft Office, the Outlook e-mail program is available. On the Mac, the high-end program is Entourage.

Doing AOL

Another popular way to access the Internet is by using America Online (AOL). A sign-up kit for AOL is shipped with just about every computer.

The advantage of AOL is that it's all over the place. Throw a cat into a crowd of people, and you will probably hit two or three AOL users. It seems that just about everyone is on AOL. Why not join them?

On the downside, AOL access to the Internet is indirect. You must first dial in to the AOL computers, which then connect you to the Internet. Also, AOL tends to be more expensive than Internet access from other national services.

Productivity Software

After the Internet, the next-most-popular form of software is generally called *productivity* software. These programs are the ones that get things done — the workhorses. Even if your main purpose for having a computer is playing games or creating graphics or just surfing the Web, you still find yourself needing at least a few productivity applications to keep yourself occupied.

Word processing

The most popular type of application on any computer is the word processor, as shown in Figure 16-1. As an office tool, the computer first replaced the type-writer. Word processors have come a long way, of course, from being just a better typewriter. Modern word processors can correct grammar and spelling as you type, and they allow you to include pictures and format your text in various and sundry ways.

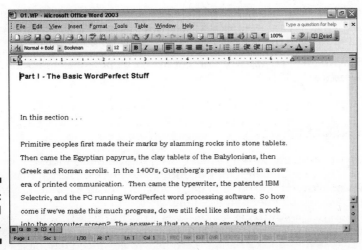

Figure 16-1:
A word
processor.

Desktop publishing

A more advanced type of word processing is *desktop publishing.* These programs combine the text produced by a word processor with graphics and other tools to create ready-to-publish documents — far better than any mortal word processor is capable of.

If you plan to do any publishing, you need desktop publishing (DTP) software in addition to your word processor and graphics applications.

The most popular desktop publishing programs are QuarkXPress and PageMaker. Unfortunately, they're also the most expensive and difficult to figure out how to use. ("Professional" software usually is.)

Other desktop publishing programs include Microsoft Publisher, AppleWorks, and Adobe InDesign.

At one time, several "levels" of word processor existed: one for beginners, one for writers, one for lawyers, and so on. However, most major programs have combined all these tools from the different levels; you pay for them whether you need them or not. That situation makes word processors full featured yet expensive.

- ✔ Most computer operating systems come with a basic word processor.

- ✔ The most popular word processor is Microsoft Word. Both PC and Mac versions of Word are available.

- ✔ Other word processors are available. For Windows, the Works word processor is popular with beginners. On the Mac, the AppleWorks program also contains an easy-to-use word processor.

- ✔ If you're into writing plays or movies, some special word-processing software has been developed especially for you. This type of software is advertised in the back of both movie and computer magazines.

- ✔ The original, arcane word processor for all personal computers was WordStar.

Databases

A *database* program is used to manipulate information, such as a listing of your record collection or a tally of unruly employees. The database software stores the information and then helps you sort it, sift it, print it, retrieve it, or mangle it in any number of interesting ways.

Many database programs are available, from simple ones that just organize your party invites and Christmas card lists to advanced databases that involve some type of programming knowledge. Whatever your needs are, you can find a database program to help you manage your stuff.

A typical and quite popular example of a database is personal organizer software, often abbreviated PIM, for *p*ersonal *i*nformation *m*anager. This type of program includes an address list, appointment calendar, and other goodies. It's basically an electronic version of the old-fashioned date book, ideal for keeping details about customers or vendors or overseas secret agents.

Home-budgeting software

Nothing helps mind the bills like a computer. For this task, you should look into two popular programs: Quicken and Microsoft Money. Both do similar things and have the same purpose: to help you balance your checkbook, write checks, manage your money, and do all those wondrous things the computer industry advertising promised in the past decade.

Some versions of programs are even available to help you manage your company or small business. These programs — as well as Quicken and Microsoft Money — also integrate into various income-tax-paying software that really saves you time when tax season arrives.

The true advantage to home-budgeting software is being able to order checks that can be printed on your computer's printer. It isn't necessary to buy these checks from the same company that produces your home-budgeting software.

Spreadsheets

A *spreadsheet* is an unusual type of program: It combines the power of a calculator with the breadth and depth of a huge table. Although spreadsheets are mostly used for "number crunching" or working with financial data, just about any information you can fit into a grid works well in a spreadsheet.

Spreadsheets rarely are considered home or personal software. However, I find them flexible enough that I take advantage of them — and this type of software typically comes with the office type of program that includes your word processor. So, if you have the program, why not use it? But, if you need the program, you will be thankful to have it.

✔ Spreadsheets aren't just for numbers. They can produce graphs, charts, and organizational charts; and spreadsheets work with any type of lists (see Figure 16-2). If your information appears in any type of grid, working with it in a spreadsheet is a breeze.

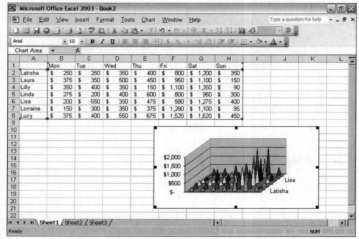

Figure 16-2:
A typical
spreadsheet,
showing off
a graph.

✔ The most popular spreadsheet program for the PC is Microsoft Excel, and Excel is also available on the Mac.

✔ AppleWorks is another popular spreadsheet program for the Macintosh.

✔ The original, prototype spreadsheet was VisiCalc. It stood for *visi*ble *calc*ulator. You may find a copy in a computer museum near you.

Graphics

Graphics software falls into two categories: drawing and painting programs. These programs enable you to create and manipulate a graphical image on the screen. Each one uses a different technique to create the image.

Drawing programs, which are much more precise than painting programs, deal with objects and vectors rather than with dots on the screen.

Painting programs are more recreational and not as accurate as drawing programs. They enable you to paint more realistic images, as shown in Figure 16-3. Drawing programs, on the other hand, are more technical in nature, just as a blueprint is more technical than a painting of the eventual structure.

Similar to painting programs are photo-editing programs. They range from the simplest programs that crop, rotate, or enlarge, to elaborate programs that let you fix common photo problems, edit images, create special effects, and do other amazing things.

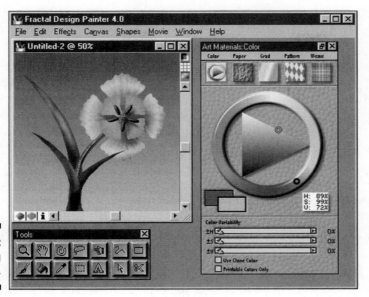

Figure 16-3:
A painting
program.

✔ If you're an engineer or architect, you probably will spend some serious
   bucks for a decent graphics system. The advantage of these systems is
   that changing a design is easy because the thing is stored in a computer.

✔ Almost every aspect of graphic arts is now done by using a computer.
   Most of the best stuff is available on the Macintosh, with some applications also available in Windows.

✔ Don't forget computer animation! Many introductory animation programs
   produce videos that rival the early computer graphics systems of the
   1990s — and at a fraction of the cost.

Recreation and Education

Though few people admit it, computers can be used to play games. Oh, and
don't forget education — although with a computer, a thin line exists between
education and entertainment; both are rather fun.

Games

This whole personal computer craze really started with the home arcade
games of the early 1980s. Although the arcade games are going strong, it's

Bundled software packages

The software industry knows that you get lots of software with your new computer. For this reason, it cuts you a break: Most of the common software you need is bundled into a productivity package or office "suite." For example, the Microsoft Office suite comes with a word processor, a spreadsheet, an e-mail program, and other applications, depending on which version of Office you get (and how much you pay).

Even better news: These bundled software packages often come "free" with the computer.

You pay for them, but the cost is built into your purchase, so the damage doesn't seem as bad.

The advantage of bundled software is that everything generally works well together. That's nice. The disadvantage is that you may get stuck with something you don't need. That's just something you have to put up with, which is why you should survey what's available before you accept one bundled package or office suite over another.

hard to compare those machines that only play games with a computer that plays games *and* does other things, like process words and browse the Internet.

Many different types of computer games are available: arcade-style (see Figure 16-4); shoot-'em-ups; classics, such as chess, Go, and Othello; adventure games; "little man" games, à la Pac Man; and simulation games (flight simulators, war simulators, and business simulators). The creativity well never runs dry with computer games.

Figure 16-4:
An arcade type of computer game.

✔ Serious gamers use PCs and not home game machines for their main systems. PCs are more customizable and easier to upgrade with the latest technology. Game machine consoles are closed boxes.

✔ The Macintosh is also a great gaming platform. The only drawback is that it takes longer for popular games to be "ported over" to the Macintosh.

✔ More and more, new games are also appearing on the Linux platform.

Education

If computers are magnets, kids are tiny balls of steel. They love computers. They're bold. And, there's a reason for that. Nope, it's not that kids now are smarter than we were. It's that kids *have no fear*. In fact, I recommend that you get your kids their own computers. Data loss means little to them.

Some great educational programs are out there, from stuff to teach toddlers their colors and numbers to encyclopedias and SAT exam simulators. Thankfully, much of what's out there is really good. Although some bad programs are out there, just ask around at a PTO meeting, and you quickly find out what's good and what stinks.

✔ Generally speaking, all the Microsoft reference titles tend to be very good.

✔ For small kids, I can recommend programs in the Jumpstart series. Also popular are the *Sesame Street* and *Dr. Seuss* programs.

Utility Programs

A special category of software is the utility program. This type of program differs from an application in that it isn't used for productivity. A utility program doesn't do your work on the computer; it works on the computer itself. A *utility* program typically does one of three things: improves performance, diagnoses problems, or repairs something.

Utilities come in bundles of several dozen programs. For example, one program may recover files you deleted, another may rescue a damaged hard drive, and another may protect your e-mail from nasty computer viruses.

✔ Utilities are also referred to as *tools*.

✔ Your computer's operating system comes with a host of utilities for doing various computer chores.

- About the oldest and most venerated set of utility programs is Norton Utilities. It's available for both the Mac and the PC.

- One of the best utilities to own is a virus scanner. This type of program ensures that your computer isn't infected with a nasty program (a *virus*) that can really foul things up. See the nearby sidebar, "Necessary utilities."

- Have you ever said "I wish I had just one little program that could. . . ." or "I keep repeating these same steps over and over — can't the computer do that for me?" If so, you need a utility. Chances are that something is available to do that specific job. If not, you can write your own computer program, as covered in the next section.

Programming

Computer programming enables you to write and run your own computer software. So, if you tire of everything in this chapter and really want something *just for you,* you can write a computer program to make that happen.

Necessary utilities

Modern computer operating systems now do just about everything and come with just about every type of program you need in order to care for your computer. In three areas, however, modern operating systems fall short. For these areas, you should consider getting three types of utilities — especially if you plan to buy a PC running Windows: antivirus, anti-spyware, and firewall.

Antivirus: This type of program helps prevent certain nasty and unwanted programs from invading your computer, compromising your security, and wreaking havoc. The most popular is Norton AntiVirus, though the McAfee utility is also popular and reliable.

Anti-spyware: This relatively new class of utility is designed to fight nasty programs on the Internet. The spyware category of software snoops on you as you use the Internet, by observing your patterns for marketing purposes. The problem with spyware is that it's often not wanted and quite hard to remove. Anti-spyware software solves that problem.

A firewall: A firewall utility is used to prevent unwanted access to your computer over the Internet. The Internet was designed during more trusting times, but now many of its weaknesses are commonly exploited. To help prevent that, a firewall can be used to help hide your computer on the Internet and prevent unwanted access.

You can purchase any or all of these utilities with the computer or afterward. In some cases, you can even find these utilities at no cost on the Internet. But, if they're available with the computer when you buy it, all the better.

Many different programming *languages* are available for the computer. Some are easy. Some are hard. The good news is that it's easy to figure out on your own. Many self-paced books and tutorials are available, and most programming languages are very helpful when it comes to spotting errors and offering suggestions on how to fix things. Perhaps the best news is that you don't have to be good at math to understand a programming language. Just having a healthy curiosity about computers helps.

✔ Don't be fooled: Writing a program, even a simple one, takes a long time. Still, you can do it. No one will stop you. It's one of the more charming things about a computer.

✔ The most popular programming language is C++. Unfortunately, it's not the easiest to master.

✔ The easiest programming language to use is BASIC. The most popular version is Microsoft Visual Basic. In a way, it lets you create a Windows program as easily as cut-and-paste.

✔ Other languages are available, each with its individual charms and detractions — plus an army of devout followers.

Software for Nothing and Almost Free

Believe it or not, not all software costs money. A good number of programs, in fact, are available for nothing or almost free. Some software may come "free" with your computer; some may be available from nice people who write software and give it away because they're eccentric geniuses and expect their rewards in the hereafter.

✔ You can find these free and almost free software programs all over the place. Computer stores sometimes have bins full of disks of free stuff (though you pay for the disks it's copied on).

✔ The most popular place to pick up free software? The Internet.

Public domain software

The freest type of free software is known as *public domain* software. It's the freest because the author of the package has donated it to the public domain: He declines ownership. Believe it or not, plenty of public domain programs are available. No cost. Ever.

- ✔ Public domain software says so, either in the program or in the documentation. Never assume that something is public domain just because someone else tells you that it is.
- ✔ Don't sell public domain software or buy it from anyone. It's free!

Freeware or open source

Freeware is software that has no cost but isn't in the public domain. The primary difference is ownership. Because public domain software has no owner, anyone could, theoretically, modify it and resell it. With freeware, the author gives the stuff away but retains ownership and control. The software may not be modified or, often, redistributed without the author's permission.

- ✔ An example of freeware is Linux. The program is given away freely. (What you pay for is a Linux distribution, not Linux itself — a weird concept a lawyer may be able to explain to you.)
- ✔ A hefty amount of Palm OS software is freeware, including the addicting Hearts game.

Shareware

A popular form of free software is referred to as *shareware,* or software that's available at no cost, just like public domain software and freeware. The exception is that if you use and enjoy the program, the author requests that you contribute a donation. After that, the software is usually "unlocked" and more features are available or the author provides free updates.

- ✔ I've used many shareware programs and pay for those I continue to use.
- ✔ The fee for buying shareware is really cheap, often $10 or less.
- ✔ Unlike with real software, which you cannot give away, shareware authors encourage you to give their programs away.

Demo software

Another category of free software is the *demo* program. These programs are special versions of major applications that you can try before you buy. Sometimes, they're the real thing and lack only a few features. At other times, the demo software self-destructs after a few weeks (the demo is over).

Beware of Illegal or Pirated Software

Though you can find lots of software available without cost, many programs still are sold through retail channels. These programs are *not* free and are not meant to be given away. Don't accept any software you can otherwise buy as free. Even if a well-meaning, innocent friend is offering you the program, don't accept it. This practice constitutes theft. Only if the software states that it's free (or it's a demo) can you legally use it without paying.

✔ Stolen versions of software are typically infected with computer viruses, or they may be nasty programs masquerading as the real thing.

✔ Pirated versions of popular games usually contain viruses or other nasty programs. Please avoid the temptation to get this software for "free."

✔ The most pirated software worldwide is Windows. In many countries on this planet, millions of computers run Windows, but only a few thousand copies have ever been sold.

Part III
Finding Your Perfect Computer

The 5th Wave   By Rich Tennant

"I'm ordering our new PC. Do you want it left-brain or right-brain-oriented?"

In this part . . .

*I*f buying groceries were as complex as buying a computer, we would all starve. Food is easy to buy in a store, probably because so many people enjoy eating. I would even bet that the first human to eat an avocado wasn't thinking about whether it was a fruit or vegetable or how many carbs it had or which vitamins it supplied or what other kinds of food would go well with it. Nope — he was thinking "Big pit."

This part of the book continues with the five-step process of buying a computer. The next several chapters continue with Steps 2 through 5: the task of hunting for software, finding hardware, searching for service and support, and, finally, buying a computer. The idea here is to remove the complexity and make computer buying as easy as grocery shopping.

Oh, and an avocado is a fruit. So is a tomato. (But, for political reasons, the United States government legally declared that a tomato is a vegetable. Go figure.)

Chapter 17

Shopping for Software

. . . .

In This Chapter

▶ Test-driving software

▶ Looking for help

▶ Checking for developer support

▶ Reading the software box

▶ Filling in the software worksheet

. . . .

See computer. See computer go. Go, computer, go! How does the computer go? Software!

After deciding what it is that you want your computer to do, the second step in buying a computer is to shop for software. After all, the *software* does the work. Even though a computer's hardware specs may look great on paper or the advertising promises the latest and greatest technology, that means nothing without the software to drive it. Gotta have that software! This chapter tells you how to find stuff that works with you and gets your job done.

How to Buy Software

Before heading off to the Mr. Software store, you should know what it is that you're about to do. I don't want you to walk around and pick up various software boxes because they're pretty or look impressively hefty. No, you need a plan of attack. Here 'tis:

✔ Take a test drive.

✔ Confirm the support that's available.

✔ Obtain product information.

✔ Fill in this book's software worksheet.

This section outlines each of the steps in your software plan of attack.

Don't buy anything just yet! You're shopping, not buying.

Some stuff about software boxes you don't have to read

Software looks great on the shelf — and there's a reason for that. It's designed to look alluring, impressive, fun, exciting, or whatever the software promises. Don't be fooled by clever packaging.

Here are some little-known facts about software in the box, on the shelf, in the store:

✔ Software boxes contain lots of air. They used to contain manuals, disks, coupons, and other stuff. Now, the typical software box contains a CD in a paper envelope and maybe a thin, pamphlet-size manual. Even so, the boxes are just as big as when the software came with a 500-page manual and a 350-page reference book.

✔ Some software boxes contain manuals and references. How can you tell? Pick the thing up and shake!

✔ All software boxes are a certain size because psychologists have determined that a given size looks good on the shelf at the software store.

✔ A theory a few years ago implied that software boxes were made intentionally larger than necessary so as to literally push the competition off the shelves!

✔ For a while, the product name on the software box appeared one-third of the way from the top. The reason was that the shelves at Egghead Software were tilted in such a way that you couldn't see the top third of the box. (Even now, the product name appears on the lower half of the software box.)

Taking a test drive

Buying software is a matter of taste. As with discovering new food, you should sit down at a computer and try out any software you plan to buy. Any store that sells software should let you do so. All you have to do is ask "Can I try out the Mobius spreadsheet?" As a buyer, you're entitled to take a test drive.

What should you look for? Look for things you like. If the program is a word processor, how easy is it for you to start typing? Do the various things on the screen look obvious to you? Is it cryptic? Does it feel slow or awkward? Make a note of these things, and if the word processor isn't to your liking, try another. You should apply this technique to all the software you test-drive.

✔ Most computer stores have machines set up on which you can test-drive the software. Some office-supply and department stores may be set up this way.

✔ Don't feel guilty about asking to test-drive! If the dealer says No, go somewhere else.

✔ Please, please don't have a salesperson demo the software; that person is often too familiar with it to do you any good. It's up to you to fiddle with the software.

✔ When you find something you like, fill out a software worksheet for it (see the sample worksheet at the end of this chapter).

Other sources for test-driving

Not everyone lives near the dream Software-o-Rama that carries everything and lets you test-drive *and* has truly knowledgeable and trustworthy employees. If you're not so lucky, you can consider some other test-driving sources:

Your guru: Having a computer-knowledgeable friend can be a boost to picking out some good software. Let your friend show you some of his or her favorite software packages. That's how I got started years ago; I basically used everything my computer guru was using on his computer. Although it wasn't what I ended up with, it was a good start.

Computer groups: Most areas have coffee groups that meet to discuss computers and hear guest speakers. These groups are listed in the newspaper or local computer circulars. Stop by and visit one to find out what people use and what their opinions are.

Buy what's popular: Another tactic some people use is to look at what's popular. If you live out in the boonies (like I do), call up a mail-order place and ask what sells best (for example, "What's the best-selling database for a philatelist like me?"). Then have the person you're talking to read the requirements from the side of the box for you. That person may also be able to fax you information, if you have access to a fax machine.

Check the Internet: If you're already blessed with a computer, or are clever enough to borrow one at the library, you can surf the Internet to visit both software stores and the manufacturer's own home page for information. Also check out online reviews at places such as www.zdnet.com and www.cnet.com.

Use school or the office: An easy way to instantly decide which software is best for you is to go with what you know. If you use WordPerfect at work, why not buy it for home? Likewise, find out what kind of software your child uses in school and buy that product to use at home.

Please make sure that you don't "borrow" software from work or school. Though it seems an easy and effortless thing to do, it's really theft. Always buy every software package you use or own, unless it states right up front that it's free or in the public domain.

TIP

Rating the games

Nothing can be as disappointing as buying what you think is a nice, engaging computer game for your 9-year old, only to find him frothing at the mouth as he controls a character on the screen who's ripping the spine from his electronic opponent. To prevent such shock (to the parent, not to the electronic opponent, who really doesn't feel a thing), two rating systems have evolved to allow parents or any PC game buyer to know what to expect before buying anything.

The Entertainment Software Review Board (ESRB) uses a five-level scale, similar to movie ratings, for its games (I would show you the graphics, but they're trademarked and I'm too lazy to get permission):

✔ **EC (Early Childhood):** Designed for young children and would probably bore a teenager to tears

✔ **E (Everyone):** A G-rated game for kids to adults

✔ **T (Teen):** Contains some violence and language, but nothing too offensive

✔ **M (Mature):** For mature audiences only, preferably 17 years old or older — the type of game the teenager *wants*

✔ **AO (Adults Only):** Contains strong sexual content or gross violence

You can get more information from the ESRB Web site, at www.esrb.org/.

How Helpful Is the Software?

Most software developers have given up on *user friendly*. Thank goodness. Whenever a developer tries to make something user friendly, it usually winds up being inane or boring. Rather than look for software that's friendly, you should examine the various ways the developer has to offer you after-sale help.

Two kinds of help are in any software package you plan to buy: in the form of online help (while the program is running) and from the software developer, in the form of phone support.

REMEMBER

✔ If you can't get help with your software, you probably bought the wrong thing in the first place (which is what this chapter tries to prevent).

✔ Because many places don't let you return computer software after you open it, make sure that you're buying the right thing in the first place.

Types of help you find in software

Programs that are nice enough to offer help come in several varieties:

Online help: Wherever you're using the program, you can press a special key to see a list of options or review the manual. This technique is good for looking up topics or seeing how things are done. (Online help is different from help on the Internet; see the end of this list.)

Contextual help: This is the same kind of help as online help, except that the helpful information you see pertains to whatever you're doing in the program. If you're about to print, for example, the helpful information is about printing. If you're about to save something to a disk, the helpful information is about saving.

Tutorial help: When you pay a bit more for a program, it usually comes with a manual for reference and a tutorial for learning. That's always a good thing. The tutorial trains you in using the program step by step. Doing the exercises is the best way to become familiar with the program. (Consider getting a good book on the product if the tutorial really reeks.)

Internet help: You can also obtain help from the Internet. The company may have an e-mail address you can use or offer support on a Web page (look for the *FAQ,* or Frequently Asked Questions). You can also find online forums in the newsgroups to get help from regular schmoes who use the program.

Don't forget support!

Some software manufacturers offer telephone support when you really get stuck. With phone support, you can call up the company and directly ask questions about the software. Strange, but true. In fact, one reason that WordPerfect shot to the top of the charts in the late 1980s was because of its wonderful toll-free phone support.

Not all software phone support is created equal. It comes in what I call the four flavors: vanilla, chocolate, carob, and fudge. These are my flavors, by the way — not an industry standard (well, maybe in the ice cream industry).

Vanilla: With this type of phone support, you pay for not only the phone call but also the support. When the software developer answers the phone, you're usually greeted with "Hi! What's your credit card number?" These developers charge you per call (often per minute) just so that you can ask questions about their products.

Chocolate: With this type of support, which is better than the vanilla type, you pay for only the phone call. After you get connected, you simply wait on hold until someone happens by to answer your question. The *answer* is free; it's just that most of these places tend to involve long-distance calls.

Carob: This type of support is like chocolate, but not as good. It starts out like chocolate: You get free support, but must pay for the phone call. After 90 days (or so), you pay for everything — the phone call *and* the support. (I call it carob because it's like chocolate, but not really as good.)

Fudge: Fudge phone support is the best. With this kind of support, you get an 800 number to call — a free phone call for free support. The only drawback is that these numbers are busy — all the time.

Tangential to this type of support is support on the Internet. For the cost of an e-mail message (next to nothing), you can write to the company and complain away. I can't properly rate this support, though. In some cases, my questions were answered immediately and properly. In other cases, my questions were outright ignored. Until this situation evens out, rate software on its phone support as I just described.

- ✔ Take note of the kind of support offered by the developer of the software you have chosen. If the type of support isn't listed on the box, ask a salesperson what type of support is available.

- ✔ The computer industry prefers selling hundreds of software packages at a time to major corporations and big businesses. Its support polices are designed mostly to please those big customers. People like you and me (and small businesses), who are intrepid enough to buy our own computers, are often left out in the cold.

- ✔ Another great source of after-sale support can be found in a computer book. Although the manual may be gone and support may cost $35 a session, for less than that you can get — and keep — a real book written by someone who really knows the program and explains it well. I recommend it!

- ✔ I find it interesting that WordPerfect started its slide from dominance at just about the same time the "suits" cut back on free support. You would think that the computer industry would learn from this, but, no.

After You Find What You Want. . . .

When you feel that you have found a software package that will get your work done much easier, don't buy it! Instead, make a note of it. Fill out a form similar to the one shown at the end of this chapter. Describe the software you have found to get the job done.

- ✔ Fill in forms for *all* the software you're interested in, even stuff you may plan to buy later. Just go nuts! The reasons for this process become obvious in Chapter 18.

- ✔ After you have found your software, wait. Buying time isn't here yet. Your next step is to find the hardware to match the software you have selected. For now, keep your software worksheets handy.

✔ Write down information about *all* the software packages you're interested in. If you can't decide between two packages, fill out a worksheet for each one. You can decide which one you want to buy later, when you buy a computer.

Stuff you find on the software box

Software comes in a box. Inside the box are the disks, perhaps a manual or getting-started booklet, and other goodies, such as registration cards, keyboard templates, bumper stickers, buttons, and more sheets of random paper than you ever find in a Publisher's Clearing House giveaway.

On the side of the box are the software program's "nutritional requirements." You should find a list of the equipment the software requires. You typically find one or more of these informational tidbits:

✔ Which computer or operating system is required. If it's an operating system, a version number may be listed.

✔ Which microprocessor is required.

✔ How much memory (RAM) it needs.

✔ How much hard drive space it needs.

✔ Which type of graphics is required (graphics memory, 3D support, and resolution, for example).

✔ Whether it has any special hardware requirements (mouse or joystick, for example).

✔ Whether any special options are required or preferred.

✔ Which kind of support is offered.

You may see even more information about even more confusing issues. Don't let that boggle you now! (If you need to, refer to Part II of this book to reacquaint yourself with computer hardware.)

✔ Information on the side of the software package tells you which type of computer runs the software best. If you eventually buy computer hardware that handily exceeds those requirements, you're doing just great.

✔ Never buy any software without first reading its box! I'm serious. Even a pro (well, myself!) should read the box before buying. I have had to return a few software packages because they were for the wrong computer or were incompatible with my equipment. Reading the box would have saved me — uh, I mean "those people" — some time.

WARNING!

Things to look out for in software descriptions

Before getting all excited, you should bear in mind a few warnings when you're reading the information on the side of a software box.

If the word *recommended* is used, beware! The box may say, for example, that it requires 64MB (megabytes) of RAM and that 160MB is recommended. This recommendation usually means that you *need* 160MB, or else the product does not perform to expectations.

Beware the "upgrade" version. Sometimes, software is sold as an *upgrade,* which means that its manufacturer assumes that you have the old or original version already on your computer. If you don't, the upgrade doesn't install properly, and you're out of luck and money. (Because upgrade versions are generally cheaper, don't think that you've found a bargain or are saving money by getting one when you don't have the original version already.)

Filling in the form: Example 1

Figure 17-1 shows the information on the side of a software box, just like you find in a store. It's from a program named Adobe GoLive, which helps you build Web pages and create online content.

System Requirements

* PowerPC G3, G4, G4 dual, or G5 dual processor

* Mac OS X v.10.2.4 through v.10.2.7 with Java Runtime Environment 1.4.1

* 128 MB of RAM (192 MB recommended)

* 200 MB of available hard-disk space

* CD-ROM drive

* QuickTime Pro 6.3 with the QuickTime 3GPP Component required for multimedia features

Figure 17-1: Software requirements on the side of the box.

This product costs $400 and has chocolate support. In addition, here's a distillation of what the software tells you about itself. You need

- ✔ A Power PC Macintosh.

- ✔ Apple system software (Mac OS X) Version 10.2.4 through 10.2.7 *and* support for the Java Runtime Environment Version 1.4.1 or a later version.

- ✔ 128MB of RAM, but 192MB is recommended, so you really need 192MB of RAM.

- ✔ At least 200MB of hard drive space.

- ✔ A computer with a CD-ROM drive.

- ✔ More software: You need QuickTime Version 6.3 with the options mentioned.

Fill in your software worksheet according to the information specified in this list. If you don't know how to fill in one of the items, leave it blank (or ask a salesperson for more information). Figure 17-2 shows how to fill out the worksheet.

- ✔ Generally, if some information isn't listed, it's probably not crucial to the operation of the software. Don't worry about it.

- ✔ Note that this product is a Macintosh product running on the Mac OS ("system software"). A PC version is, doubtless, available as well. If you're undecided between PC and Mac, take down information for *both* versions — including price.

- ✔ The Java Runtime Environment and QuickTime options are potential operating system upgrades for the Macintosh. Generally speaking, these types of options are checked when the software is installed. Otherwise, you can easily obtain new versions over the Internet.

Filling in the form: Example 2

Microsoft is anything but brief. Its description for the requirements to run Microsoft Office 2003 isn't exactly an example of brevity, as shown in Figure 17-3. You can decipher what's there, though. Assume that this package costs $499 and that Microsoft is famous for its carob level of support.

Software Worksheet

Product name: <u>Adobe GoLive CS</u>

Developer: <u>Adobe</u>

Price: <u>$400</u>

Category:
Office	Word processing	Spreadsheet	Presentation
Utility	Database	Graphics	Education
(Internet)	Networking	Programming	Financial
Multimedia	Entertainment	Reference	Other

Type of support: Vanilla (Chocolate) Carob Fudge

Operating systems: Windows 2000 / NT XP Home / Pro
Macintosh OS X
Linux: _____
Other: _____

Microprocessor: Pentium: _____
(G4) G5 Other Mac: _____
Alpha
Speed: _____ MHz

Memory (RAM) needed: _____ megabytes

Hard disk storage: _____ gigabytes

Media: (CD-ROM) DVD Other: _____

Graphics: Memory: _____ megabytes GPU 3D
PCI AGP
ATI NVIDIA

Printer: _____

Other: _____

Notes : <u>Java Runtime Environment 1.4.1 / QuickTime 6.3</u>

Figure 17-2:
A filled-out
software
worksheet.

Microsoft Office Standard Edition 2003 system requirements

Computer and processor
Personal computer with an Intel Pentium 233 MHz or faster processor
(Pentium III recommended)

Memory
128 MB of RAM or greater

Hard disk
260 MB of available hard-disk space; optional installation files cache
(recommended) requires an additional 250 MB of available hard-disk space

Drive
CD-ROM or DVD drive

Display
Super VGA (800 x 600) or higher-resolution monitor

Operating system
Microsoft Windows® 2000 with Service Pack 3 (SP3), and Windows XP or later

Other
Microsoft Exchange Server is required for certain advanced functionality in
Microsoft Office Outlook; Microsoft Windows Server 2003 running
Microsoft Windows SharePoint Services is required for certain advanced
collaboration functionality; certain inking features require running Microsoft
Office on the Microsoft Windows XP Tablet PC Edition; speech recognition
functionality requires a Pentium II 400 MHz or faster processor and a
close-talk microphone and audio output device

Internet Connection
Internet functionality requires dial-up or broadband Internet access
(provided separately); local or long-distance charges may apply

Figure 17-3:
Software
require-
ments.

✔ You need a Pentium running at 233 MHz or higher, though a Pentium III is recommended.

✔ You need 128MB of RAM, although . . .

✔ . . . this product can run on Windows 2000 Professional or Windows XP, either the Pro or Home version. For those operating systems, 256MB of RAM is recommended.

✔ You need 260MB of disk space, but that extra-250MB-of-space thing has me worried. I would just add both figures, for 510MB, to be safe.

✔ You need a CD-ROM drive or DVD drive.

> ✔ The Other category contains a lot of information about specific features. The only one pertaining to hardware is regarding speech recognition, where a faster microprocessor (400 MHz) is recommended.
>
> ✔ The fact that Internet Connection is listed as a category is a red flag to me. That term means that it's important enough to weigh in when you're comparing this product to others. I would consider it a tiebreaker.

Figure 17-4 shows how you could fill in the software worksheet for Microsoft Office 2003, Standard Edition.

Software Worksheet

Product name: _Office 2003, Standard Edition_

Developer: _Microsoft_

Price: _$599_

Category: (Office)   Word processing   Spreadsheet   Presentation
Utility   Database   Graphics   Education
Internet   Networking   Programming   Financial
Multimedia   Entertainment   Reference   Other

Type of support: Vanilla   Chocolate   (Carob)   Fudge

Operating systems: (Windows)   2000 / NT   XP Home / Pro
Macintosh OS X
Linux: _____
Other: _____

Microprocessor: (Pentium:) _233 MHz or greater_
G4   G5   Other Mac:
Alpha
Speed: _____ MHz

Memory (RAM) needed: _128_ megabytes

Hard disk storage: _.510_ gigabytes

Media: CD-ROM   DVD   Other: _____

Graphics: Memory: _____ megabytes   GPU   3D
PCI   AGP
ATI   NVIDIA

Printer: _____

Other: _____

Notes: _Need 400MHz Pentium for voice recognition_

Figure 17-4: A software worksheet for Office 2003.

At last: The software worksheet

Figure 17-5 shows you the software worksheet before it has been filled out. You should use a sheet like it when you software-shop. You can even customize it, by adding special items you find along the way. In fact, you may find that a stack of 3-x-5 cards works better. The idea is to document as much information as you can from a software box.

Fill out the sheets as you software-shop. Look for stuff you like, stuff you need now, and stuff you're thinking about for later. Then, get ready to move on to the next step in the buying process.

Software Worksheet

Product name: _____

Developer: _____

Price: _____

Category:

Office	Word processing	Spreadsheet	Presentation
Utility	Database	Graphics	Education
Internet	Networking	Programming	Financial
Multimedia	Entertainment	Reference	Other

Type of support: Vanilla   Chocolate   Carob   Fudge

Operating systems: Windows   2000 / NT   XP Home / Pro
Macintosh OS X
Linux: _____
Other: _____

Microprocessor: Pentium: _____
G4   G5   Other Mac: _____
Alpha
Speed: _____ MHz

Memory (RAM) needed: _____ megabytes

Hard disk storage: _____ gigabytes

Media: CD-ROM   DVD   Other: _____

Graphics: Memory: _____ megabytes   GPU   3D
PCI   AGP
ATI   NVIDIA

Printer: _____

Other: _____

Notes : _____

Figure 17-5: The software worksheet (or something similar).

Chapter 18

Matching Hardware to Your Software

In This Chapter

▶ Using the hardware worksheet

▶ Filling in the worksheet

▶ Examining a sample worksheet

*W*hen you know about the software you will run, you can better gauge how much hardware you need. This technique is superior to guessing; by gathering information about the software (refer to Chapter 17), you're more than prepared to know exactly what type of hardware you need in order to successfully run that software, both now and well into the future. The battle is half over.

This chapter covers how to select the hardware you need in your new computer. The chapter centers on filling in the computer-buying hardware worksheet. Filling that in is the third step toward buying a computer.

✔ Buying a computer is still two steps away, so don't get ahead of yourself!

✔ Please continue to avoid brand names and part numbers at this stage.

The Hardware Worksheet

Your software gets the job done for you, but only if you find the hardware horsepower to make the software happy. That's the second-biggest mistake people make when they're buying a computer: not getting enough hardware. Fortunately, that mistake won't happen to you.

Figure 18-1 shows the hardware worksheet. When you fill out this worksheet properly, it tells you exactly which type of computer you need. It doesn't tell you a brand name, and it doesn't recommend a store. That stuff comes later.

Hardware Worksheet

Operating system Windows: _____

Macintosh: _____

Linux: _____

Microprocessor: Pentium   G4/G5   Other:
Speed: _____ MHz

Memory (RAM): _____ megabytes

Hard drive storage: _____ gigabytes   Second hard drive   GB

Removable media: Floppy / No floppy
Digital media: _____
Other: _____

Optical media: CD-ROM   CD-R   CD-RW
DVD   DVD-R   DVD-RW   plus / minus
Combination drive   Other:

Graphics adapter: _____ megabytes   GPU   3D
PCI / AGP   ATI / NVIDIA
Other: _____

Monitor: Size: _____ inches   CRT / LCD
Other: _____

Modem: Internal   External
Dial-up   DSL   Cable   Satellite
Speed: _____ (Kbps)

Mouse/pointing device: Standard   Optical   Wireless   Wheel
Trackball   Other:

Ports: COM   Printer (LPT1)
USB   IEEE (FireWire)   Ethernet (RJ45)
Other:

Printer: Brand: _____
Laser   Ink   Impact
Color   Photo   All-in-one
Options: _____

Figure 18-1:
The
hardware
worksheet.

With the worksheet filled out and in your hand, you can visit any computer
store in the land and find a computer that's perfect for you.

Filling in the worksheet (step by step)

Start with a blank piece of paper. You use this piece of paper to create your own copy of the hardware worksheet, by putting on it what's necessary and needed for your personal computer. As you go through each of the following subsections, write down the information you have gathered from your various software worksheets or 3-x-5 cards (whichever is the case).

If you're still "up in the air" between a Macintosh and a PC, create two hardware worksheets. (The same advice applies for any two types of computer systems, though the decisions aren't as varied for game consoles and portable computers.)

You may also want to keep a calculator handy.

Choose an operating system

Look over all your software worksheets, and locate the most advanced operating system listed. That's the operating system you need on your new computer. Granted, you have a few things to note:

- All Macintosh computers come with the latest version of the Mac OS (or "Apple system software"). If you're leaning toward a Macintosh, just circle Macintosh on that form.

- If any program specifies Windows XP Home Edition or is compatible with older versions of Windows, such as Windows 98, you need Windows XP Home Edition. (This advice applies mostly to games that don't run on Windows XP Professional Edition.)

- Any software requiring Windows NT is considered to be Windows 2000 compatible.

- If the software has no written restrictions, get Windows XP Pro.

- Linux software supposedly runs on all distributions of Linux. Be sure to pay attention if special Linux distributions (Red Hat or Mandrake, for example) are mentioned.

Write down your operating system selection.

Pick a microprocessor

You want the latest and fastest microprocessor you can afford. For the sake of filling out this worksheet, however, write down the latest microprocessor your software specifies.

For example, you may get these results:

- Pentium or better
- Pentium 4
- Pentium 4 at 2 GHz

The latest, greatest system in that bunch is a Pentium 4 running at 2 GHz (minimum). That's what you want.

For processor speed, write down the fastest rating specified by any software package. For example, if some game program says that it needs at least an 800 MHz Pentium, write down that value.

- Yes, yes: You will probably get something much faster, and maybe fancier, than the minimum requirements you're writing on the hardware worksheet. Be patient.
- All Macintosh G5 computers are compatible with G4 and all Power Macintosh software. But, if the box says that it needs G4, get at least a G4. Likewise, if the box says that it needs *dual* G5s, you need a computer with two G5 microprocessors.

Calculate your memory needs

To find out how much memory your computer should have, look for the *highest* value specified on your software worksheets. Don't add up the values; simply note the highest one.

Suppose that the memory requirements from various software packages are 128MB, 256MB, 64MB, and 148MB. You pick the highest value, which is 256MB. That's the *minimum* amount of memory your new computer should have.

Note that despite an application's memory needs, memory is packed into a computer in predetermined chunks, such as

- 128MB
- 256MB
- 512MB
- 1024MB or 1GB

If one of your applications needs 148MB of RAM, for example, you have to get a computer with at least 256MB of RAM. Likewise, if an application needs 640MB of RAM, a computer with 1024MB of RAM is in the cards.

As with the microprocessor, if you can afford more memory, get it. The value you calculate here merely tells you a good *minimum* amount of memory you should have. Calculate that value and enter it on your hardware worksheet.

- ✔ More memory is better.

- ✔ The amount of memory the software needs should be *less* than the total amount of memory in your computer. You never want to cut this value short.

- ✔ Windows XP requires at least 256MB of RAM to run, so most Windows XP systems can run any program that has RAM requirements of 256MB or less.

- ✔ If a memory size is *recommended,* always go with it. The minimum memory size is put there by marketing types who want the package to have the widest appeal. The engineers who design the software set the recommended value.

Calculate your hard drive storage

Unlike computer memory, hard disk storage is a cumulative thing. It adds up. And you will, eventually, run out of hard drive storage. The idea is to put that day off as far as possible.

Add all the hard disk storage requirements from all your software work-sheets. If the package doesn't list the storage requirements, use the value 100MB. Total 'em all up.

Suppose that you have the following storage requirements (the two for 100MB are from two packages that don't list hard drive storage requirements):

131MB

100MB

100MB

26MB

65MB

210MB

The total of those values is 632MB.

After you add the values, double the result. In this example, the amount is 1264MB. If you're using a database or graphics program, double the number again. The result is approximately the *minimum* amount of disk space you need in order to use your computer.

That's just for programs. You must also consider the data files you plan to create.

If you plan to use your computer for Internet access, e-mail, and the Web, and perhaps word processing and home accounting, add 4GB to the amount of hard drive storage you need.

If you plan to use your computer for digital photography, add another 20GB to your storage needs.

If you plan to use your computer to play music, add 20GB to your hard drive needs.

If you plan to store computer video on your system, add another 40GB of storage.

Note that these are just wild estimates. The idea is to have a hard drive that has enough room for you in the future. The last thing you want is to have to upgrade a six-month-old computer with a new hard drive because of a lack of planning before the purchase.

- ✔ Relatively speaking, hard drive storage is cheap.

- ✔ Disk storage is different from memory storage. A program uses memory only when it runs. Every program, however, as well as the files and documents the program creates, has to be stored on the hard disk.

More storage decisions

Chances are that your software doesn't require any specific type of disk drive, such as a CD-R or DVD. If it does, jot down that information. Otherwise, you probably can get by with whatever comes with the computer.

- ✔ Don't lament the iMac's lack of a floppy disk drive. You can always add a USB floppy drive later, if you discover that you *really* need one. Ditto for any other floppy-drive-less computer.

- ✔ Write down the fastest CD-ROM rating listed on your software worksheets. If one program requires a 48X CD-ROM, for example, write down that value. Otherwise, you can leave this item blank; whatever the dealer gives you should be fast enough.

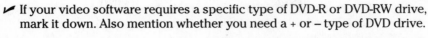

- ✔ If your video software requires a specific type of DVD-R or DVD-RW drive, mark it down. Also mention whether you need a + or – type of DVD drive.

- ✔ If you can, try to specify the *tray* type of CD-ROM, where a tray slides out and you lay the disc in the tray. Personally, I find that method of sticking CDs into the drive easier than using the slot-type of CD-ROM drives (like you have in your car). If this issue is important to you, mark it on the worksheet.

Other hardware stuff

After your memory and storage requirements, the rest of a computer system tends to fall into place without many heavy decisions on your part. Here's a rundown of almost everything left in your computer system:

Graphics: Write down any specific graphics requirements your software lists — for example, "256 color display" or "64MB video memory recommended." If the game you want to play requires a specific graphics processor unit (GPU), note it on the worksheet. You must make sure that whatever graphics adapter you buy is capable of accomplishing at least those feats.

Monitor: A monitor is a personal-preference item. I recommend getting an LCD monitor if you can afford it. Bigger monitors, LCD or CRT, are more expensive.

Make sure that you get a multiscanning, noninterlaced monitor. If you can't afford it, that's okay. I recommend it, though. Also make sure that the dot pitch is at least .28 mm or *smaller*.

Modem: Unless you're planning to get DSL or cable Internet access, you need a dial-up modem. You can use it, at a minimum, as a fax machine on your computer.

- ✔ By not getting a modem, you may save a few dollars on the purchase price.

- ✔ Note that your Internet service provider (ISP) provides you with, or sells you, a DSL or cable modem; these items aren't purchased with the basic computer setup you're buying now.

Mouse: You can have many fancy mice, so make sure that you visit a computer store to see what's available. The dealer will probably give you a choice.

Remember to get a fancy mouse, such as the wheel mouse, only if your software knows what to do with it.

Sound: Most sound cards sold with computers are generally compatible with all the games out there. Only if your software requests a specific sound card should you write it down on the worksheet.

Be sure that your computer comes with external speakers. For extra money, you can get the subwoofer option, which beefs up your computer's sound. All this equipment is extra and not truly required. If your money is tight, you should spend it elsewhere.

Ports: Ensure that the computer has at least two USB ports. Some PCs don't come with an IEEE port, so if you need one, it's an add-on extra.

Other options: Specify any other items your PC may need: a scanner, backup power supply, graphics tablet, or whatever else your software programs may specify.

Part II has more specific information about the hardware mentioned in this list.

A Sample for You to Review

Figure 18-2 shows how a sample worksheet may be filled in. Your sheet should look something like this one when you're through reviewing your software requirements. (Or, you may have two sheets: one for a future Mac and another for a future PC.)

- ✔ The first thing to notice is that not every item is required.

- ✔ Remember that you're configuring a minimal computer. The model you get will probably have more stuff in it.

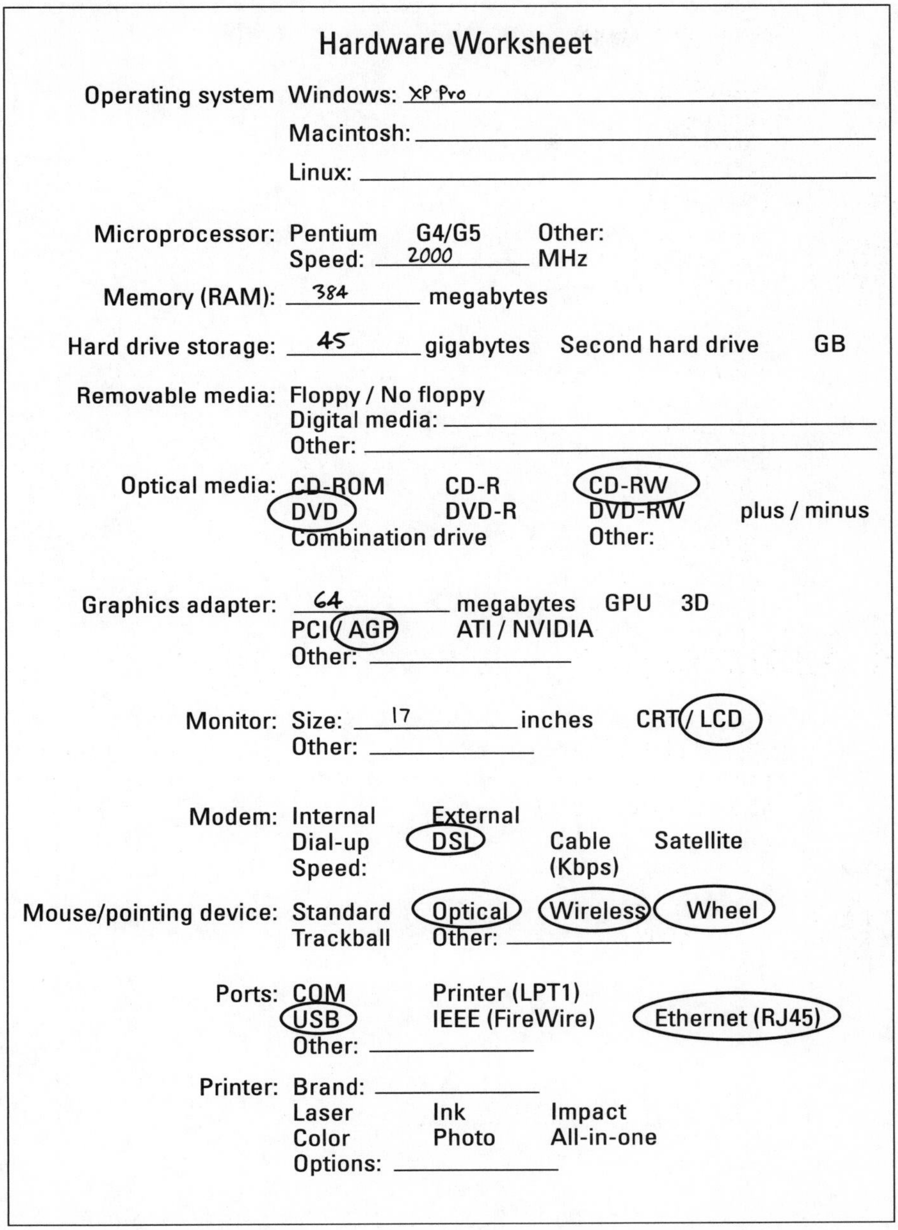

Hardware Worksheet

Operating system Windows: _XP Pro_____

Macintosh: _____

Linux: _____

Microprocessor: Pentium   G4/G5   Other:
Speed: ___2000___ MHz

Memory (RAM): ___384___ megabytes

Hard drive storage: ___45___ gigabytes   Second hard drive   GB

Removable media: Floppy / No floppy
Digital media: _____
Other: _____

Optical media: CD-ROM   CD-R   (CD-RW)
(DVD)   DVD-R   DVD-RW   plus / minus
Combination drive   Other:

Graphics adapter: ___64___ megabytes   GPU   3D
PCI /(AGP)   ATI / NVIDIA
Other: _____

Monitor: Size: ___17___ inches   CRT /(LCD)
Other: _____

Modem: Internal   External
Dial-up   (DSL)   Cable   Satellite
Speed: (Kbps)

Mouse/pointing device: Standard (Optical) (Wireless) (Wheel)
Trackball   Other: _____

Ports: COM   Printer (LPT1)
(USB)   IEEE (FireWire)   (Ethernet (RJ45))
Other: _____

Printer: Brand: _____
Laser   Ink   Impact
Color   Photo   All-in-one
Options: _____

Figure 18-2:
A sample,
filled-in
hardware
worksheet.

Chapter 19

Surveying the Shopping Landscape

They sell computers everywhere, so finding one to purchase isn't a big issue. "Two slurpies, a Lotto ticket, and one of those mini–Macs, please." Of course, you don't want to walk into just anywhere to buy your computer.

Lots and lots of places sell computers. Some are dedicated computer stores, some are mom-'n'-pop places, some do mail order, some sell directly from the factory, and some places even sell washers and dryers right next to the iMacs. This chapter describes each place and gives you an idea of what to expect when you walk in.

Where do you start? Probably by picking up the paper and reading the computer ads. Heck, you have probably been doing that already. Now, find out what it all really means.

Reading a Computer Ad

The first step in buying that computer is to look at computer ads. Although this process can be boring, it's definitely not as boring as bewildered browsing in a warehouse-size computer store. After all, because you're reading this book, you'll show up knowing exactly what you need; you don't have to be sold anything. Computer stores aren't really set up for that kind of customer (just look around the next time you visit one of the stores).

Finding computer advertisements

You can find computer ads in computer magazines, your local newspaper, and freebie computer fliers.

Newspapers: Look in the sports section on Saturday (don't ask me why). That's usually where you find some computer-related ads from local stores. You may also want to check the business section throughout the week. Some newspapers even have computer-specific inserts.

Computer magazines: Visit a magazine rack and look for computer magazines. It doesn't matter how technical they are; you are doing research at this point and are using the magazines for their advertising. The library is a great place for this kind of research.

Free circulars: Many communities have free computer magazines or tabloids published locally. They're crammed full of ads from local vendors with some prices — plus service and support — that meet your needs.

Dissecting an ad

Figure 19-1 shows a computer ad I mocked up myself this morning. It lists various "systems" along with their hardware contents and prices. It's typical of what you might see from most local dealers.

Systems displayed in ads such as the one shown in Figure 19-1 are set up primarily for price comparison with competitors. This statement doesn't imply that your choices are limited to what's displayed. Feel free to mix and match components in a system as you need them. If the dealer doesn't do that, shop elsewhere.

Figure 19-1:
A typical
computer
ad.

Don't fear abbreviations! Although I'm sure that some fondness for computer jargon is responsible, space restrictions are the most likely reason that the ads say *RAM* rather than *memory* and *GB* or *G* rather than *gigabytes*. You may even see *HDD* used in place of *hard disk drive*. *VRAM* means *video RAM* or *video memory.* You often find customized products, such as the "clackity" keyboard or maybe some special type of mouse.

One important abbreviation you often see is $CALL. It means that the advertiser wants you to phone up to see what price it offers. You can interpret $CALL in several ways: The price is too ridiculously cheap to advertise (which happens), the price changes frequently (that happens too), or someone there just wants to talk to someone on the phone (not often).

Note that some items are missing from the computer descriptions. Most important, *where's the monitor?* Those prices may look cheap, but all PCs need a monitor.

Always note, in any ad, the phone number *and* address. Although just about any place lists its phone number, you know that a dealer is legit if it has a street address. (Some fly-by-night operations never give addresses.)

Finally, don't forget service and support! The ad may not say anything about what's offered, so be sure to phone or visit the store before you make a decision.

✔ Name-brand manufacturers (Dell, for example) also have ads similar to the one shown in Figure 19-1. Even though your system may not be listed, remember that you can mix and match.

✔ Macintosh and PC rarely mix. If you cannot find specific information about Macintosh computers, buy a Macintosh-specific magazine, like *MacWorld.*

Recognizing common tricks used to make an advertised price look really cheap

Because the competition is fierce, computer dealers go to great lengths to make their systems look cheaper than the other guys'. Here are some common tricks you may want to look for or inquire about when you find a ridiculous price:

✔ The price of the monitor isn't included (the most common trick).

✔ The price of the microprocessor isn't included. (Although this practice sounds ridiculous, it happens.)

✔ No memory is included in the computer. Look for 0MB RAM in the ads, or see whether the memory value is missing.

✔ Manufacturer's rebate coupons are included, which lower the price only *after* you turn them in.

✔ Support or service is omitted!

✔ An unrelated illustration is shown — usually, a picture of a computer that may or may not look like what's being advertised. For example, watch out for "Model 400 shown" or "Optional monitor shown" written in tiny print below the illustration.

The myth of the free (or almost free) computer

The final trick you find lurking out there is the free, $0, or $100 computer. Basically, they make the price so low by preselling you several years' worth of Internet service with the computer. So, the Internet provider is buying your computer in exchange for your subscribing to its service.

It works like this: When you buy the computer, you sign up for three years of Internet service. You get, in exchange, a certificate for $300 to $600 off the purchase price of your computer. You walk home with a new PC or Macintosh, having paid only $100. And then, the bills come.

Every month for 36 months to come, you have to pay your Internet provider $20 or so a month. It's part of your purchase agreement. That's great if you're planning to do so anyway, but if you want to change Internet providers, you still have to pay for 36 months. Or, if you don't like the computer and it ends up in the closet, you're still paying $20 for 36 months ($720 total).

My advice? If — and that's a big *if* — the computer is exactly what you need according to this book *and* you have the proper service and support for it, consider the "free" or cheap computer as an option. However, also keep in mind that I'm not recommending it to any of my friends, not even as a joke.

Some Q&A before You Rush Out to Buy

In keeping with the theme of the preceding section, you may have even more buying questions right now. This section lists some general questions and answers (the preceding section is specific to the free-computer phenomenon). Hopefully, the one question you want to ask is among the following.

"Should I get a quote?"

I wouldn't. The margins on computers are so low today that the dealer is probably giving you the best price it can muster. If you can find something cheaper — and I mean a lot cheaper — it's probably refurbished or sold without any support. Remember, support is more important than price, especially for your first purchase.

An exception to this rule is when you go shopping on the Internet (as covered in Chapter 20). In that case, you can use some handy tools to compare prices on exactly the same pieces of hardware and often find a deal.

Don't forget to factor in the cost of support, especially if you're buying your first computer. Even if you have a computer but haven't been shopping in many years, support is worth the extra price.

"Can I haggle?"

Don't bother haggling over the price unless you're buying many computers at a time. Otherwise, you just irritate the dealer.

The competition between computer stores is too great to allow for any haggling. The price you see advertised is usually what it sells for. Computers still have a manufacturer's suggested retail price (MSRP), and you may see that ridiculous value listed above the store's "discount." Whatever. Don't expect to get any more breaks than that.

"Should I get a discount off the manufacturer's suggested retail price?"

Yes, especially on software. The "street price" of all computer whatnots is always less than the manufacturer's price — a weird holdover from the days of haggling.

"Isn't there any way to get a deal on a computer?"

Yes, if you don't mind buying something that's going out of style. For example, yesterday's top-of-the-line computer is certainly a deal today! Computer stores push that inventory out at a discount just to get rid of it and make way for the newer, better, faster computers. But my advice is not to wait for such deals and instead buy the best computer you can afford today.

"Is it better to buy from a noncommissioned salesperson?"

I have been buying computers for more than 25 years and have yet to find a commissioned salesperson. Because most stores are either discount or locally owned, there's no commission to be made. I would guess that only the manufacturer's direct-sales reps who sell to major accounts get commissions, although I doubt that even that's the case any more.

If commissioned salespeople bug you, you can always consider going elsewhere.

"What about buying a used computer?"

A used computer is a bad idea for a first-time buyer. Why? Because you're cutting off your service and support, for not only the hardware but also any software they throw in. You get no guarantees or warranties with used equipment. For a second purchase, sure, but not when you're just starting out.

"What about refurbished stuff?"

I have purchased a few refurbished computers, but only because they came with a manufacturer's warranty. The equipment was older, but because it served the purpose I had in mind, it was fine for me. And, it was cheap!

Watch out for refurbished stuff masquerading as new equipment. Always read the fine print. The dealer must tell you that it's refurbished, but it doesn't have to shout its lungs out at you.

"You didn't say anything about the swap meet"

The reason I don't mention swap meets — even computer swap meets — is that no service and support are available. True, if you find a local dealer that is simply making its presence known at the swap meet, that's okay — as long as the dealer has local service and classes or some kind of support.

Swap meets are havens for fly-by-night outfits and jerks who sell stolen or substandard crap from the back of pickup trucks. I don't mean that everyone there is shifty; some reputable dealers do show up. If you do business with a jerk, though, don't expect him to be there the next weekend.

Where to Buy

Looking over the computer ads gives you an idea of what's out there. Eventually, however, you have to pick a few places to phone or visit and get a more lasting impression. You don't want to shop by price alone. A store's reputation is based on service and support, which you can't determine over the phone.

When it comes time to narrow your choices, you can buy your computer from several types of places:

- A local computer store
- A national chain
- A megastore
- Mail order

Any of these options is fine by me for buying a first-time computer. Even mail-order places offer service and support, though the support takes place over the phone rather than in a classroom.

One additional place to buy a computer is the Internet. Obviously, you need a computer to use the Internet, so if you don't yet have one, that choice doesn't do you any good right now. Still, Chapter 20 covers the topic of online buying if you already have Internet access.

Your locally owned and operated computer store

If you're one to support your local economy, a locally owned store is probably your first choice for buying a computer. These places may look tacky. Although they may have stuff on folding tables and boxes stacked in back, they may also have fair prices and owners who offer more personal support than their Big Brother competitors.

The most serious issue about a local store is how long it has been in business. Any store that has been around for three years or more probably has an excellent reputation (or at least a reputation you can verify). Give new places a chance, but consider hanging out in the lobby or checking the service counter to see whether it has any disgruntled customers. You may also ask for a list of satisfied customers to confirm its reputation.

- ✔ I often go to local stores to pick up something quick: a keyboard, a modem, or some piece of software that they have in stock.

- ✔ Some smaller stores may have to order your computer or assemble it. Although this process takes time, you're getting a custom computer. Larger stores tend to sell things "off the rack."

- ✔ Another type of local store is a university bookstore, but don't think that it's cheaper! Some computer manufacturers used to offer decent discounts to students who bought computers at their school bookstores. That may not be the case any more. Never assume that the school bookstore is cheaper than a local store.

National chains

National computer chains have been replaced by computer megastores (see the next section). However, some national stores that aren't necessarily computer stores carry computers: Wal-Mart, Sears, Radio Shack, Kmart, Costco, Sam's Club, and other places sell computers, right next to stereos and DVDs.

The big benefit of buying a computer at a national chain is that it's everywhere. Unlike with local dealers, you never have to worry about finding a Wal-Mart because it's all over the place.

The big drawback to national chains is that they're not geared specifically toward helping people buy computers. Although some places are exceptions, it's hard to expect sincere support from the guy who sells you a computer, a hair dryer, and a country-and-western CD. These places don't have a classroom to teach you about AppleWorks or Windows, and don't expect to get far when you phone up to ask a question about formatting a disk.

The megastore

Megastores are those super computer stores, some bigger than a grocery store, that have everything and anything to do with a computer. You can browse, check out new hardware, ask questions, take classes, and spend money until you have to take out a third mortgage.

One downfall of these stores is that their sales staff turns over quickly. Just as I start a relationship with someone, he's off to another job. This quibble is a minor one as long as the new clerk is just as knowledgeable as the guy he's replacing.

Before you commit to one of these megastores, be sure to check on its warranties and return policies, and double-check on its service and support. Also find out *who* fixes the stuff. Is it fixed there, or does the store just ship broken stuff to some factory in another state?

Mail-order brand names

Welcome to the 21st century, where you can have just about anything mailed to your house — including a computer! You typically order from a catalog or magazine article; someone quotes you a price; and a few days or weeks later, your computer shows up, ready to go.

(Okay, the computer shows up in a box, and you have to set it up. Don't worry — this book shows you how! See Chapter 23.)

Mail-order computers offer the same things as your local dealer or megastore. The only difference is that the computer is sent to your home or office rather than to a loading dock. The price is often cheaper because you aren't charged an in-store markup, and often you can dodge your state's sales tax (though those days are rapidly drawing to a close).

Many people are concerned about mail-order computers showing up dead or damaged. Before you order, make sure that you get a no-questions-asked return policy and that the manufacturer pays (or reimburses you) for shipping. Most places have these types of polices, and, even so, rarely does equipment arrive damaged.

About the only downside to mail-order computers is that their support takes place over the phone. Most places offer an 800 number you can call at just about any time to ask a question. If you're more comfortable with in-person support, however, consider a local dealer or megastore.

One other perk to look for is free on-site service. This service is especially important if you live or work in the boonies, as I do. Make sure that this service is offered even after the warranty period expires, and double-check that your city and state are included in the on-site service deal.

Mail-order pieces' parts

There's a difference between a mail-order brand-name computer and what I call "mail-order pieces' parts": No one should buy a mail-order pieces' parts computer as a first computer. Instead, if you take the mail-order route, buy a brand name you know: Apple, Dell, IBM, or one of a host of others I don't have time to list.

The main way you can recognize a pieces' parts mail-order outfit is that it sells pieces' parts in addition to complete computer systems. Right along with its main Pentium systems, you see a list of hard drives, memory, video cards, modems, printers, and other stock, ready to roll. Sure, those prices look good, but if the outfit doesn't offer the kind of service and support you need, why bother?

What about Building Your Own Computer?

Do you want to build your own computer from scratch? It certainly is possible for the PC (Macs are made only by Apple). Many places sell the parts, and everything plugs in or is screwed in to one thing or another. It's not hard.

The big problem with "rolling your own" PC is that you get no service or support. Even if you're gutsy enough to try, you have no one to turn to when something doesn't work right. Individual parts, but not the complete unit, may be covered by a warranty.

Despite the lack of support, I must tell you that building your own computer is cheaper. The last three PCs I bought were assembled right on my kitchen table and cost me about half what a similar system would have cost from a dealer or directly from the manufacturer.

I don't recommend building your own PC as a first-time purchase. But, if you're handy with electronics, know which end of a screwdriver is which, and you can follow directions, building a PC is entirely possible and can be kind of fun. Here are some tips and pointers:

✔ Buy a bare-bones system if you're just starting out. That includes the console case and motherboard. The CPU and memory required by the motherboard should be documented, so picking out the right things isn't difficult.

✔ The motherboard requires a specific type of microprocessor as well as specific memory. This information isn't easy to find when you're buying the parts, so be sure to confirm that all three things — motherboard, CPU, and RAM — work together before you buy.

✔ Follow the directions in this book to figure out which hardware you need. Ensure that the console case you select is big enough for all that stuff.

✔ Heat and noise are the big issues with home-built computers. Ensure that the console case is properly ventilated and not too noisy.

✔ Good luck!

Chapter 20

Tips for Online Shopping

. . . .

In This Chapter

▶ Buying a computer on the Web

▶ Using a catalog store

▶ Building your own PC on a Web site

▶ Computer-buying tips

▶ Using a shopping agent

▶ Tracking your order

. . . .

*Y*ou may find it odd that computers are required in order to buy computers, but that's the way it works on the World Wide Web. It makes sense:
In the early days of radio, the items advertised the most were new radios. So,
why not sell computers on the Web?

If you have access to the Internet, you can use it as a resource for computer
shopping. Every major computer manufacturer and nearly all the national catalogs, plus many local stores, have an Internet presence. The advantages and
disadvantages of this new approach are covered in this chapter, along with
other, related information for anyone willing to computer-shop on the Web.

Buying on the World Wide Web

Can you buy a computer on the Web? Certainly! Every computer I have
bought in the past five years has been purchased through the Web. The last
time I phoned in a computer order from a catalog was in 1997. (The last time I
bought a computer in a store was in 1988!) But, that's me. What about you?

If you're new to buying a computer, I don't recommend getting your first computer from the Internet. Why? Because you're undercutting the kind of service
and support that would be available to you otherwise. Finding those things is

hard enough when you're shopping locally; imagine trying to find them on the Internet!

For people already bathed in the computer experience, buying online has some real advantages. For example, if you know *exactly* what you want, you can easily find it online rather than search a catalog or waste time on the phone or in a computer warehouse.

- ✔ Service and support *are* available from the Internet. Chapter 21 covers this issue.
- ✔ Buying on the Internet is often cheaper because you're not paying for overhead.
- ✔ If you already have a computer, you can easily buy peripherals or upgrades on the Internet.
- ✔ Buying online isn't foolproof. I have never had trouble with any computer company, but other online retailers have turned out to be rotten apples. As usual, if you have a recommendation from a friend or reliable source, go with it.

Finding a place to buy

Every major computer manufacturer, most catalogs, and even local dealers have a presence on the Web. Therefore, finding them on the Internet is as easy as knowing their names.

Generally speaking, you find two types of stores on the Internet. One, the catalog store, is essentially an electronic version of the same type of catalog you may receive as junk mail from time to time. Another type of store lets you configure your computer the way you want, similar to the traditional walk-in computer store model.

The catalog store: Catalog stores are merely electronic representations of their pagebound junk mail brothers. A Web page catalog usually opens with a list of bargains or popular deals. You should find somewhere on the page a list of categories to browse or a place where you can search for specific hardware. Products may be listed by manufacturer, type of microprocessor, or price.

Note that nearly all the products listed in a catalog are sold as is. Generally speaking, with a catalog-type Web page, you cannot reconfigure items, and your choice of options is limited to what the manufacturer provides. The price is therefore cheaper than if you have special requests, but your choices are limited.

Manufacturers' Web stores: Another way to shop (a way more in tune with how this book is set up) is to select the items you want for your own computer. That usually happens with manufacturers' Web pages and their online stores.

The manufacturer begins with a basic system setup. Then you use the Web page to select various options and see how that affects the bottom-line price. For example, adding another 256MB of memory may cost $70, and selecting a smaller monitor may save $100.

As you work the steps on a manufacturer's Web page, the cost of the computer configuration is updated, calculated, and displayed. You then select an operating system and software and shipping options.

If you make an error, such as selecting an incompatible piece of hardware, the Web page lets you know.

Even if you're not buying right now, a manufacturer's Web page can really help you get an idea of what each option costs and how much you can save if you change a configuration.

✔ Use the hardware worksheet in Chapter 18 to help you get the best possible computer to match your software. Buying more hardware than you need (if you can afford it) is great!

✔ You can find a complete list of online computer retailers at Yahoo!:

```
http://shopping.yahoo.com/computers/
```

✔ Ensure that the vendor has a phone number and street address. You don't want to get stuck online and have to fumble with e-mail to get satisfaction. It just doesn't work.

Placing your order

Eventually, you reach a place on the Web page where you have to place your order. It's either the Checkout button or the Shopping Cart button or some other obvious means to tell the Web page that you're done shopping and are ready to buy.

When you're ready to check out, review the items in your order. Confirm items and quantities or remove items from the list. Use the Update button if you change quantities or remove items. When you're ready to buy, click the Checkout button or Continue button. The next few Web pages contain forms you must fill out.

Some Web pages want you to *log in* at this point, which is merely a handy way to recognize a returning customer. If you have never been to the Web page, you should create a new account. Then you don't have to reenter information each time you buy something.

You need to list your billing and shipping address. Eventually, you have to cough up a credit card number and expiration date. You gotta pay for it, you know.

After filling in everything and clicking the proper buttons, you eventually see an order confirmation page. *Print this page.* The page contains your order number, the items you ordered, plus the final damage to your credit card. If you cannot print the page, carefully copy down the order number. Do this step for future reference.

Many online retailers send an e-mail confirmation of your order. Print it.

Now, you just sit and wait for the computer to arrive. You did opt for the express delivery option, right?

✔ If you're afraid to order online, look for an option that lets you print or e-mail the order form. You can then phone in the order by using an order ID number or simply quoting the catalog numbers over the phone. Nothing is wrong with ordering online. As long as you heed my advice in this book, you should have a pleasant experience and be able to quickly handle any problems that may crop up.

✔ Never has a reported case of credit card fraud involved an online retailer. Never! Buying online is as safe as, if not safer than, ordering from a catalog or buying something in a store.

✔ Always pay with a credit card when you buy online. Though no reported fraud has ever taken place, I would be leery of a company wanting your bank account or Social Security number to buy a computer. They're absolutely not required.

✔ Avoid places that require your credit card number *before* you have selected anything to buy.

✔ You can check up on a potential dealer online by visiting the Better Business Bureau, at www.bbbonline.org. Note that not all businesses are listed with the BBB.

✔ When you create an account for an online retailer, use a common user name or ID for yourself and a unique password. Do *not* use your credit card number as a password.

✔ Have your order shipped by a company that tracks its shipments. I cover order tracking at the end of this chapter.

✔ To be honest with you, I have had trouble buying things on the Internet two times. The first was a company (now out of business) that charged my credit card *before* shipping my order. The second was a company that didn't list any phone number, so when my order never arrived, I had only e-mail to communicate with them — which didn't work. As long as you follow my advice in this chapter, you should never have similar problems when you shop online.

Comparison shopping

Buying a computer isn't about getting the lowest price. But, if you have discovered that the computer you want is a common model — like a Presario or an iMac — you can take advantage of the Web to search for the lowest possible price, at www.froogle.com, for example.

The Froogle site doesn't sell anything. It collects items and prices from various online retailers and shows you what comes up. This option obviously isn't my recommended method for computer shopping. Only (and it's a big *only*) if your hardware worksheets show that you can have a generic type of prepackaged computer does this site help you find the best price. Otherwise, you may need to stick with a build-your-own method, similar to the one offered by most manufacturers' sites, as described earlier in this chapter.

✔ Technically, such price searching Web sites are known as a *shopping agents*.

✔ Here are some other shopping agents worth looking into:

```
pricewatch.com
fatwallet.com
mysimon.com
roboshopper.com
```

Sleazy tricks used by online retailers

Not every online retailer is a jerk. Many offer quality stuff at low prices and ship it cheap. Some places cut corners to save money or to look better than their competition. The following list warns of some well-known tactics used by less-reputable online dealers (even more tricks exist, but keep in mind that mail-order catalogs and local dealers can do many sneaky, nasty things too):

✔ **Bait-and-switch:** A very cheap computer or component is advertised, but — oh, no! — it's suddenly out of stock or back-ordered when you check into it. An alternative is offered instead, for a much higher price.

✔ **Repackaged goods are sold without any warning:** Although nothing is wrong with returns or refurbished equipment, you should have the option of buying either them or new stuff, if you like. Refurbished goods should be clearly marked.

✔ **Handling charges or exorbitant shipping charges:** The cheapest price may not be the least you spend! Some sleazy dealers add "handling" charges to your purchase, which jacks up the price. Be sure that you understand all charges you will pay before you buy.

✔ **Credit cards are charged at the time of order rather than at the time of shipping:** If this is the case, you don't have to pay. Inform your credit card company, and it will be happy to hold the charge for you. If you want to place the charge *in dispute,* instructions are on the back of every credit card bill. You don't have to pay for something you didn't receive or for receiving something you didn't order. It's fraud, and it's illegal.

✔ **Your stuff is shipped elsewhere, and it's your fault:** Shipping problems, such as damaged goods or goof-ups where your stuff gets sent to the wrong location, are a problem for the shipping companies. Inspect your packages before signing for them. And, if your stuff is sent to the wrong place, the shipping company has to fix the situation for you; it's not your fault!

Tracking Your Order

You probably just can't wait to get your new computer. Although anticipation is half the fun, you can while away the time by monitoring your purchase's progress on the Web.

Most retailers have internal tracking, which lets you monitor your computer's progress as it's assembled, tested, and eventually shipped. That can be fun. Even more fun is tracking the delivery as it hops around the United States. Get a shipment tracking number from the Web site as soon as your order ships. Then you can use the delivery service's Web page to see where your shipment is and when it's due to arrive.

Some Web sites automatically link you to a shipper's tracking service. If not, I list some common shipping companies; armed with a tracking number, you can visit these sites to see exactly where your new stuff is and when you will finally get your hot little hands on it (after you get to the site, click the Track or Tracking link on the main page — in some cases, you may have to select your country first):

✔ **DHL:** www.dhl.com

✔ **Federal Express:** www.fedex.com

✔ **UPS:** www.ups.com/tracking/tracking.html

✔ **U.S. Postal Service:** http://www.usps.com/shipping/trackandconfirm.htm

Chapter 21

Searching for Service and Support

A common mistake new computer buyers make is spending all their time worrying about the brand name of a computer or the size of its monitor. But, you can't overlook one extremely important factor: the service and support you need after you set up your computer.

Step 4 in the buying process is to shop for service and support, which is covered in this chapter. If you know anyone who has had a bad computer-buying experience, that person probably forgot this step. After reading this chapter, you won't be the one making that mistake.

How to Find Service and Support

In this section, I make some enemies: Large warehouse stores and department stores are the worst places to buy a computer. Sure, the price may be nice, but after you buy your computer, you're on your own, and that's a mighty lonely place to be if you have a computer question with nowhere to go to get help. It's almost sad, really. My eyes are welling up now, just thinking about it (sniff, sniff).

The moral to this pathetic story is that shopping for service and computer support is just as important as shopping for the computer itself — more so if you're buying your first computer and don't want to feel lost.

Use the list of questions in the next section to grill your prospective computer salesperson. If the salesperson answers most of the questions to your satisfaction, you have found your service and support. If not, buy somewhere else.

✔ Price isn't the most important part of buying a computer. You need service and support more than you need a deal.

✔ Not all warehouse or department stores have awful-to-no service and support. It helps to ask, though, so that you don't become one of the legions who discovers a lack of it later.

Service Questions

Service means "Where does my computer get fixed?" and also "Who pays for it?" Consider asking the questions in this section.

"How long is your warranty?"

A typical computer warranty is only about half a page long, but that's not important. What is important is the length of *time* the warranty covers your computer.

All major computer manufacturers offer some type of warranty, from a few months to several years. Does the dealer support that warranty and offer additional coverage? Consider it a plus.

✔ Computer warranties may seem rather short — 90 days? But, really, that's enough to cover it. Electronic things, like computers, break early in their life cycles if anything is wrong. Otherwise, after 90 days of smooth operation, your computer should be good for at least 4 or 5 years.

✔ Be sure to check whether the warranty is a replacement or repair warranty. Replacement is better; few things on a computer can be repaired in a cost-effective way.

✔ After four or five years, the hard drive tends to die and the computer's internal battery needs replacing.

"Do you fix the computers at your shop?"

If the place that sells your computer fixes them too, that's great. If your dealer has to send your computer to Taiwan to have it fixed, buy it somewhere else.

Note that many dealers don't fix the computers they sell. Instead, you must contact your computer's manufacturer directly. They don't even accept bad equipment, and rarely do they ship it for you. This isn't a plus.

Extended-service policies?
Don't bother, unless. . . .

I don't recommend that anyone purchase an extended-service policy for a computer. The reason is simple: Computers are electronics. If it's going to break, it breaks during the first few weeks of use. If your computer can survive that long, it should be around for its full lifetime, which should be anywhere from four to five years — longer if you take good care of your equipment.

The same rule applies for in-store warranties. These are offered by the store in addition to the manufacturer's warranty. The salesperson applies a lot of pressure when selling those in-store warranties, mostly because the salesperson makes all the money from the warranty. Again, such a thing is not necessary when you

buy a computer. In fact, if they're too pushy on such a thing, I would consider buying a computer elsewhere.

The exception for extended service policies is for laptop computers. Because their internal parts are, by their nature, expensive and more integrated than desktop systems, definitely consider getting an extended warranty for as long as you expect to keep your laptop. Paying a few hundred dollars now beats having to pay $1,000 later to replace a laptop's motherboard. In that case, the extended warranty is worth every penny. But, also note that the in-store warranty is still not needed in this case. Again, run screaming for the door when they start talking about in-store warranties!

"Can you fix my computer at my home or office?"

Because I live in a remote part of northern Idaho, I always insist that any computer I buy comes with an on-site service policy. When one of my computers broke a while back, a representative from the company came to my home and fixed it right there on my kitchen table. (And, the service rep had a great view of the lake while fixing my computer.)

On-site service is a bonus, well worth it if you have to pay extra for it — especially if you live way out of town, like in Idaho.

Support Questions

Support is help after the sale. It's not help in fixing the computer; it's help for you as a computer user.

A sample support question to ask

If you're unsure about whether a dealer truly allows you to ask questions after the sale, call up before you buy, and ask this question:

"I'm installing a game, and it says that I need to 'swap disks.' What does that mean?"

The answer to this question is something along the lines of "Take one disk out of the disk drive and put the next disk into the disk drive." It works just like changing CDs in your car radio. If the dealer makes it sound easy on the phone, you have found good support. If the person sounds annoyed by the question or tells you to call the game developer, buy your computer somewhere else.

For your software, you use the developer's phone support — or buy a good book. For some hardware, you may have to call the hardware manufacturer directly; for what you buy from your dealer, however, you should be able to call someone there. (Some supernice dealers even help you with your software questions.)

"Can I phone someone to ask questions?"

This question is important. Does the dealer have someone available to help you? Many superdiscount places lack the proper support staff to deal with your after-sale troubles. Nothing is more frustrating than to plunk down Big Bucks for a computer and have the dealer ignore you when you come back for help 24 hours later.

 ✔ *Hint:* Any place that also sells TV sets and jeans next to its computers probably doesn't give you much after-sale service and support.

 ✔ Your salesperson may not be the person you end up calling for support. Salespeople sell. Support people answer questions. (Although sometimes your salesperson may help, don't count on it.)

 ✔ Test the dealer! See the nearby sidebar "A sample support question to ask," just to make sure that the sales rep is being honest about phone support.

"Do you offer classes?"

All the better computer dealers have a classroom with a real live, human teacher right there, ready to help you do something bizarre, such as run Windows. It's a major plus. Some dealers have classes in conjunction with local universities or high schools. Great.

- Expect to pay perhaps a little more for the support, hand-holding, and general warm-fuzzy feeling you want. The price you pay is more than offset by removing after-sale anxiety.

- Obviously, buying from a catalog or on the Internet means that you don't have any classroom handy. That's right! It's a good reason to consider paying a bit more for local service and support.

- I first went out to buy a computer with $1,500 in my pocket. I waited and waited in the showroom, and eventually grabbed a salesman by the arm and asked, "What can you tell me about this Apple II computer?" He asked, "Why don't you just go out and buy a book on it?" Needless to say, I bought my first computer elsewhere.

Support Issues for Buying on the Internet

Buying on the Internet is just like mail order when it comes to getting support. Depending on what you bought and where, you could end up with an 800 number, on-site service, or the lonely echoes of your palpitating heart. But, with buying online, you have to *dig* to find out which type of support is available and how the service works. Here are my suggestions:

- Always buy from places offering toll-free tech support. Many online dealers have a support line for everything they sell. Some have you call the manufacturer, which can be a letdown. Avoid a dealer that offers help only through its Web page.

- Ensure that the dealer supports what it sells and that it doesn't redirect you elsewhere. This is a "fine print" issue. Always read all the conditions when you buy. Sometimes, you have to click a special link to discover what the conditions are. Beware!

- If possible, try to sign up for on-site service.

- Scour that Web page! Look for support issues like a FAQ (Frequently Asked Questions) list, troubleshooting guide, comment location, feedback, or even maybe a chat room. Often, you can find common problems and their solutions on a vendor's Web page.

- E-mail support works, but it's spotty. When I ordered a computer online and the monitor was bad, I e-mailed the vendor. It replied quickly and sent me a new monitor along with a shipping tag. I put the old monitor in the new monitor's box and shipped it back. It cost me nothing, and I never spoke with a person. To me, that was amazing.

- On the flip side of e-mail support is the runaround issue. You can e-mail Microsoft all you want about its software bundled with your new computer, but Microsoft will tell you that it's up to the dealer to give you support. The dealer will claim that it's Microsoft's job. And so it goes.

- If buying on the Internet worries you in any way, don't!

Chapter 22

Buying the Computer

· ·

In This Chapter

▶ A quick review of the buying process

▶ Spending your "extra" money

▶ Taking the plunge and making the purchase

▶ Remembering some last-minute buying tips

· ·

F ind someone whose fingernails have been chewed to the nubs, and he has probably been looking for a computer. Simply mention "buying a computer" to anyone, especially someone who is now looking, and he will probably faint — maybe even die.

This book arms you with all the knowledge you need in order to know what a computer does. You have been braced, studied, quizzed, and oriented. It's time to buy. A whole chapter for that? Yup. Buying is the big move that many people put off. This chapter is devoted entirely to motivating you to go for it.

A Review of the Five Steps

Buying a computer is cinchy, as long as you follow the five steps as outlined in Chapter 1. As a review, here they are:

1. **Identify your computer needs.**

    This step is easy. What do you want the computer to do? Answer that question, and everything else falls into place.

2. **Find the software to meet those needs.**

    This step is where you software-shop, which is covered in Chapter 17. The software boxes themselves describe the hardware that's required in order to run the software. (Remember that it's the software that's more important.) Filling out your software worksheets marks the end of this step.

3. **Find the hardware to run your software.**

   Part II of this book reviews all the hardware and software issues for you. Matching up all your software worksheets to the hardware worksheet is covered in Chapter 18.

4. **Locate a place you can do business with — some outfit with both the service and support you need.**

   This step is the most neglected. If you ever have any problems buying a computer, or know of anyone who relates a horror story, the problem was in omitting this important step.

5. **Buy the computer.**

   Do it!

Why is this last step so hard? Because buying a computer frightens many people. Hopefully, those people will turn to this chapter first and then read the previous chapters to bone up on what's important. After that, this last step should be a snap.

What to Spend "Extra" Money On

Buying anything above and beyond what you have written on your worksheets depends on how much you can afford. The real question is "Where should I spend my money first?"

Without a doubt, spend any "extra" money you may have on the following items, in this order:

- **Microprocessor:** First and foremost, buy yourself the fastest microprocessor you can afford. This is a must. If your software craves a Pentium 4 at 2.40 GHz, but you can afford the fastest Pentium 4, spend your money there. You won't regret it.

- **Memory:** Second, get more memory. If your software can get by with 256MB, 512MB is even better. If you can afford it, get 1GB or even 2GB. Computers just love extra memory!

- **Hard drive:** Third, buy a higher-capacity hard drive. If you have followed the hard drive size calculation from Chapter 18 and can afford a larger hard drive, buy it.

- **Monitor:** One word: LCD.

The idea is to spend more money on the things that are the hardest to upgrade later. Everything on a computer can be swapped out for something faster and better, although some things are more easily swapped than others.

The most difficult upgrade is the microprocessor, so that gets first priority. Then come the hard drive and the memory. Most computers can sport a second hard drive, and memory is easy to upgrade. Doing so first, however, saves you the trouble later (especially if you have the money now). Finally, you can replace a monitor at any time.

Often, the second or third item from the top is the best bargain. For example, rather than get the top-of-the-line hard drive or microprocessor, get the model that's one or two notches below that. There, you will find a bargain because you're not paying merely for the boasting rights of having the (current) top-of-the-line stuff.

"When Do I Get My Computer?"

You can go to buy a computer and walk out of the store with it that day. Most home and personal systems can be found this way. The iMac, for example, comes in its own, friendly box, as do numerous low-end and home PCs. The iMac has everything you need! But, if you have ordered a special configuration, receiving it may take longer.

Most of the time, plan on waiting anywhere from a couple of hours to several days for your computer, depending on how busy the dealer is and whether the dealer runs tests on your computer before giving it to you. (Read more about that subject in the "What about the 'burn-in' period" sidebar, later in this chapter.)

Mail-order computers may arrive right away, or they may take anywhere from a week to three weeks to arrive. The amount of time depends on how busy the dealer is and whether the parts you need are in stock. Always ask! Never assume that the Federal Express driver is sitting there with his engine idling and waiting to unload your new computer.

✔ Computer sales are seasonal, like most things. End-of-the year, back-to-school, and Christmas are the busiest times to order and the longest times to wait for custom systems.

✔ High demand means that you have to wait.

✔ Custom computers also take time to build. I have waited up to three weeks before one of my systems was waiting for pickup on the dock. (I tracked its progress on the Web, as outlined in Chapter 20.)

Don't Ever Put a Deposit on a Computer!

When someone asks you for a deposit up front for your computer, run like the wind! Up-front deposits are one surefire way to find a shady computer dealer. You should never put down a deposit on a computer. The best way to be sure is to always pay by credit card.

Not everyone is out to rip you off. Most classic computer-store scams, however, involve a "rob Peter to pay Paul" scheme. Writing a check for your computer at this type of place usually means that you lose your money.

Paying with a credit card is the best option because you can always cancel your order. Most dealers don't charge your card until the computer ships or you pick it up. If you don't receive your computer and the charge shows up on your bill, call the dealer and ask what's up. If the answers or attitude don't sit well with you, immediately phone your credit card company and place the charge "in dispute." The credit card company will tell you what to do from there.

Don't fret over having to put a deposit down to hold a special on-order item. For example, you may need some special piece of equipment that's not in stock. If so, a 5 to 20 percent deposit is okay to hold it. Again, use the dealer's reputation as the deciding factor and pay by credit card.

Hey, Bud! You're Ready to Buy

It's time to take the plunge. Jump in with both feet, and get that computer. As always, you need to take into consideration and remember some things when you're buying your dream computer:

✔ Don't forget software! You need software to make your computer hardware go. Software is expensive; you eventually spend as much on software as you spend on your computer.

✔ You may want to get other items for your computer: a printer, scanner, or digital camera or other "toys." Worry about them later. For now, concentrate on using the computer itself. You have enough to deal with when you get it!

✔ If your dealer offers classes, now would be a good time to sign up for one. Give yourself a week or so alone with your computer before you show up (with your yellow pad full of questions).

What about the "burn-in" period?

Some people wonder about "burn in" when it comes to computers and high-tech equipment. This term has nothing to do with setting the computer on fire.

The *burn-in* is a test: The dealer assembles the computer and turns it on to ensure that everything is working. Then the computer is kept on for a length of time to ensure that everything *keeps* working. The system may be turned off and on a few times. The idea behind the burn-in period is to find any bad hardware before you take the system home.

Few places now do burn-in tests. The reason is simple: Computer hardware is just too darn reliable! The failure rate for computer hardware is so low as to be insignificant. Computer dealers have therefore determined that the burn-in period is a waste of time and that you would rather have your new computer sooner than later.

A few last-minute buying tips

Never worry about technology making your computer obsolete. For example, you may hear a rumor that Apple is coming up with a new, more powerful line of iMacs — so what? Buy your iMac now, and start using it now. The difference between today and tomorrow's computer is so slight that it's not worth mentioning. (Today's computer versus *next year's* computer is another issue, but you won't be waiting that long.)

Computer ads are riddled with cryptograms and small words that may earn you big points in Scrabble but confuse the heck out of any first-time computer buyer. Check any unfamiliar terms with this book's index.

Never pay for a computer with a check; use a credit card. Credit card users are granted certain rights and protections that aren't given to people who write checks.

Try not to buy your computer on a Saturday. This advice has nothing to do with the zodiac. It's just that Saturday tends to be the busiest day for buying a computer. Also, most computer stores close on Sunday, so if you get stuck the first night, you have no one to call.

Allow yourself time to get to know your computer. Don't expect to rush home and instantly be brilliant with it. These things take time.

The final step is to. . . .

Go for it! When you're finally ready to buy, take a deep breath and buy your computer!

Part IV
Living with Your Computer

"I don't really care how user-friendly the spin cycle is—I think we're getting away from our core business."

EZ PCs

In this part . . .

Wouldn't it be great if expedient and cheery young people in white lab coats would set up your new computer for you and make everything just so? Not only that, but they could also sing show tunes while they snappily danced around your home or office. The reality of opening a new computer is honestly quite close to that fantasy.

Today's computers come nearly ready to go, right out of the box. You have only a few things to assemble, a smattering of cables to connect. And, is the buying process over? No! You have still more to do, and this book is here to help you do it.

This part of the book is devoted to after-sale euphoria — or despair. There's no sense in being left in a lurch, with boxes to unpack, parts to assemble, and things to work out. So, this part of the book takes you through the stages of computer assembly and getting it up and running. Then, it covers other things you need, or may want, for your computer, along with some good advice on how to maintain your computer for years to come.

Chapter 23

Helpful Hints for Computer Setup

. . . .

In This Chapter

▶ Opening the boxes and unpacking everything

▶ Finding a place for your computer

▶ Setting up the console

▶ Setting up the monitor

▶ Turning the computer on

▶ Turning the computer off

▶ Dealing with hardware and software

▶ Understanding your computer

. . . .

*N*othing can be more pleasing than opening up something new. Computer marketing types even have a name for it: the *out-of-box experience*. It almost sounds religious.

"Yes, Doctor, I had an out-of-box experience. For a moment, I saw our old bread machine, and then the water heater that blew up last year. It told me that I had to go back . . . go back to assemble my computer."

Sheesh.

If you haven't yet put your computer together, this chapter offers some helpful hints and strategies. If your computer is fully assembled and up and running, skim to the section "Breaking It In: The Burn-In Test," later in this chapter, for some helpful hints for putting your computer's wee li'l rubber feet to the fire.

Check the Shipment

First things first. When you get your computer, review the packing slip. Compare it with your order. Ensure that everything you're due has come.

If you ordered from a catalog or the Internet, review the boxes before signing the delivery sheet. The friendly delivery service guy even helps you out if you notice a damaged box. Most services return the box immediately if it appears damaged. Just remember *not* to sign for damaged material!

- ✔ Count the boxes! An iMac comes in one box, and most other computers come in two — one for the monitor and another for the console. If you have ordered a printer, scanner, or other peripheral (like mondo speakers), it probably comes in an extra box as well.

- ✔ Sometimes, packing lists come separately, or you may have an invoice. Either way, make sure that you have all the boxes you need.

Setting Up the Computer

Unless the nice person you bought your computer from sets it up right there on your desk, you have to do it yourself. It's much easier than it was in the early days. The first Apple computer (which cost $666 in 1977, by the way) came as a bag of electronic parts. You had to solder the whole thing together from scratch!

Now, assembling a computer is easy, often easier than assembling a stereo or hooking up a DVD player (but not by much). You don't even need a screwdriver.

Open the boxes

Setting up a computer starts with opening big boxes. If one box screams "Open me first!" open it first. It probably contains instructions. Otherwise, open the console box and look for the setup instructions.

After you find the instructions, locate the sheet that lists all the parts that came with your computer. Try to find all the parts to make sure that you have everything. Nothing is more distressing than discovering on Saturday that you're missing a part and having to wait until late in the day on Monday to use your computer.

If you bought any expansion options — extra memory or a network card, for example — the dealer will have installed them. You don't have to plug them in on your own.

Also, don't panic if you can't find some small computer part (like the keyboard) when you're unpacking your computer. These beasts come in lots of boxes and in boxes within boxes. Look everywhere before calling your dealer and accusing him of omitting something.

✔ Some boxes have opening instructions. I kid you not! My huge 21-inch CRT monitor had to be opened on top and then turned upside down so that I could lift the box off the monitor. Remember that gravity can be your friend.

✔ You have no easy way to ensure that the stuff installed inside the computer is really what you paid for. Generally speaking, however, news of improperly installed hardware, or "switcheroos," travels quickly. Your computer guru can quickly tell you whether your computer's console contains all the guts you have paid for.

✔ Some dealers install internal components in the console and then place those components' empty boxes inside the console box to demonstrate that the gizmo has been installed. Don't think that you have been ripped off if you find an empty network card adapter box; it probably means the adapter was installed and they just tossed in the box because they know how much you enjoy empty boxes.

✔ Always keep the phone numbers of your dealer and computer manufacturer handy. (Space is provided on the Cheat Sheet in the front of this book.) Also, look out for special support numbers; some manufacturers offer a 24-hour, toll-free support number. Write 'dem numbers down!

Box-opening etiquette

Be careful when you're opening any box. The "grab and rip" approach can be dangerous because those massive ugly staples used to close the box can fling off and give you an unwanted body piercing. (It's fashionable in parts of Silicon Valley to have a large staple through your eyebrow.)

The same advice holds true with using a box knife: Use a small blade because you don't want to slice through or into anything electronic — or fleshy, for that matter.

"What can I toss out?"

Nothing yet.

"What do I do with all this stuff?"

You can unpack most of the material in the boxes now, if you like, and set each item aside. You probably have several stacks:

- ✔ The monitor, with its cables
- ✔ The console
- ✔ The power cable
- ✔ The mouse
- ✔ The keyboard
- ✔ A stack of disks
- ✔ A stack of "free" offers and other paperwork
- ✔ Reference material

Just keep everything in its stack for now. You need each item as you build your computer. Eventually, after a few days or weeks, you can review all the stuff that came with your computer and decide what you want to keep. Some "free" offers can get tossed right away, but wait before throwing anything out until you *know* what it is.

"Should I keep the boxes?"

Computers are shipped with a great deal of packing material: plastic bags, twist ties, rubber bands, nylons, Hershey bars, and so on. For now, keep *everything*.

You have two reasons to keep the boxes and packing materials: to return a bum computer to the dealer and for when you move.

If the computer dies on you, you need something in which to ship it back. Believe me, it's worth it to keep the original boxes. Some dealers claim that not shipping the computer in its original box voids your warranty. That's not good.

If you move frequently, you should keep the boxes. Many moving companies don't insure your computers unless they're in the original packing material, with the original foam peanuts and Hershey bars.

✔ Also, be on the lookout for boxes within boxes! Don't toss out any box until you've examined it thoroughly for anything you may need.

✔ The boxes do make for clutter. After a year, I throw my boxes out. A year is usually well past the time a computer or monitor may turn sour, so then it's okay. (Back when I moved often, though, I kept all my boxes forever.)

"Do I have to read the manuals?"

Nope. I recommend looking over all the manuals, though, just to see what you have. You may get a humorous tutorial or guide for assembling your computer. Keep all the manuals together in one spot so that you can read them later — if you dare!

✔ Most computers don't come with real manuals any more. If any information is to be found, the computer itself displays it. (This doesn't help you much when the power goes out, though.)

✔ I have a special shelf in my office where I keep all my computer discs and manuals. Each computer has its own area on the shelf and, I admit, it looks junky. But, at least I know where all the material is located.

✔ Also consider getting one of those folder-organizer boxes from an office supply store. You can put your computer's manuals, disks, and other detritus in one of those for long-term safekeeping.

Putting It Together

Now that you know where the computer goes and you have everything situated for optimal computer use, go ahead and put it together. How? Although each computer is different, you put everything together in some standard ways.

The whole operation takes about half an hour, or more if you have additional items, such as printers or scanners, to install.

✔ Be patient. Take care. Give yourself plenty of room and time.

✔ Keep pets and small children at a distance when you set up your computer. If you keep a cold beverage handy, put it in a safe place (like in another time zone), where spilling it won't be a problem.

✔ You may need a flashlight to see behind your computer after it's set up.

Where will Mr. Computer live?

Find a home for your computer. Clear off your desk or tabletop, and allow enough room for the computer and keyboard. Remember that your computer will have an octopus of cables and peripherals around it. Make room for all that stuff too.

The computer must live somewhere near a power outlet, preferably an independent circuit with a grounded plug.

- ✔ Computers need room to breathe. Don't put your computer in a closet, box, recessed vault, grotto, or other cavelike place with poor ventilation.

- ✔ Don't put your computer by a sunny window because that heats up the computer and gives it anxiety.

- ✔ If you can sit on the table, the table can support the computer. Don't put Mr. Computer on a wobbly table or anything you wouldn't sit on yourself (like the cat).

- ✔ The obvious place to set the computer is on a well-supported computer desk.

- ✔ An *independent circuit* is one not shared by other devices in your home or office. For example, if you plug your computer into the same circuit as the refrigerator or air conditioner, it may blow a fuse when either of those devices turns on.

- ✔ If you have a desktop computer, you can set the monitor on top of the console. If you have a minitower, set the monitor to the side. The minitower can even go on the floor, if you like.

- ✔ Try to position the computer so that no lights shine directly into the monitor. Your eyes can get frazzled from the glare of the lights or the sun. My eye doctor tells me that monitor glare is, in fact, the biggest cause of eye fatigue from using a computer.

- ✔ Today's computers don't draw as much power as the computer systems of yesterday. Even so, I highly recommend that you put your computer system on an independent, 20-amp circuit, especially if you're using a laser printer. Most 15-amp household circuits do fine, but 20 amp is better. (If this amp stuff confuses you, never mind.)

Preparing to plug things in

Just about everything on a computer has a plug that plugs into the wall socket. Your monitor, computer box, printer, and anything else that's peripheral (such as a modem) have to plug into a wall socket. Find that wall socket now!

- ✔ I recommend buying one of those *power strips* that lets you plug four, six, or more items into one receptacle.

- ✔ Make sure that the power strip is *off*. That way, whenever you plug something into it, the something doesn't turn itself on (which you don't want at this point).

- ✔ An even better deal is to get a surge suppressor or a UPS (uninterruptible power supply). A *surge suppressor* protects your computer against power surges, and a *UPS* gives you time to save your work when the power goes down. Check out the nearby sidebar "Ode to plugging things into the wall" for more information.

- ✔ A laptop computer doesn't need a UPS. It has its own battery, which immediately powers the computer if the power from the wall is ever cut off.

Setting up the console

The first thing you're most likely to set up is the *console,* which is the box that everything else plugs into. It's the least mobile of the units you unpack, so setting it up first gives you a good starting base.

Remove the console from its plastic bag, if you haven't already done so.

Don't slide the console against the back of the desk just yet. In fact, twist the console around 90 degrees so that it's facing right or left. You need access to the back of it.

Plug the power cable into the console and then — after ensuring that the console is turned off — plug the power cable into the wall. If you hear the console switch on after you plug it in, no problem: Just turn it off.

A map or large sheet of paper may come with your computer. That sheet tells you how and where to plug various things in. Refer to that sheet as you work through the following sections.

Attaching the mouse and keyboard

Plug the mouse and keyboard into the console.

On a PC, the mouse and keyboard each has its own, tiny hole into which it plugs. Each one plugs in only one way (you have to line up the pins with the holes). You have to push hard to plug one in wrong, so don't force things.

String the mouse cable out on your desk to ensure that it's not tangled or looped.

Set the keyboard and mouse out of the way so that you can attach other devices.

On the Mac, the keyboard plugs into the console, and then the mouse plugs into the keyboard.

Attaching other devices

If your computer has special external speakers, plug them in now. Locate the speaker holes on the computer. Plug the speakers in.

If you see left and right speaker holes, great! Otherwise, you need to plug in one speaker and then plug the second speaker's cord into the back of the first speaker. If you have a woofer unit, everything probably plugs into it first.

Ode to plugging things into the wall

Nearly everything that comes with a computer should be plugged into the wall or some similar wall-socket-like device. Ideally, the console and monitor should be plugged into a UPS, or uninterruptible power supply — a power source capable of running the computer during brief power outages.

Other devices should be plugged into a power strip or surge protector.

Printers can also be plugged into a power strip. A laser printer, however, should be plugged directly into the wall. (Printers don't need to be plugged into a UPS; just wait until the power comes on again to print.)

Here are some other power and electrical issues and rules:

✔ Never use an extension cord to meet your power needs. People trip over extension cords and routinely unplug them.

✔ If you need more sockets, use a power strip or one of those multisocket adapters that plugs *and screws* into an existing wall socket. Avoid those plus-shaped extensions because they easily fall out of the wall socket when burdened with cables.

✔ Computers need grounded sockets, which must have three prongs in them.

✔ If a UPS has extra sockets, plug in your desk clock or an external modem.

✔ Not every UPS has full UPS sockets. For example, some UPS devices may have two full UPS sockets and two surge-protected sockets that aren't backed up by battery.

If the speakers need electrical power, ensure that the speakers are turned off and then plug them into the power strip.

Setting up the monitor

If your monitor is separate from the console, set the monitor beside the console. That isn't its final resting place — it's merely a way to set it down while you work.

Plug the monitor into the console.

Ensure that the monitor is turned off, and then plug it into a power receptacle. If you have a UPS, plug the monitor into the UPS.

Plugging in other stuff

Finally, anything else you bought also has to be plugged into the computer box. For example, an *external* modem (one that lives outside your computer) has a cable that connects the modem to your computer. The modem also has a cable that connects to a phone jack in the wall, plus a place for you to plug your desktop phone into the modem. (Yes, this process is complex, but if it weren't, it wouldn't be a computer!)

If you already have a printer, plug its printer cable into its back. Then plug the other end of the cable into the back of the console.

Plug in anything else as well.

If the modem plugs into a router, connect the router to your PC, as directed by the modem's or router's instructions.

Finishing up

Plug all the power cords into the wall socket. Ensure that everything is switched off, and then plug it all in.

Reorient the console so that it's facing forward and the ugly cables are 'round back. (Do this gently so that you don't unplug anything.)

If you have a desktop computer, you can set the monitor on top of the computer now.

Set up everything just the way you want.

✔ Don't set a large (19 inches or larger) CRT monitor on top of a desktop PC unit. The heavy monitor may crush the console, which is designed to support only lighter-weight monitors.

✔ If you don't have enough cable to put the keyboard and monitor to one side of the console, you can buy extension cables at your favorite computer store.

✔ Some monitors come with a tilt-and-swivel base, which enables you to move the monitor to various orientations, albeit stiffly. This type of base is also an option you can buy for the monitor, if it's not already built in.

✔ As with the console, the monitor needs to breathe. Don't set anything on top of the monitor or cover its wee tiny air vents in any way.

Turning the Thing On

To use your computer, turn everything on!

What to turn on first?

Almost everything connected to a computer has an on–off switch. So, the question is obviously "Which thing do I turn on first?" An equally valid question is "What do I turn off last?" Decisions, decisions. . . .

The answer? Seriously, turn on the console *last*. Turning everything on at one time is okay, but if you have a choice, make the console the last thing you turn on. That way, it "sees" and recognizes all the devices plugged into it.

Turning it off

On both the Mac and the PC, you must properly shut down the computer. This process involves selecting a Shutdown command from the operating system's menu. Where it can be found depends on which version of Windows, Linux, or Mac OS you're using.

If the computer shuts down by itself, great. The console turns itself off, and you can turn off everything else by flipping its switch. If the console doesn't switch off automatically, flip its switch (or punch its button).

Breaking It In: The Burn-In Test

One way to ensure that your new equipment is up to snuff is to put it through a special test — the *burn-in test*. The object of this test is to break in your new computer during its warranty period. If something is amiss, you want to know about it before the warranty expires.

The desktop burn-in test

When you take your new computer home, follow these two instructions:

✔ Keep your computer turned on 24 hours a day for 2 weeks.

✔ Once a day, turn the machine off, wait for a full minute, and then turn it back on.

Because of the way electronic components are designed, faulty chips usually go bad within their first 48 hours of use. By testing your computer this way, you're certain to find any faults immediately. Turning the power supply off and on each day helps to ensure that it's tough enough to stand the load.

After the two-week test, you can obey whatever on–off habits you have deemed proper for your computer. At that point, in fact, it will probably behave itself for years.

The laptop burn-in test

Laptops should be burned in, just like desktops, though with the laptop computer, you also want to stretch the battery's legs. Here's what I recommend:

✔ After initially charging the laptop's battery, use the laptop on battery power only. Use the laptop until the battery fully drains and the computer tells you to recharge.

✔ Recharge the battery, either while you're using the laptop or with the laptop turned off.

✔ Repeat the charge-drain cycle at least five times.

✔ At least once a day, while using the laptop on battery power and while using it plugged in, close the laptop lid to ensure that Standby mode is activated and the laptop "sleeps."

✔ At least once during the burn-in test, try the operating system's Hibernation option.

Hopefully, these tests reveal any immediate problems the laptop may have, either with the system itself or with the battery and power-management hardware. If a problem occurs, you can immediately get the laptop fixed or replaced, well before the warranty period is over.

After a week or two of testing, feel free to use your laptop as you normally would. Note that if you don't plan to use the battery for an extended period, you should remove the battery from the laptop and store it in a nonmetallic (or conducting) container. The battery drains over time, but it lasts longer outside of the laptop than it does when it's fully charged and never used inside the laptop.

What's Next?

With the computer all set up and ready to roll, you're probably tempted to turn it on. Wait. You should look for a few things before you steamroller ahead:

- ✔ Find any manuals that came with your computer. Look for the ones that contain directions and troubleshooting help. Keep these manuals handy.

- ✔ Always retain the manuals that come with your computer and any software manuals. Keep any disks and their software manuals together.

- ✔ You can throw away most of the little scraps of paper now. Don't throw away anything that has a phone number on it until you have written the number down — in the manual, for example, or just on a piece of paper — and stored it in a safe place.

- ✔ Mail in your registration or warranty card. Make a note of the computer's serial number, and file it away. In an office situation, you should keep track of all your equipment's serial numbers.

Dealing with software

You may have purchased some software with your computer. If so, great. However, leave all those boxes alone for now. One mistake many beginners make is overwhelming themselves with computer software. Although it's okay to buy lots of software (if you haven't, you will probably buy more later), using it all right away is counterproductive.

- ✔ Your computer's operating system is the most important piece of software you have. Find out about it first.

- ✔ Refer to Chapter 15 for more information about operating systems.

✔ If you have anything you must do — a priority project, for example — set aside the software you need from the rest of your stuff. For example, if finding out how to use Quicken, Word, or QuarkXPress is your top priority, set aside the software and get ready to find out how to use it first. Everything else can wait.

✔ Remember that no job can be done immediately. No matter how annoying your boss is, you must find out how to use software before you can be productive with it. Give yourself at least two weeks before you squeeze something brilliant from a computer.

Dealing with other hardware

You may have purchased other hardware goodies, each waiting for hookup and installation. Put them on hold for now. Trying to understand too much can boggle you. Handle the basics first, and install extra hardware later.

✔ You add hardware to a computer either internally or externally.

✔ Installing internal hardware requires some type of computer nerd. True, you can do it yourself. Many books and magazine articles go into the details, if you want to bother with installing internal hardware. My advice is to force someone else to do it.

✔ External hardware requires a power cable and some type of cable to connect it with the computer. A few devices don't use a power cable (they run off your brain waves). Also, you may need special software to run the external hardware; a scanner requires scanning software, and a modem requires communications software.

Understanding Your System

Give yourself time to read about your system, time to play, and time to relax and have fun with your computer. Believe it or not, the best way to understand how to use a computer system is to play around with it. Poke around. Test things. Try weird options, and see what they do. As long as you're not rushed to start your serious work, you have time to easily grow with the system. After the workload comes, you will feel good about the system, and, lo, that expected and much-rumored frustration won't be there.

✔ After you have used your software for about a month, go back and reread the manual; you will be surprised at how much clearer it seems. It makes sense! (People who write manuals are overly familiar with the product and forget what it's like to be a novice.)

- ✔ By reading the manual a second time, you pick up a few more tips and some shortcuts. This trick is just another one the experts use to become experts.

- ✔ As a kind word of advice, give yourself two weeks to find out about your software before you start doing serious work with it.

- ✔ The more time you have to play with and figure out how to use your software, the more productive you become.

- ✔ Give yourself three weeks (if you have it) to become used to your new computer system. Then when you're ready to get to work, you will know some tricks, and you should proceed smoothly. Heck, you may be a computer wizard by then!

Chapter 24

Time to Get a Printer

Your new computer needs a printer. It's a necessary part of the purchase — like software. You can buy the computer and the printer together, or you can come back for the printer later. Either way, every computer needs a printer eventually.

This chapter covers the printer purchase. Fortunately, if you already have your computer and its software, picking a printer is a snap. As with the computer, it's software that controls your printer. Your software can instantly help you narrow your printer choices and options.

Different Printers for Different Printing

Forget brand names. When it comes to printers, you can choose from three basic printer models:

✔ Laser

✔ Inkjet

✔ All-in-one

Each type of printer gets the job done. They can all do color. Choosing one really depends on your printing needs.

✔ The all-in-one printer is really an inkjet. It can also be used as a scanner. Depending on the manufacturer, the printer may also double as a fax machine or photocopier. Amazingly, all those things work well together.

✔ Inkjet printers are the most popular. They're fast, quiet, and relatively inexpensive — and they print in color.

✔ A laser printer is a must if you're in business. Its chief advantage is that it's faster than an inkjet.

✔ If you want color, go with an inkjet printer. Color lasers have dropped in price, but you still pay a premium — for both the printer and its supplies.

✔ A special type of inkjet printer is the photo printer, but be careful when you buy one! Any inkjet printer can print photographs. But, photo printers should come with extra ink — specifically, six ink colors rather than the standard four. If the printer doesn't use six ink colors, it's not a true photo printer.

✔ Other types of printers exist. For example, you can get an impact printer for printing on multipart forms, as well as a battery-powered bubble or LED printer designed for portability and use with a laptop on the road.

Printer speed

A printer's speed is measured in pages per minute, or ppm. The higher the value, the better. Some laser printers can manage 30 ppm, under optimal conditions, of course (usually repeatedly printing the same page of simple text). The more complex the graphics, the slower the printer goes.

✔ Most inkjet printers manage between 8 ppm and 22 ppm.

✔ Color laser printers are very slow, typically dribbling out 6 ppm or fewer.

✔ Photo printers are very slow, though the manufacturers would prefer it if I said *meticulous* rather than slow.

✔ The printer speed you see in the ads is an optimal value. The pages-per-minute values you experience will doubtless be less.

The print quality

Print quality is judged by how well the printer produces an image on paper, which depends on how many tiny dots the printer can squeeze on a square inch of paper. The more dots, the higher the printer's resolution and the better the image.

Early laser printers could print 300 dots horizontally by 300 dots vertically. Today's models can easily manage 600 x 600 dots in a square inch. Some models can manage 1,200 dots per inch (dpi), which is the same resolution as a professional typesetting machine.

Inkjet printers have similar dots-per-inch values. Higher resolution is available, but you pay more for it. Also, the print quality on an inkjet printer depends greatly on the paper quality. Special inkjet printer paper is available and produces a much better image (the paper literally absorbs the image).

How much?

Printers range in price from less than $100 for a cheap model that I wouldn't wish on anyone to $2,000 for a high-quality color laser printer. You will probably pay anywhere from $150 to $600 or more for your printer, depending on what you get.

Several things affect a printer's price. The top two are quality and speed. But, among the various models, you find subtle differences based on these factors:

- **Memory:** Some printers come with their own memory, sometimes as much as a megabyte or more. The more memory you add to a printer, the faster it goes — especially for graphics. In fact, if you plan to print lots of graphics, pay the extra money and load your printer up with RAM.

- **Brains:** Some printers are actually computers, ones specifically designed to print on paper (not foul up your phone bill). Cheaper printers? They're cheap because they don't have brains.

  For example, you may notice that one color ink printer costs $390 and another model — just as technically good — costs $120. The difference? The $390 model has a brain. The $120 model uses your computer as its brain, which means that it takes that model longer to print *and* your computer slows down while the printer is printing.

- **PostScript:** The PostScript printer is essentially a computer customized for printing high-quality images. The printer does all the thinking on its own. Your software merely says "Do this," and the printer does the rest, which frees up the computer to do other things.

  PostScript printers originally appeared for the Macintosh computer. Although you can get one for your PC as well, you have two pills to swallow. The first is that PostScript printers are expensive. All them thar PostScript brains cost money. The second pill to swallow is that PostScript printers work best with software that produces PostScript output — primarily, graphics applications, though you can look on the side of any software box to see whether it's PostScript-happy.

✔ **Networking:** Printers, like computers, can sport their own networking adapter, or NIC. If so, you can hook the printer right up to your computer network. That way, each computer has equal access to the printer. Again, you pay extra for this feature.

✔ **Other stuff:** Oh, and other factors determine a printer's price: whether it has a wider paper-feed mechanism for printing "sideways," an alternative paper tray for legal paper, a duplex device for printing on both sides of a sheet of paper, and other details too technical to bore you with here.

✔ Refer to Chapter 12 for more information on networking computers and what hardware is required.

✔ For some reason, the USB version of a printer costs more than the printer port version of the same printer.

✔ I recommend getting a USB printer, one that you can continue to use even if your future computers don't have a printer port.

✔ Some broadband routers and wireless base stations have a special USB port for plugging in a printer. If you take advantage of that port, all computers on the network can share the USB printer.

✔ All Macintoshes now use USB printers. If you want a printer for your Mac, get a USB printer.

Laser Printers Go "Fwoom Pkt Shhh!"

Laser printers (see Figure 24-1) are similar to the old desktop copying machines, and they work on the same principles. The difference is that a laser printer receives its information from the computer instead of using a reflected image, which is how the copy machine does it. A laser beam is used to draw the image.

Laser printers have really come down in price over the past decade. Today's models are cheap and reliable and don't use all the watts required of the earlier models.

To print an image, a laser printer uses a toner cartridge. This item can be expensive! If you have a choice between two laser printers of similar quality, check the cost of the toner cartridge. You may think that you're saving money on a printer now, but if it costs you $150 a year (or more often) to replace the toner cartridge, are you really saving money?

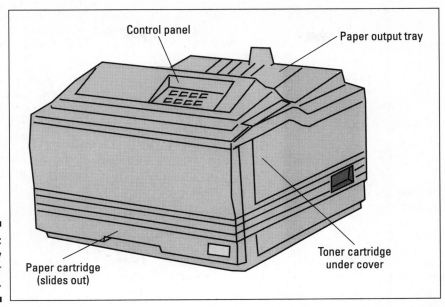

Control panel

Paper output tray

Figure 24-1:
A chunky
type of laser
printer.

Paper cartridge
(slides out)

Toner cartridge
under cover

Color laser printers? They use *four* toner cartridges (black, magenta, cyan, and yellow). That can get spendy over time.

Ink Printers Go "Thwip Sft-Sft-Sft Clunk!"

Up front, here's what you fear: Ink printers work by spewing ink all over paper, similar to the way a 3-year-old spits water on his little brother in the bathtub.

Now, the truth: An *inkjet printer* works by lobbing a tiny ball of ink precisely at the paper and forming a teensy-tiny dot on the page. The ink dries instantly, and the resulting piece of paper doesn't smudge. In many cases, the paper looks *exactly* like it came from a high-priced laser printer. Figure 24-2 illustrates a typical inkjet printer.

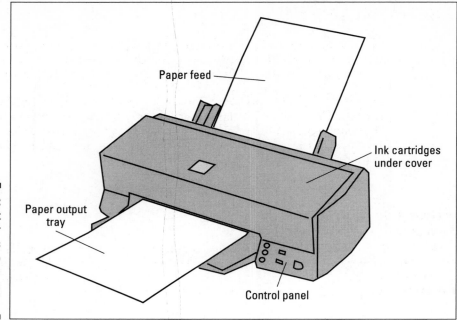

Figure 24-2:
An inkjet printer stands ready to cost you a fortune in ink "carts."

Paper feed

Ink cartridges under cover

Paper output tray

Control panel

The only downside to the ink printer is the cost of the replacement ink cartridges. In two words, these cartridges are outrageously expensive! Not only that, but the cartridges also run dry when you print often, which forces you to continually pay for newer cartridges! It's an endless cycle!

- Odds are pretty good that you will get an ink printer for your first computer purchase. It's a good way to go.

- Inkjet printers use two ink cartridges. One is for black, and a separate cartridge contains the color inks: magenta, cyan, and yellow.

- No, the colors aren't red, blue, yellow. The names come from photography; magenta and cyan combine to make more colors than red and blue.

- If you can afford it, get an inkjet printer that uses separate ink cartridges for each of the four color inks: black, cyan, yellow, and magenta.

- Because little mechanical movement is involved, inkjet printers are quiet. Sometimes, the brand name implies something about the printer's silence: Quietwriter, Whisperwriter, and Gaspingforairwriter, for example.

- When you buy the printer, make sure to buy some spare ink cartridges.

- That special photographic paper is expensive. I just bought a box of eight sheets for $15. (Call me dumb, but it's what I do for a living.) The output on that paper, however, is almost the same as an 8-x-10-inch photograph.

The All-in-One

The most popular computer printer sold now is the *all-in-one*. Basically it's an inkjet printer that can also be used as a scanner, fax, copier, it can walk the dog and get you a beer — if you pay enough money and buy the right model.

Seriously, the all-in-one is fine if you need a printer and only occasionally could use the services of a fax, scanner, or copier. If so, the price is right and the printer works surprisingly well. If you're into high-end graphics, however, I recommend that you get a separate scanner. Refer to Chapter 13 for what to look for in a scanner.

The Photo Printer

If you plan on doing digital photography, look into getting a special type of ink printer known as a *photo printer*. This type of printer is far superior to either the standard inkjet printer or even a color laser printer when it comes to reproducing photo-quality output.

The key difference between a photo printer and a standard ink printer is the number of inks used. The standard ink printer uses four inks: *c*yan, *y*ellow, *m*agenta, and blac*k* (CMYK). The photo ink printer uses six inks, by adding second shades of magenta and yellow to the standard ink colors. The extra ink enables the printer to better render certain colors, which makes the photo printer's output nearly photographic!

The downside to photo printers is that they're slow. You can pay more to get a faster model (which I recommend). Also consider the higher cost of the ink when you're making your decision.

Buying the Printer

You can buy a printer at the time you buy a computer or later, after you have toyed with the computer a while. No rule says that every computer must have a printer. And, you don't have to print everything you do on the computer.

- ✔ Your computer manufacturer's brand-name printer isn't required for your brand-name computer. Just about any computer can have any printer attached. It doesn't matter.
- ✔ Printers can be added to a computer at any time.
- ✔ Your computer has the ability to control more than one printer at a time. You can add many printers via the USB cable. On a PC without USB, you must add additional printer ports to connect more than one printer.

What does your software say?

To find out which printer works best for you, check your software.

Not all software has specific printer suggestions. Some software merely says on the box, "Any PC– or Windows–compatible printer." But, some types of software, especially graphics programs, say "Any compatible printer or PostScript printer." In that case, you should look into getting a PostScript printer for the best possible (and fastest) output.

Printer shopping

You don't have to buy the printer at the same place you bought the computer. It's nice, for example, if you had a pleasant buying experience and want to honor that place with repeat business. But, if its price is too high or it doesn't sell what you want, feel free to go elsewhere.

   ✔ If you're set on a specific make and model of printer, consider using the Internet to shop — after all, you have a computer now! Use a shopping agent, like mySimon (as described in Chapter 20), to help you find the cheapest printer.

   ✔ The same rules for buying a computer — or buying any extra hardware — apply for buying a printer.

Printers don't come with cables!

Before diving in to the fast and exciting world of printer types, you should note one little-known axiom of the computer-buying world: Printers don't come with cables. Gasp!

Unlike a stereo or VCR, which comes with all the required cables, a computer printer doesn't come with everything you need to hook it up to your computer. The reason is simple: Not all printers are hooked up to the same type of computer.

   ✔ The printer cable can't be more than 20 feet long, which is kind of common sense because the best place for your printer should be within arm's reach — or did you know that? Well, now you do.

   ✔ A USB printer cable should be 3 meters (9 feet) or less in length.

✔ Note that a USB cable has A and B connectors. Ensure that you get the proper one for your printer to plug into your computer.

✔ Most computers are now sold with a smart *(bidirectional)* printer port. If your printer takes advantage of the smart printer port, ensure that you buy a smart printer cable. Some cheaper printer cables lack the smart feature (which is merely a few extra lines of data).

Printers don't come with paper, either!

It almost goes without saying that your printer needs paper. Laser printers eat regular copy-machine paper, or you can pay more to get special high-quality paper.

Inkjet printers can print on any paper as well, although you should do yourself a favor and get special ink printer paper. It costs more, but the quality is worth it. Also, specialty papers are available for creating photographic-quality output as well as iron-on T-shirt transfers, transparencies, and other fancy time wasters.

Don't bother with fanfold paper (the kind with the sheets connected to each other) unless you have a printer that has a proper paper feeder. Some ink printers have them, and nearly all impact (dot matrix) printers have them, but laser printers don't.

✔ Always buy the proper paper for your printer. Look in the documentation that came with your printer. Sometimes, printer manufacturers recommend the kind of paper that's best for your printer.

✔ Stock up on paper! Nothing is worse than running out of paper and not having any backup. Go to a discount paper warehouse place, if one is near you, and buy a whole box.

Buy some extra ink

As long as you're at it, buy your printer a second toner cartridge or backup ink supply. That way, if you run out quicker than you expected, you have the replacement handy.

Setting Up the Printer

Setting up a printer is a snap. As with most things, you have a hardware part and a software part to add a printer to your computer system.

Initially, you set up the printer similarly to the way you set up everything else: Take it out of the box, unpack it, and then set it where you want it. Put the printer near the computer — the nearer, the better — although it doesn't need to be too close.

- ✔ Keeping the printer at arm's length can come in handy.
- ✔ Be sure to look inside the printer box for its software discs (CDs), manuals, font cartridges, and other stuff the printer needs.

Printer pieces' parts

Printers come in many pieces. You have the printer itself, the ribbon or toner cartridge, and the thing that holds the paper. An instruction sheet that comes with the printer explains what goes where. Find that sheet and heed its instructions.

Basic printer setup requires yanking a few shipping items from the printer's insides, installing the ribbon and toner cartridge, setting up the paper-feeding mechanism or paper tray, adding any font cards, and plugging in the cables.

- ✔ *Si la feuille du mode d'emploi a l'air français, c'est peut-être parce que c'est écrit en français. La plupart des modes d'emploi ont des directives en plusieurs langues. Il faut chercher la version en anglais.*

  If the instruction sheet reads like it's written in French, it probably is. Most instruction sheets list instructions in several languages. Look for the English version.

- ✔ Some printers may require a detailed internal setup, which means that you yank out several plastic doohickeys, peel tape, and apply salve to the printer's aching foot pads. Those parts hold the printer's insides inside during shipment. You don't need to keep them; freely toss them out (even if you plan to move the printer later).

- ✔ If you purchased extra memory for your printer, install it before you turn the printer on. Better still, have your dealer install it for you.

Connecting the printer cables

Printers have two required cables: the power cable, which plugs into a wall socket, and the printer cable, which plugs into the computer. (Congress

Sharing one printer between two computers

It's possible — and often cheaper — to share one printer between two or more computers. So, although it may seem nifty to have a printer for each computer, it's really not practical. The better solution is to *network* your computers and then share the printer between them.

Networking involves both h~~~~~~ ~~~~ ~oft-ware. You need the ~~~~~~~~~~~~ ~~n-nect bot~~~

software ensures that the computers can talk with each other, share files, and do other nice networky things. Connect the printer to one or the other computer, and inform the operating system that the printer is to be shared; then both computers can access it.

For more information on networking, refer to a good networking book or general PC reference.

that every computing device have, at

the computer's printer port. Aren't

and serial port options, use the

Macintosh standard of today: All

ut the printer

The computer know about it. You do th the printer.

The pr sequence of steps. For example, some pr plugged into the computer. At that point, the comp the printer and set things up automatically. Most of th wever, you do a manual setup.

Because each operating system handles printers differently, refer to your own operating system's manual or a good book for information on the soft-ware side of on setting up a printer.

Chapter 25

From the Old Computer to the New One

*O*ftentimes, your new computer purchase is really a replacement computer purchase. For example, you were computing in the Stone Age with an old Packard Bell, or maybe you're upgrading your first Pentium to a brand-spanking-new Pentium 4 powerhouse. I upgrade my office computers every four years. It's a thrill!

Although the new computer may delight you, what do you do with all the *stuff* on your old computer? Does it just sit there? Or, can you move it over to the new system? The answers lie in this chapter, which covers moving both hardware and software to your new computer system.

Moving Over Hardware

If your main reason for buying a new computer is to replace an older computer, consider what really needs replacing. Quite a bit of an older computer's hardware may find a home inside or alongside the new computer. It all depends on the shape of the older system's components. This section illuminates what can, may, and shouldn't be moved to the new system.

Antiques: Don't bother

If your early computer is older than six years, the thing probably has no hardware that would serve the new computer well. For example, I have an old, old Macintosh Quadra. Nothing inside that computer would work with a new Mac system. Nope, nothing. Ditto for older PCs versus newer systems.

- ✔ If you have purchased any new peripherals or monitors for an older system, they may be able to be passed on to the new system. See the following subsections.

- ✔ So, the hardware is crummy — but, don't forget your data and software! See the sections later in this chapter for moving over your software.

- ✔ Honestly, computers never really go out of date as long as they work. New computers are faster, but, given the choice between using an old clunky IBM PC/AT, DOS, and WordPerfect 4.2 versus a typewriter, I would take the old clunky PC any day of the week.

Monitors

CRT monitors tend to fade and fuzz out with time. If your older computer's monitor is doing well or you just bought yourself a new LCD monitor, you can move it over to your new computer. Not buying a monitor can shave a few hundred dollars from a new computer's purchase price.

As an example, I purchased a new LCD monitor for an older computer whose monitor was in its dying days. When I replaced that computer a few years later, I simply bought a new console and moved the LCD monitor over to the new computer.

- ✔ As long as the monitor is in good shape, use it!

- ✔ Even if you already have a monitor for your new computer, you can add a second monitor to your system. Most computers support dual monitors. Note that you need a second video adapter to make this happen.

Disk drives

I don't recommend removing older hard drives and installing them in new computers. The hard drive is one of the first things to go on an older system, so relying on it for a new computer is risky. Even installing the older hard drive as a "backup" is questionable. No, you're better off just getting the information from the hard drive and using a newer unit.

External disk drives can easily be moved to a new computer, simply by plugging them in. Always make sure that you have the original installation discs, which helps the new computer recognize your older hardware.

Some internal disk drives, such as a new DVD or CD-R you added can be moved over to the new system — no problem. Again, remember the original software installation disc so that the operating system recognizes the new hardware.

Memory

Memory is something that you generally cannot move from computer to computer. The reason is that older memory is probably much "fatter" than your new computer can handle. By fatter, I mean that the memory is probably of lower capacity and slower speed; a new computer probably needs higher-capacity memory (256MB versus 64MB SIMMS, for example) and faster access times. No, moving over memory is a waste of time.

Expansion cards

Some expansion cards may work in the newer system; some may not. The best advice I can offer is that if you have recently purchased an expansion card for the older system *and* it offers some feature that the newer system lacks, consider the move.

Suppose that you just bought a USB expansion card for your old PC, and the new PC also lacks USB ports. Moving over the old USB expansion card could be a good move. Ditto for newer network cards and high-end graphics adapters.

- ✔ Refer to Chapter 10 for more information on expansion cards.
- ✔ PCI and AGP cards are the best candidates for transfer to a new computer.
- ✔ Also worthwhile are specialty cards: video input cards for any video-editing software you own, sound synthesis, and special waveform cards, as well as anything else you need with your software.

Printers

The easiest thing to move from an older computer to a newer model is a printer. This makes total sense: There's no point in buying a whole new printer just because you have a new computer. As long as the printer is working just fine, keep it!

    ✔ Don't forget your printer's original software disc! You may need it to install the software drivers for your new computer.

    ✔ My main printer has been used with four different computers. It's a robust little guy who has served me well for more than ten years!

Modems

Internal modems need to stay internal. Don't even bother removing one from your old computer. If you have followed my buying advice, your new computer already has an internal modem. For cable and DSL or external dial-up modems — yes! — most definitely, move them over to your new system.

Other peripherals

Peripherals can easily be moved from an old computer to a newer model. For example, I'm typing these words on a classic IBM keyboard that I have been using for almost ten years now — even though this computer is only four years old. (I'm picky when it comes to computer keyboards.) This IBM keyboard, if it lasts, may even find its way to whichever computer replaces my current model.

Scanners can also be passed from computer to computer, as can most other peripherals. As long as you always have a way to connect the device to the computer, and you still have the software and installation manuals, reinstalling the peripheral for the new system is a snap.

    ✔ No, you have no reason to buy a new scanner for a new computer if your old scanner works just fine.

    ✔ This peripheral-keeping and -sharing will become even more popular as USB devices take over the world.

    ✔ As you get more adept at using and upgrading computers, you may find yourself ordering the minimum when you buy. Just transplant your favorite items from the old system to the new model, and you're off and running in no time!

Transferring Your Software

The software you transfer to your new computer has two parts: the programs you have accumulated — programs you want to install on the new system — and the data you have created, as well as your e-mail address book, favorite Web pages, and personalized settings, for example. You may want to keep all that stuff as well — which, in many cases, is probably more important than all that old software anyway!

Reinstalling applications

Because you're an honest person, you purchased all your software from a retail store, or the software was included with your computer purchase. Whatever the case, you have the original box, manuals, and discs that came with the software. (That stuff is important — pray tell you didn't toss it out!)

When you move to the new system, you need to "move over" your old software: Simply reinstall each program on your new computer.

You *must* reinstall the software. You cannot simply copy the program files from one computer to another. These days, software has to be installed properly for it to work. If you copy the programs from the old computer (however that's done), things most likely will not work to your expectations.

I suggest installing the software as you need it. For example, if the first thing you want to try with your new computer is your word processor, install it. Ditto for a game or an "office" suite or any software you use.

✔ Some software has to be uninstalled and reregistered before you can reinstall it on your new system. This process typically involves a phone call to the developer.

✔ Some software may need corresponding hardware installed. For example, your imaging software may yearn for the presence of a scanner. Better install that scanner first.

✔ Older software may not be compatible with the newer computer or its operating system. Oops! If you see any sort of error message or get a warning about incompatibilities — *ka-ching!* — you need to pay for an upgraded version of the program. Yes, this happens.

✔ Some applications on your old computer may be "upgrade" or "OEM" versions. For example, the version of Microsoft Word that came with your old PC may be an OEM-only version (it was supplied by the computer manufacturer), and you may have trouble installing it on a new computer. My advice: Try your best! If it doesn't install, you have to go out and buy the program. Yes, I know that this is unfair, but it's how it works.

✔ Occasionally, an upgrade merely needs to "see" the preceding version's disc in order to install the upgrade. That's a good reason for hanging on to your old software manuals and discs.

✔ Don't be surprised if that old game doesn't work on the computer! Some games are geared to work best and work only with the technology available at the time.

Moving over data

Ah! Here's the tricky part. On your older computer, you probably have lots of files you have created — documents, images, and other information you need and use every day. I call them "data files." The goal is to get those data files over to your new computer — if not all of it, at least the stuff you really, *really* need.

Here are the methods you can use to move over your data files:

By disk: Copy all your data files from the old computer to a CD-R or Zip disc. Then move the files over to the new computer, by copying them from the removable disc to the hard drive. Yes, this process is lots of work. (I have done it many times.)

By network: If your computers are connected by a network, you can easily access the files on the old system and *beam* them to your new computer. This method is by far the easiest and most efficient way to do things. In my office, I typically keep the old system up on the network for months to ensure that I have pulled off every single file I need.

By cable: Second best to the network method of transferring files is to directly connect both computers by using a special data-transfer cable, available at most computer and office supply stores. You can then use software that came with your computer to help you move the files (for example, the Data Migration Wizard that comes with Windows XP; Mac OS X has a similar utility).

By gizmo: You can also use solid-state USB drives, as well as any removable memory card or other media, to transfer files. I prefer something like the Lexar Media (www.lexarmedia.com) USB drive, which you can plug into any computer with a USB port. You can use this palm-size device to copy files from the older computer to the new one, with no cables or disk swapping needed.

However you make the connection — disc or cable — moving over the files is an important part of making the move. I miss the files I have left behind on various computers over the years.

> ✔ An interesting piece of software to check out is Unicenter Desktop DNA. It grabs not only software but also personalized settings and other options, which allows you to move your old computer's "personality" to the new system. Refer to the Computer Associates Web page for more information: www.ca.com.

> ✔ Also available is the Personality Transport Pro program, from Tranxition Corporation (www.tranxition.com).

Eliminating the preinstalled bonus crap

Most computers sold today come with prepackaged *stuff.* I find this practice most unnerving.

Sometimes, the stuff is useful; for example, you get a new computer and a brand-new version of Microsoft Office. Or, maybe you have your choice of Office versus a home package (including Quicken and maybe Word) or a gamers' package with a ton of nifty games. That's fine.

What's not fine are the bonus programs they give you that you don't want and will never use. That's bunk. And, it junks up your hard drive. Of course, the question looms about what is really junk that you can remove versus which programs are valuable and keep the computer running.

 ✔ **Stuff you can freely delete:** I have noticed that most, if not all, new PCs and Macs come with programs to connect you with various online ser-vices. If you want to try them, swell! If not, delete them. Ditto for any other offer for online services or Internet connections that you don't want or feel that you will never use. Zap 'em away.

 ✔ **Free trials:** These trials include anything you get that's offered as a free trial or demo version of some program you can zap away. Bother with keeping something to check it out only if you're interested. If you're not interested, remove it.

Be careful how you remove things! In Windows, always use the Control Panel's Add/Remove Software icon. Peruse the list that's displayed, and unin-stall anything there that you don't want. If you're unsure about something, phone the dealer and ask what it is or whether you need it. Then, uninstall!

This problem isn't as pervasive on the Macintosh as it is on the PC. Only Apple makes the Mac, and Apple has not (at least since 1986, when I bought my first Mac) preinstalled junk the way junk is preinstalled on a PC.

Still, you may notice, for example, both Netscape and Internet Explorer avail-able on your Mac. If you use one, drag the other's folder to the Trash. Ditto for AOL and other online service sign-up icons. If you don't need 'em, drag 'em to the Trash.

Chapter 26

Selecting an ISP

. . . .

In This Chapter

▶ Getting on the Internet

▶ Paying for the Internet

▶ Finding an ISP

▶ Getting the service and support you need

. . . .

1 n addition to choosing basic hardware and software, you should now consider that all computers have a third element: Internet access. In some
cases, your company, the university you attend, or maybe some local organization provides Internet access. But, for the small office or home, Internet
service is *another* purchase you need to make. Just like buying more hardware or software for your computer, you should look for certain things when
you're selecting an Internet service provider, or ISP.

This chapter covers the items you should look for when you're selecting an
ISP. Your computer probably comes with dozens of offers from national ISPs
or online services, like AOL, and you may occasionally find newspaper fliers
or junk mail (regular mail) for local ISPs and their offerings. This chapter
helps you sift through all that stuff, to find an ISP that suits your needs to a T.

What You Need in Order to "Do" the Internet

The Internet isn't a single computer or a piece of software. Instead, it's lots of
computers, all connected to one another. They store and exchange information. To "get on" the Internet, you need to connect your computer to another
computer already on the Internet. That computer is usually owned by a company that provides Internet access — an ISP.

What you need

To access the Internet, you need a computer with the necessary hardware and software, plus an account at an ISP or other Internet service provider. Basically, it boils down to five items:

A computer: You most likely have this item, if you have worked through the various chapters in this book designed to get you a computer. Congratulations.

A modem: This gizmo connects your computer to the Internet. It can be a dial-up modem or a high-speed modem. Refer to Chapter 11 for the details on buying a modem.

Internet software: All modern computer operating systems have built-in programs and the software required in order to access the Internet. Honestly, you have nothing to buy here. Even if your computer seems to lack this or that program, you can find the software you need on the Internet by using the tools the operating system provides.

An ISP: This type of company provides Internet access. Unless your computer already has Internet access through your company or university, you need an ISP to grant you access.

Money: Ah, yes. Nothing is free. Even if Internet access just happens to be free in your part of the world, you're still paying for it somehow. Most people need to pay an ISP for access.

You probably have three of these five items already. All you need, most likely, are the ISP and the money. This section helps with the ISP. The money . . . I'll leave it up to you to figure that part out!

- ✔ A good way to get money is to *work*. Most people who have money also have a job.

- ✔ Some handheld computers require special Internet software, though if you're serious about Internet access, you probably have a desktop or laptop system that serves as your main Internet computer.

- ✔ The pundits predict that, eventually, all Internet access will be free, which means that it will be heavily subsidized by obnoxious advertising. I pray that will be an option; I prefer to pay *not* to see obnoxious advertising.

What the ISP gives you

In exchange for your hard-earned coin, an ISP should provide you with the following services. Remember that the *S* in ISP stands for *service*:

A dial-up number: You need a number to call so that your computer can access the Internet. This number, along with other basic account information, is given to the Internet connection program that configures your computer for the Internet.

For high-speed access, the ISP provides you with the technical nuts and bolts to make that connection work.

An e-mailbox: This item is very important. You should receive, as part of your account at the ISP, an e-mail address and a mailbox for receiving messages on the Internet. It's a must! Avoid any ISP that doesn't offer e-mail as a basic service.

Some kind of getting-started booklet: Even the pros need some of the basic, and often technical, information required to connect to the Internet. The booklet should tell you about the ISP's service, what's offered, general information (like phone numbers and tech support), plus lots of how-tos and some Q&As.

If the ISP is really on the ball, you may also get some or all of the following items. They may be offered at an additional charge, or they may be included with the base price:

Classes: Not only should classes be offered on basic Internet, Web browsing, and e-mail, but some ISPs may also offer classes that cover Web page design or even using a shell account. The beginning classes should be free or included with your sign-up fee. You may be charged for the advanced classes, or classes may be offered in conjunction with a local community college. No problem there.

Software: Some ISPs may have special software available, including a Web browser, an e-mail program, and other programs. The getting-started booklet (mentioned a few paragraphs ago) should tell you about the software.

Web space: This location on the ISP's server is reserved for your use in case you ever decide to create and post your own Web page on the Internet. Sometimes, this space involves an extra cost, and sometimes it's included with your account.

Newsgroup access: Some ISPs offer newsgroup (also known as USENET) access with regular accounts. Others may offer newsgroup access separately or for an extra fee. Having an ISP that provides all the newsgroups is a bonus.

Personal domain name: If you're interested in having your own dot-com or dot-org or dot-whatever Web page, ask whether your ISP can provide it. Some can — at an extra charge, of course.

Programming services: Some ISPs also offer programming for Web pages, if you want such a Web page. This service and others are usually reserved for businesses that need these types of facilities.

Overall, what you really need are the number to dial, basic account information, and an e-mailbox. That's really enough to get you started. Having the other options available may help down the road. For example, your home business may blossom into the next eBay, in which case it would be nice to be connected with an ISP that can provide you with that kind of service.

How much should it cost?

The price for Internet access ranges anywhere from free to several hundred dollars a month, depending on which services you're getting or whether you're just getting screwed.

A sign-up fee: This fee may involve a connection fee or other one-time fee to get you started. Some places have them, and some don't. Sign-up fees can also be waived. Mostly, use them for comparison: If one ISP has a sign-up fee and another doesn't, go with the cheaper of the two.

Monthly fees: These fees can range from as low as a couple of dollars to several hundred a month. Typically, Internet access is about $20 a month.

Contracts: In these deals, you sign up for a large amount of Internet time for a lower price. These contracts can be good or bad, depending on your needs.

As an example, my company buys Internet time one year in advance. By paying for the full year upfront, I get a heck of a discount. On the other hand, that's a big check I write. It also means that I'm stuck with that ISP for a full year.

Avoid long-term contracts at all costs, such as the two- or three-year contracts that come with "free" computers. At $20 per month, the cost adds up. Besides, you should be getting a hefty discount for a three-year contract. Plus, a back-out clause would be nice. Please don't be fooled by these offers.

Always review your billing options. Never assume that the rate you signed up for is eternal. For example, you may have signed on for service for $20 per month and then discover that the $4.95 rate suits your needs just as well. If so, change! Don't pay more for services you don't use. Refer to the ISP's current rate information, or phone up its support crew for information and try to save yourself some money.

TIP

Changing ISPs

Unlike cable TV service, it's entirely possible to change ISPs without moving your house. If you're dissatisfied with the service or somehow feel ripped off, you can sign up to a new ISP and dump the old one, just like you can start shopping at a new grocery store.

If you plan to switch, sign up with the new ISP before you dump the old one. Make your connection, and let your e-mail buddies know your new e-mail address. Then cancel the old account. That way, you don't miss anything.

Finding an ISP

Most cities and even towns and hamlets have their own ISPs. I highly recommend that you go with a local outfit, not some large, impersonal organization like — well, for legal reasons, I can't mention them. No, service is important in an ISP, and nothing beats the local Ma-and-Pa Internet Shop.

If your area is blessed with more than one ISP, shop around. Find the one that gives you the best deal. Often times, the cheapest ISP lacks lots of features that other ISPs offer (but it doesn't tell you that unless you know what you're missing). Also, paying quarterly or annually (if you can afford it) is cheaper than paying monthly. These places can wheel and deal with you — if you know a bit about what you want.

✔ You can find ISPs in the Yellow Pages, under *Internet*. Some of them even advertise on TV, usually late at night along with the 1-900 psychic hot-tub-babe hotlines.

✔ I might add that ISPs with 24-hour service rank high on my list. If your e-mail dies at 11 p.m. and you need to get online, it's nice to have someone there who can help you.

✔ Don't be afraid to change ISPs if yours doesn't work out. I have done it twice. Please don't put up with crummy service; change ISPs if you need to.

Is AOL an ISP?

AOL has its fans, but I'm not one of them. For the price, I think AOL is a rip-off. Yet, if you enjoy AOL and feel that you're getting your money's worth — great. Before moving on, however, consider some arguments both pro and con for AOL as your ISP:

Pro: AOL is great if you're just starting out. The software is free (but not the monthly service fee), and it's easy to set up. Access is available all over, which means that you can get your mail and go online when you travel. AOL is widely supported by many companies, news organizations, and online retailers. If you're happy with AOL, why rock the boat?

Con: Using AOL is *slower* than connecting directly to the Internet through an ISP. You're limited by the AOL software, through which Web pages are funneled, as opposed to viewing them directly with a true Internet Web browser. AOL e-mail is nonstandard, which means that some attachments cannot be received. Though the AOL phone lines may not be as busy as in days past, AOL is still subject to outages. The AOL help system is impersonal and bad.

I favor a local ISP because you often get hometown service and the fastest Internet access possible. All your Internet software works, and you're not restricted to certain places or prevented access because the system is busy. Because of that, this book doesn't cover AOL.

The S Means Service

Remember that the *S* in ISP means service. An ISP should not be judged merely on the fact that it gives you a phone number and Internet access. And, never buy into an ISP's plan just because it's the cheapest. There should be more.

Beyond classes, I would give high marks to any ISP that offers 24-hour human tech support (a person on the phone). Nothing is more helpful than a human voice when you're experiencing Something Weird on the Internet at 1 a.m.

Ensure that the ISP has plenty of phone lines. Ask how well connected it is; the more connections it has to the Internet, the more likely you can still use the Internet in the event of a crash (the Internet does crash from time to time).

Make sure that the people at the ISP are those with whom you're willing to work. Having their personal e-mail addresses available is a major plus, almost like having a favorite salesperson in the store.

Chapter 27

When to Buy, When to Sell, When to Upgrade

*N*othing lasts forever. Well, except for death and taxes (but you die only once). Diamonds last a while. But, most things have a life span. For example, rubber spatulas seem to last about three months before they get all melted and cracked. Cars? Maybe five or seven years (just enough time to pay off the loan). Computers? They have life spans too.

Expect your computer to last at least four to seven years. Although a computer can last longer, technology advances so much and software demands new technology so strongly that after four years, your new computer is seriously outdated. What should you do? Should you sell it? Should you upgrade it? Should you buy a new one? This chapter helps you make those decisions.

Unlike Wine and Cheese, Computers Don't Age Well

Nothing is more disappointing than reading a computer ad six months after you buy a computer and discovering that you could have had, for the same money, a much better computer. Don't get discouraged! This situation happens *all the time*, which is why I say "Buy!" when you're ready to buy. You have your computer. You're using it. That's much better than waiting.

When exactly does your computer become a true geezer? Generally, after four or five years of duty. After that time, two things generally happen: The hardware becomes much better and cheaper, and the software starts craving that better hardware. A third thing also happens: Your computer starts to go south. The hard drive may start making a louder noise, especially when the system first starts up. It's a sign that the bearings are starting to go. (It's not an emergency; the drive may still have years of life left.)

Should You Upgrade?

One of the joys of owning a computer is that you can upgrade or replace any of its components at any time — as long as the computer is turned off when you do so.

Upgrading is an easy alternative to tossing out a fairly good computer and spending more money on a new one. Upgrades are inexpensive. And, often, all you need is a simple upgrade: more memory, another monitor, another hard drive. A few twists of the screwdriver later, and you have an almost-new computer again. Upgrading should come from some serious need: Software demands more memory, you run out of disk storage, or something breaks.

Which hardware to upgrade first

What you upgrade first depends on your needs. Does your software need more memory? Upgrade it. Is your monitor shot? Buy another one. Out of hard drive storage? Add another.

Memory: As long as your computer is properly configured for memory (refer to Chapter 6), plugging in another 256MB, or even 1GB, of RAM is relatively easy. This upgrade often solves a number of problems you may have with a sluggish computer.

Hard drive: Although plugging in another hard drive is easy, getting it going can be a pain. Hard drives must be formatted, and it's hard to find out exactly how that's done. Better leave this upgrade to your dealer.

The best part about upgrading a hard drive is that you can add a second hard drive of immense size. If you miscalculate and find that 40GB of storage isn't enough, for example, buy an 80GB hard drive! You can install it right inside the console. Upgrading the hard drive is more expensive than upgrading memory. Because humans tend to collect things, however, you will enjoy the extra space right away.

Monitor: Buying another monitor is cinchy: Buy it! Turn your computer off, unplug the old monitor, and plug in the new one. Done!

Old monitors don't keep their value. You cannot sell them, and you shouldn't toss them out in the trash. Instead, refer to your locality's disposal people for the proper method of tossing out an old computer monitor.

Other stuff: Just about everything in your computer can be upgraded. You can upgrade, in addition to the preceding items, your CD-ROM player, a floppy drive, a video adapter, or virtually any component in your computer.

Watch your upgrade costs! Sure, it may be fun to buy your computer a present in the form of an upgrade. Tally what you spend, though. If you're not careful, you may wind up spending more on your old computer than it would cost to buy a new one.

My $.02 on upgrading your microprocessor

Another hardware upgrade touted in the computer magazines is the microprocessor upgrade. It's not hard to do: The microprocessor slides or clips into a socket. Most computers are designed that way. I don't recommend it, though, for several reasons:

- **Cost:** When your dealer buys microprocessors to plug into his computers, he buys them by the truckload. He gets a discount; you don't. You pay top dollar for a new microprocessor, which can be a several-hundred-dollar premium for the current top-of-the-line model. Spending your money on a memory upgrade may give you better results anyway.

- **Compatibility:** Although the new microprocessor may plug into the old one's slot, is the computer's circuitry geared to work with it? Motherboards are designed around specific microprocessors running at specific speeds. Although the new one may function, it may be crippled or inhibited by the older circuitry on the motherboard. What's the point of having a faster microprocessor when it has to slow down to access your computer's old memory, for example?

- **The whole motherboard upgrade:** This upgrade involves another microprocessor upgrade, which directly addresses the issue of compatibility, but not price! New motherboards (your computer's main circuitry) are spendy. If you go that route, you may as well buy a new case and a new hard drive and — hey! — you have a new computer! You have the old one too, gutted out and not good for anything.

Upgrading software

You're often bombarded with developers' propaganda for upgrading their software. Hurry! Version 4.02 is available! It's only $69 because you're a registered user and *we like you!*

When should you upgrade your software? As with everything else, the answer is "according to your needs." Do you *need* the new features the software offers? Does the new version fix the bugs that annoyed you? If so, buy it.

> ✔ It's possible and quite common to skip software upgrades. For example, skipping from Version 3.2 to Version 4.1 can save money *and* keep you current.
>
> ✔ If you're using the same software at home as you are at work, upgrade when your office does. If you don't, your older software at home may not be capable of reading the documents the newer software at work produces.
>
> ✔ A good argument to eventually upgrade any application, in fact, is to keep compatible with any new document formats. Eventually, you may find that others are using the software and that your older application cannot read those newer document formats.

Upgrading your operating system

Like all software, your operating system eventually will have a new version. In days of yore, this situation caused a debate: Everything worked fine with the current operating system, so why upgrade? Even if the new version had exciting features, the upgrade may not have been compatible. It was a puzzle. Generally speaking, I can give you this advice:

Never upgrade your operating system.

The best way to get the next version of an operating system is to wait until you need to buy a new computer. The new version comes installed on that computer. Otherwise, you risk a great deal by upgrading your current operating system — primarily, that some of your older software may not be compatible, which would force you into paying lots of money for upgrades.

You may eventually encounter new software that requires the newest operating system. Traditionally, however, that doesn't happen until the new operating system is about two years old. Why? The answer is that because software developers don't want to lose you as a customer, they don't write a specific version of their applications until *everyone* has upgraded. So, don't panic.

Should You Sell Your Beloved Computer?

I remember when friends of mine in the mid-1980s tried to sell their computers. They had sold cars, so they tried to figure the price of their used computers in the same way. The stuff never sold.

Used computers have no value. If you wait four or five years, the new stuff is so much better that you never can recover any value from your original purchase. I have my accountant rapid-depreciate my computers, in fact, because they just don't hold any value.

If you do try to sell your computer, ask only $50 to $100 for it; use a higher price if it's a recent system, but don't expect to walk away with a profit. The best buyer is someone who already has that type of computer and wants to buy another one.

Sell everything that comes with the computer when you sell. Make the computer system as complete as you can. You can throw in software too, although that doesn't add to the price of the computer. (Old software has no value.)

Ask for either cash (because it won't be that much) or a cashier's check for your old computer. The last insult you want is to sell something you paid $2,000 for to a guy who writes you a rubber check.

What about the hard drive and all your personal data?

When you get rid of your old computer, don't get rid of your personal data as well! The most secure thing to do is keep the hard drive. Offer your used system without a hard drive, or, if you really want it to sell, buy a replacement hard drive for the computer. That's the safest way to ensure that your data doesn't get abused. (Companies that are serious about security remove hard drives from their old computers and have those drives physically destroyed.)

If physically removing the hard drive isn't practical, you can use software that "bulk-erases" the disk. This type of program comes with Norton Utilities (or Norton SystemWorks). It's called *Wipe Disk.* Use it to utterly erase everything on your PC's hard drive so that none of your personal information is sold with your computer.

Other programs that can erase your hard drive include OnTrack's Data Eraser (www. ontrack.com) and Jetico's BCWipe (www. jetico.com).

A better thing to do with your old computers is to donate them to charities or private schools. Give them as much computer as you can, including a printer. Give them your software manuals and discs. And, ask for a receipt based on the computer's fair market value (see an accountant for more information). You get more from the computer that way, as a tax deduction, and you give something back to your community.

Buying a Used Computer

You may have many reasons for buying an old computer. The most common is that you have a computer exactly like it and want another as a spare. Or, maybe your software just runs better with an older system. If so, buying a used computer saves you hundreds of dollars over buying a state-of-the-art system whose power just isn't needed.

Test-drive a used computer before you buy it. Take some software with you and load it up. Make sure that it runs. Save something to disk. Print something. If it works, the used computer is worthy.

Used computers, unless they have been used less than a year, are worth only a couple hundred dollars — max. Don't overpay! Check the classified ads to see what's being asked for used equipment. Then check the prices of new equipment and compare. Obviously, paying $200 for an old Pentium PC makes no sense with new PC models selling for $400.

Someone may tell you, "Oh, but you also get $2,000 worth of software for only $200!" Just laugh at the person. "Ha-ha!" Old software has no value. Sure, the guy may have paid $2,000 for it originally, but it's worth nothing now. Insist that the seller include all the boxes (if they're available), original software, and documentation.

Part V
The Part of Tens

The 5th Wave   By Rich Tennant

In this part . . .

Lists are fun to make and share, and often useful. For example, astronauts have dozens of lists to check off and work through to ensure that their billion-dollar spaceship, supplied by the lowest bidder and assembled by government employees, doesn't blow all to hell. When it comes to buying a computer, you have lists to peruse as well, but without all that blowing up stuff.

The chapters in this part of the book contain lists of ten items (sometimes more, sometimes less), which you should review at various stages in the buying process. It's all good advice. Read it and heed it.

Chapter 28

Ten Common Mistakes Made by First-Time Computer Buyers

. . . .

In This Chapter

▶ Buying hardware rather than software

▶ Shopping for brand names

▶ Shopping for the cheapest system

▶ Being unprepared for the sale

▶ Forgetting the "extras"

▶ Paying by check or cash

▶ Not reading the setup manuals

▶ Forgetting that software is expensive

▶ Buying too much

▶ Not counting learning time

. . . .

*I*f you have followed this book's advice, you won't (I hope) fall into the trap of making one of the following ever-so-common mistakes. It's worth putting them in a list, just as a reminder.

Buying Hardware before Software

Software controls the hardware by telling it what to do. Don't be tempted by marvelous hardware features. Don't be lured into buying one brand or the other by some advertising campaign. Without software, the hardware is next to useless. Buy your hardware to support your software.

Dropping Brand Names

When people find out what I do, they usually want my advice about buying a computer. "Dan," they say, as they puff up their chests, about to impress me with some trivial tidbit, "I've been looking at the UltraDork computer. What do you think about it?"

"Big mistake," I answer. It doesn't matter which brand they mention; I always say the same thing. Software is more important than hardware. Most people don't see that, so I'm not rude when I tell them. But, thinking about brand names rather than what the computer can do is a big mistake.

Shopping for the Cheapest Computer System

When you buy a *bargain system,* you will probably wind up with a competent and functional computer. When things go wrong, you want the dealer to provide service to get your system fixed. That bargain price often doesn't include service, however. Look for a dealer you can grow friendly with. The dealer's reputation, which is more important than price, is how it stays in business.

Being Unprepared for the Sale

Computers have different jargon (in case you haven't noticed). Don't expect a computer salesperson to be able to explain to you all the subtleties of things like GPU, scan rate, MHz, and IEEE. Some disreputable salespeople may even dupe you into paying more money for obsolete and unnecessary technology.

Forgetting Some Extra Items

The ad says $600, and you have just a hair over that — enough to pay the sales tax. Alas, you didn't read the fine print: That $600 computer doesn't come with a monitor. Oops!

Ensure that you buy a complete computer system! Double- and triple-check the ads for any missing pieces. You need a monitor, a keyboard, memory, a hard drive, and operating system software to make a computer system.

Not Paying by Credit Card

Never pay for a computer with a check. Never pay cash. Always pay with a credit card. Why? Because credit charges can be put into dispute if anything nasty happens between you and the dealer. Credit card companies support their clients. If someone sells you junk, the credit card company doesn't force you to pay for it (as long as you have taken legitimate steps to resolve the problem).

Most banks don't let you reverse the charges on a check. If you pay cash to a shady dealer, your money is gone forever. Computer-dealer scams aren't as popular as they used to be, although they still exist.

Not Reading the Setup Manuals

As a general rule of advice from a self-proclaimed computer guru: Read things over before trying them. If you make a mistake or something doesn't happen right, read the instructions again and try a second time. Consider it a last resort to make that phone call to your dealer. Don't substitute the phone for the manual.

Forgetting That Software Can Be Expensive

Contrary to what you may think, computer hardware is only half your cost. The computer software that your computer needs probably costs the same amount as what you paid for your computer (over time, of course). Piece by piece, package by package, software is expensive.

Buying Too Much

Start simple. If you buy too much stuff too quickly, you may go overboard and never find out all about your system. My recipe for becoming a computer guru, in fact, involves starting with a minimal system. After you have that mastered, upgrade slowly and learn as you go.

Not Counting Learning Time

If you have just figured out that you need a computer "yesterday," you're too late. I advise everyone (businesspersons, students, or just the idle curious) to give themselves at least three weeks to use and become comfortable with their computer system before the real work starts.

Chapter 29

Ten Warning Signs

If all people were good, wholesome folks with high morals and standards and a strong sense of customer support, I wouldn't have to write this chapter. Because this chapter is here, though, I suppose that you will have a better understanding of human nature.

Because the computer industry is full of terms and standards that only real computer geeks have knowledge of or an understanding of, it's rather easy to pull the wool over your eyes. I don't want that to happen. The best thing I can do is educate you on what to be aware of. Consider this chapter a computer-buying self-defense class.

Hi-yah!

Industry "Standards" versus the Ads

Beware of computer hype! You may read about "groundbreaking" technology, but, honestly, unless you see that technology available in a computer ad, forget it.

Any new hardware technology takes time to become accepted. Wait until something "fabulously new" is available on most new computer systems before you decide whether to buy one. Remember that software controls the hardware. You need software in order to use the new hardware, regardless of whether every computer has the new hardware.

Out-of-Date Stock

Computer dealers like to sell stuff they don't have to fix. No one — neither you nor the dealer — likes to see you come back with your computer in the box because it doesn't work. I don't mean, however, that shady dealers don't try to sell you old stuff just to get rid of it.

Do your research (like reading this book) before you walk into a store. Be aware of what's appropriate for your needs and what the computer industry suggests as standard (which you determine by reading the ads). You don't want a pushy salesman convincing you that a CRT monitor is better than an LCD simply because he has three dozen stacked up in the storage room and the boss told him to get rid of them.

(I worked *one day* at a computer store. During my only sales meeting, we were told to "unload" an ailing computer, to steer customers to it first regardless of what their true needs were. Like I said, I worked there only one day.)

Money Down Required

For what possible reason would anyone need money down on a computer? It's just not necessary. Don't believe them if they pull this bit: "We need the down payment to ensure that you're committed to buying this computer." Computers are selling like hotcakes, so it's not like they would build a computer and be stuck with it forever if you didn't take it. Someone else will buy it.

- ✔ Never put money down, especially cash, on a computer.
- ✔ Always pay for your purchase with a credit card.

Missing Pieces

If you open the box and everything isn't there, take it back immediately! Chances are good that you were sold a computer someone else returned and everything wasn't put back properly. Tell the people at the computer store that you want another computer. Don't accept their giving you the missing parts. Unless someone there told you that you were buying a refurbished computer, he cannot legally sell it to you. Check the laws in your state about selling refurbished equipment.

No Address in the Mail-Order Ad

It's an easy scam: Someone opens a business with a rented postal box, places an ad in a circular (and doesn't pay for it), and has an 800 number. The orders fly in because the prices in the ad are just too good to be true. That's because they are; two days later, the "business" doesn't exist and folks are out thousands of dollars in cash.

Reputable dealers post their physical addresses in their ads, along with their local phone numbers.

Salespeople Too Busy to Help

My theory has always been that if people are too busy to take my money, I don't want to give it to them anyway. Go someplace else, to wherever you find someone who's willing to answer your questions and take the time to fully explain what they have to offer you.

Salespeople in the Store Ignore You

If the salespeople in the store are ignoring you, one of two things is going on: Either no one knows enough to walk up and help you, or no one gives a hoot whether you buy a computer. Apathy and ignorance are two qualities you don't ever want to do business with, regardless of whether you're buying a computer, a car, or some shoes.

(I was ready to plunk down $800 for a new hard drive in a local store, and *everyone* in the store ignored me. The salesperson didn't know what a SCSI drive was. The techie commented only on the SCSI drive and didn't tell me whether it was in stock or available for sale. It was a nice store, too; it had a classroom in back and competitive prices. Because the people in there were jerks, though, I bought my $800 hard drive by mail order.)

Also, be wary of any salesperson who refers to you behind your back as a "mark" — unless, of course, your name is Mark.

No Classroom

If a store doesn't offer some kind of computer class to help you with your new purchase, the folks there really aren't concerned with giving you complete customer service. They're more concerned with making a sale.

If you're a first-time computer buyer, taking a class gives you a better sense of confidence to go exploring with your computer, and your frustration level is much lower.

No Software Documentation

All software comes with some kind of documentation: installation instructions, information on how to play or work the software, and maybe even some technical notes. This stuff is all-important. If the software documentation doesn't come with the computer, chances are that the software is stolen. Don't leave the store without seeing that documentation. If someone makes any of the following comments, leave the store!

- ✔ "The software doesn't come with any documentation."
- ✔ "Oh, you'll be able to figure it out."
- ✔ "The program tells you what to do as you go along."

All software must be sold with documentation! Even if it's just a CD, that CD must have a serial number on it — or, sometimes, the entire manual!

Chapter 30

Ten Other Things You Should Buy

T his chapter is dedicated to the ten additional things, whatnots, and items you need to buy that will help with your whole computer-using experience. Buying these things isn't optional. You really need them.

Mousepad and Wristpad

Ever try to use a mouse with a dirty ball? No, really, I'm serious. The mouse has a ball that it rolls on, and if that ball becomes dirty, it doesn't roll smoothly and you have a heck of a time trying to get it to point, drag, or do anything.

A *mousepad* is a screen-size piece of foam rubber that sits on your desk and that the mighty mouse rolls on. A mousepad makes the mouse roll more smoothly and keeps that mouse ball clean (as long as you don't drop cookie crumbs all over it).

- ✔ You get the best performance from your mouse if you buy a mousepad that's slightly textured. Smooth pads don't work as well.

- ✔ Optical mice don't need mousepads, but, still, having a mousepad is nice; it keeps a portion of your desktop clean for the mouse to slide around in.

Buying a wristpad is more of a health measure than a technical one. Lazy key-boarders drop their wrists to an unnatural position, which eventually causes stress on their wrists and their infamous carpal tunnels. This condition, of course, can be painful.

The purpose of a wristpad is to keep your arms and hands in a normal, healthy position. It fits right below your keyboard, and your wrists gently lie on it.

Wristpads are also available for your mousepad, sometimes both in one unit.

Neither a mousepad nor a wristpad is expensive, and you can get creative with a mousepad. Kinko's has a process in which you can put your kids' pic-tures (or pictures of your cats, if you don't like kids) on your mousepad.

Power Strip

Not until you start putting together your computer and all its various gadgets does it occur to you that home builders truly underestimate the need for wall outlets.

You have to plug in your computer, printer, modem, scanner, lamp, clock, and answering machine. The list can get pretty long, and you're probably looking at one, maybe two, plugs to accommodate all this stuff.

Power strips are like short extension cords, except that they have several out-lets to accommodate your computer paraphernalia.

The Kensington SmartSockets brand of power strip has a large, wide area that allows more room for the AC converters that often come on computer peripherals. I recommend this brand.

Surge Protector

A *surge protector* is merely a dooded-up power strip. It's like a power strip with a fuse to even out the electricity in times of power glitches, which can crash your computer and make you lose everything you have been working on.

✔ A power strip can also be a surge protector. Some just have extra outlets. Others have surge protection in them, like the SmartSockets, mentioned in the preceding section.

✔ Some surge protectors also come with filters for protecting your phone line and network cable.

✔ The more you pay for a surge protector, the better its protection. The highest level of protection is *spike protection,* which protects your computer from lightning strikes.

✔ Sorry — you can't get any "wrath of God" protection.

UPS

UPS (not the delivery service) stands for *uninterruptible power supply.* It keeps the computer on (for a while) during a power outage.

By plugging your computer and monitor into the UPS, you have enough time to safely save and close all your documents before turning off your computer. The UPS also has surge protection, but you don't really have to plug *everything* into it. After all, who cares whether your modem or your printer goes off during an outage? The data in your computer is more important, and that's what the UPS protects.

✔ If you plug too much stuff into a UPS, your computer doesn't have enough power to last long enough to save any of your work. Plug just the computer and monitor into the UPS.

✔ Never plug a printer into a UPS; printing can wait until after the power comes back on.

✔ If possible, try to find a UPS that supports swappable batteries. That way, you can replace only the battery if the unit ever gets sluggish and not have to buy a whole new UPS.

✔ Most UPS systems are good for around five minutes, so don't dawdle! Save your work, and then turn off your computer!

Printer Cable

Printers don't come with printer cables, which has always amazed me because you can't get your printer to work unless a cable connects your printer to your computer. It's like buying a television without a cord to plug into the wall. Ugh.

The only thing you need to worry about with printer cables is that your printer can be no farther than 20 feet away from your computer. Information tends to get lost at that distance. The most common length for printer cable is 6 feet.

(Note that the 20-foot limit applies to parallel printer cables. For USB printers, the limit is theoretically 3 meters, or about 10 feet.)

Printer Paper

Paper. You gotta have it for the printer, or else the darn thing is kind of useless. Only a few rules apply when it comes to paper:

✔ Don't use *bond* paper in a laser printer. Bond paper may have a type of dust on it, which clogs up the printer.

✔ Don't use erasable typing paper. This type of paper is good for manual typewriters, where you have to erase all your typing mistakes; with a computer, the dust on the erasable typing paper can clog up the printer's internals.

✔ Buy a whole box when you go to buy paper. You will use it. Nothing is more frustrating than printing a report, running out of paper in the middle of it, and then realizing that you don't have any more.

More Inky Stuff

Printers, like ink pens, run out of ink — except that with a pen, you're more likely to throw the darn thing away and buy another one. You don't want to do that with a printer. That could get costly. Instead, you have to buy more ink.

Printer ink comes in various containers and exists in various states, depending on your printer.

✔ Inkjet printers use little containers of ink that are really supereasy to change (but very expensive!)

✔ Laser printers use a drop-in toner cartridge. These cartridges are fairly easy to install if you follow the directions.

✔ Impact (or dot matrix) printers use a ribbon.

Because all these printers require you to handle the ribbon or cartridge, you run the risk of getting this stuff on your hands. Be careful! It's ink. It doesn't come off easily. It kind of wears off more than it washes off. To help prevent that, wear some rubber gloves when you change the toner or ribbon in your printer.

Removable Disks

Even though your hard drive has a huge capacity to store information, you still need removable disks. You use them for transferring information from one computer to another.

If your PC has a floppy drive and you actually use it, get some floppy disks. Buy a box of preformatted disks. Ensure that they're "IBM formatted," which means they're ready for use in a PC.

If you have a specialty drive, like a Zip drive, get some of those disks too.

CD-R and CD-RW drives deserve to have their own media as well. Stock up on those discs because buying them in bulk is often cheaper than buying them one at a time.

- ✔ Zip disks are expensive. Buying them three or more at a time saves you some money.
- ✔ If possible, try to get the green-gold type of CD-R discs. They tend to be more reliable and compatible than the cheaper CD-R discs.

CD Caddy

Software comes on CDs, and you will probably create your own CDs (both music and backup) and have music CDs handy by your computer. The best way to store these is to get one of those plastic or wire CD-holding tray things. You can find them at music stores as well as at office supply stores.

A Roll of Paper Towels

Paper towels? You're surprised, right? Even though one of the rules for computer use is that you don't eat or drink by your computer, you will. It's inevitable. You will succumb to temptation and grab a cup of coffee to keep you company.

Paper towels are for those times when you spill your beverage of choice. Spilling liquid of any kind can cause havoc with your computer, so either don't drink and compute or keep those paper towels close by.

Getting your keyboard wet fries the keyboard (metaphorically speaking — it's not like smoke and stuff billows out of the keyboard). You can try to let it dry out or use those paper towels to try to wipe up the liquid before it does too much damage.

Chapter 31

Ten Tips and Suggestions

. . . .

In This Chapter

▶ Your computer's clock

▶ Get a second phone line

▶ Reread your manuals

▶ Put a timer on the Internet

▶ Get antivirus software

▶ Subscribe to a computer magazine

▶ Join a users' group

▶ Buy some computer books

▶ Don't let the computer ruin your life

▶ Have fun!

. . . .

No one wants any surprises when they're using a computer. Imagine buying a new car, signing your name, being handed the keys, and then the salesperson saying, "Oh, I forgot to tell you — this thing runs only on 110 octane super-dooper premium" or "Always hold your steering wheel with your left hand because the car pulls to the right." Fortunately, owning a computer doesn't involve many surprises along those lines.

This chapter contains a list of ten tips, suggestions, and warnings. They're nothing major; they're just some last-minute items you may not know about — by-the-way sort of things to wrap up this book.

Your Computer Has a Clock

You may not notice at first, but your computer keeps track of the time. And, it remembers the time even when you turn off your computer or unplug it. The reason is that the computer has a battery that helps it remember the time as well as a few other items.

Someday, in about five years, your computer's battery will die. You will notice it because not only will your computer have lost track of the time, but you may also see an error message when the computer starts up. When that happens, phone your dealer and get a new battery installed.

Even though your computer has a clock, it makes a lousy timepiece. No two computers can keep track of the same time. Some are fast; most are slow. You have to reset your system's clock every month or so. If not, your computer could be lagging by as much as 20 or 30 minutes by the end of the year.

Get a Second Phone Line

If you plan to use a computer and a dial-up modem, do yourself and everyone else a favor and get the computer its own phone line. I tried to phone up a friend one night, and his phone was busy for *three hours*. He was on the Internet and utterly unaware that anyone was trying to call.

- ✔ If the second line from the phone company costs too much, consider getting a digital cellular phone instead. Often, the monthly bill for the cellphone (especially a digital model) is much less than buying a second phone line. And, you can take the cellphone with you.

- ✔ Cable and DSL modems don't need a separate phone line. In fact, DSL "shares" a phone line with your regular telephone. (You need a DSL doohickey on the phone line that isn't connected to the DSL modem.)

After a While, Reread the Manuals

Although computer manuals are horrid, they may begin to make sense a few weeks after you use your computer. Use any program for a while, and try to figure it out. Then go back and read the manuals. Don't do it right away; take some time, and do something with the program. Figure out how it works. After that, for some reason, the manual tends to make sense. I follow this simple advice, and for some reason, everyone thinks that I'm a computer genius.

Put a Timer on That Internet

If you plan to be on the Internet, set a clock! The Internet sucks up time like a black hole in space. Limit yourself to 30 minutes or an hour for your Internet browsing, or else you will see the sun rise some morning.

Get Defensive Software

If you're going to be on the Internet, you need antivirus and anti-spyware software. They aren't just options. Viruses and other nasty programs proliferate on the Internet. If you don't take defensive action, your computer will become infected, overrun, or otherwise disabled. You didn't just plunk down good money to have that happen, right?

Some new computers come with antivirus software as part of the "free" software that comes with the computer. If not, buy antivirus software *at once!*

Anti-spyware software can be found on the Internet, freely available. I recommend either Spybot (`www.safer-networking.org`) or Ad-Aware (`www.lava soft.de`).

I also recommend getting a firewall, though the best firewall to get is one included with your broadband router. Refer to Chapters 11 and 12 for more information.

Subscribe to a Computer Magazine

Now that you have a computer, it makes sense to get a computer magazine. That's where you find advice, tips, and information about computer things. The magazine keeps you up-to-date and informed better than dealers and developers, who put their own interests above yours.

Several levels of computer magazines are available, from novice magazines to hard-core nerd publications. Most bookstores have racks full of them, so take a few minutes to browse, and pick up a few of the ones that interest you.

Join a Computer Users' Group

Sociologists tell us that injured people tend to cluster after a catastrophe. It's a force of nature. Just like those walking wounded, computer users — dazed and bewildered — gather in small groups in cities across the land. They discuss. They share. They learn.

Refer to your local newspaper events column to see when and where any computer groups meet in your area.

Buy a Great Book

I can't recommend books enough! Some great titles are out there to help you find out about anything you can do on a computer. When your dealer support craps out, when the developers admit that they loathe the customer, and when you have exhausted your friends and computer buddies, buy a good book.

As with magazines, be aware that different levels of books — beginner, intermediate, and advanced — are available for different computer users: You can get reference books, and you can get tutorial books. Buy what suits you best.

Remember That You're in Charge

The biggest problem that most new owners have with a computer is taking it too seriously. Life is just too important to take anything seriously, especially a computer.

Above all, never think that it's your fault when something goes wrong. If you always blame yourself, you have a horrid time computing. The truth is that computers are dumb. They foul up all the time. It's not your fault.

Don't Let the Computer Run Your Life

Computers are *not* a big deal. They're tools. You use them to extend your own abilities. They aren't important. Human beings don't live to serve the computer.

If you find yourself overly enamored with your computer, make it a point to take a break every so often. Walk outside. Get some fresh air. Talk to a human being. If the universe has a center, it's not powered by a microprocessor.

Have fun.

Index

• C •

• X •

• Z •

Software Worksheet

Product name: _____

Developer: _____

Price: _____

Category: | Office | Word processing | Spreadsheet | Presentation |
Utility	Database	Graphics	Education
Internet	Networking	Programming	Financial
Multimedia	Entertainment	Reference	Other

Type of support: | Vanilla | Chocolate | Carob | Fudge |

Operating systems: Windows   2000 / NT   XP Home / Pro
Macintosh OS X
Linux: _____
Other: _____

Microprocessor: Pentium: _____
G4   G5   Other Mac:
Alpha
Speed: _____ MHz

Memory (RAM) needed: _____ megabytes

Hard disk storage: _____ gigabytes

Media: CD-ROM   DVD   Other: _____

Graphics: Memory: _____ megabytes   GPU   3D
PCI   AGP
ATI   NVIDIA

Printer: _____

Other: _____

Notes : _____

Software Worksheet

Product name: _____

Developer: _____

Price: _____

Category:
Office	Word processing	Spreadsheet	Presentation
Utility	Database	Graphics	Education
Internet	Networking	Programming	Financial
Multimedia	Entertainment	Reference	Other

Type of support: Vanilla   Chocolate   Carob   Fudge

Operating systems: Windows   2000 / NT   XP Home / Pro
                  Macintosh OS X
                  Linux: _____
                  Other: _____

Microprocessor: Pentium: _____
               G4   G5   Other Mac:
               Alpha
               Speed: _____ MHz

Memory (RAM) needed: _____ megabytes

Hard disk storage: _____ gigabytes

Media: CD-ROM   DVD   Other: _____

Graphics: Memory: _____ megabytes   GPU   3D
           PCI   AGP
           ATI   NVIDIA

Printer: _____

Other: _____

Notes : _____

Software Worksheet

Product name: _____

Developer: _____

Price: _____

Category: Office   Word processing   Spreadsheet   Presentation
Utility   Database   Graphics   Education
Internet   Networking   Programming   Financial
Multimedia   Entertainment   Reference   Other

Type of support: Vanilla   Chocolate   Carob   Fudge

Operating systems: Windows   2000 / NT   XP Home / Pro
Macintosh OS X
Linux: _____
Other: _____

Microprocessor: Pentium: _____
G4   G5   Other Mac:
Alpha
Speed: _____ MHz

Memory (RAM) needed: _____ megabytes

Hard disk storage: _____ gigabytes

Media: CD-ROM   DVD   Other: _____

Graphics: Memory: _____ megabytes   GPU   3D
PCI   AGP
ATI   NVIDIA

Printer: _____

Other: _____

Notes : _____

Software Worksheet

Product name: _____

Developer: _____

Price: _____

Category:
Office	Word processing	Spreadsheet	Presentation
Utility	Database	Graphics	Education
Internet	Networking	Programming	Financial
Multimedia	Entertainment	Reference	Other

Type of support: Vanilla   Chocolate   Carob   Fudge

Operating systems: Windows   2000 / NT   XP Home / Pro
Macintosh OS X
Linux: _____
Other: _____

Microprocessor: Pentium: _____
G4   G5   Other Mac:
Alpha
Speed: _____ MHz

Memory (RAM) needed: _____ megabytes

Hard disk storage: _____ gigabytes

Media: CD-ROM   DVD   Other: _____

Graphics: Memory: _____ megabytes   GPU   3D
PCI   AGP
ATI   NVIDIA

Printer: _____

Other: _____

Notes : _____

Software Worksheet

Product name: _____

Developer: _____

Price: _____

Category:	Office	Word processing	Spreadsheet	Presentation
	Utility	Database	Graphics	Education
	Internet	Networking	Programming	Financial
	Multimedia	Entertainment	Reference	Other

Type of support: Vanilla   Chocolate   Carob   Fudge

Operating systems: Windows   2000 / NT   XP Home / Pro
Macintosh OS X
Linux: _____
Other: _____

Microprocessor: Pentium: _____
G4   G5   Other Mac:
Alpha
Speed: _____ MHz

Memory (RAM) needed: _____ megabytes

Hard disk storage: _____ gigabytes

Media: CD-ROM   DVD   Other: _____

Graphics: Memory: _____ megabytes   GPU   3D
PCI   AGP
ATI   NVIDIA

Printer: _____

Other: _____

Notes : _____

Software Worksheet

Product name: _____

Developer: _____

Price: _____

Category:
Office	Word processing	Spreadsheet	Presentation
Utility	Database	Graphics	Education
Internet	Networking	Programming	Financial
Multimedia	Entertainment	Reference	Other

Type of support: Vanilla   Chocolate   Carob   Fudge

Operating systems: Windows   2000 / NT   XP Home / Pro
Macintosh OS X
Linux: _____
Other: _____

Microprocessor: Pentium: _____
G4   G5   Other Mac:
Alpha
Speed: _____ MHz

Memory (RAM) needed: _____ megabytes

Hard disk storage: _____ gigabytes

Media: CD-ROM   DVD   Other: _____

Graphics: Memory: _____ megabytes   GPU   3D
PCI   AGP
ATI   NVIDIA

Printer: _____

Other: _____

Notes : _____

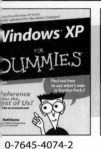

SPORTS, FITNESS, PARENTING, RELIGION & SPIRITUALITY

0-7645-5146-9

Parenting FOR DUMMIES

0-7645-5418-2

Also available:
- Adoption For Dummies
  0-7645-5488-3
- Basketball For Dummies
  0-7645-5248-1
- The Bible For Dummies
  0-7645-5296-1
- Buddhism For Dummies
  0-7645-5359-3
- Catholicism For Dummies
  0-7645-5391-7
- Hockey For Dummies
  0-7645-5228-7

- Judaism For Dummies
  0-7645-5299-6
- Martial Arts For Dummies
  0-7645-5358-5
- Pilates For Dummies
  0-7645-5397-6
- Religion For Dummies
  0-7645-5264-3
- Teaching Kids to Read For Dumm
  0-7645-4043-2
- Weight Training For Dummies
  0-7645-5168-X
- Yoga For Dummies
  0-7645-5117-5

TRAVEL

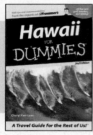

0-7645-5438-7

0-7645-5453-0

Also available:
- Alaska For Dummies
  0-7645-1761-9
- Arizona For Dummies
  0-7645-6938-4
- Cancún and the Yucatán For Dummies
  0-7645-2437-2
- Cruise Vacations For Dummies
  0-7645-6941-4
- Europe For Dummies
  0-7645-5456-5
- Ireland For Dummies
  0-7645-5455-7

- Las Vegas For Dummies
  0-7645-5448-4
- London For Dummies
  0-7645-4277-X
- New York City For Dummies
  0-7645-6945-7
- Paris For Dummies
  0-7645-5494-8
- RV Vacations For Dummies
  0-7645-5443-3
- Walt Disney World & Orlando For Dum
  0-7645-6943-0

GRAPHICS, DESIGN & WEB DEVELOPMENT

0-7645-4345-8

0-7645-5589-8

Also available:
- Adobe Acrobat 6 PDF For Dummies
  0-7645-3760-1
- Building a Web Site For Dummies
  0-7645-7144-3
- Dreamweaver MX 2004 For Dummies
  0-7645-4342-3
- FrontPage 2003 For Dummies
  0-7645-3882-9
- HTML 4 For Dummies
  0-7645-1995-6
- Illustrator CS For Dummies
  0-7645-4084-X

- Macromedia Flash MX 2004 For Dum
  0-7645-4358-X
- Photoshop 7 All-in-One Desk
  Reference For Dummies
  0-7645-1667-1
- Photoshop CS Timesaving Technic
  For Dummies
  0-7645-6782-9
- PHP 5 For Dummies
  0-7645-4166-8
- PowerPoint 2003 For Dummies
  0-7645-3908-6
- QuarkXPress 6 For Dummies
  0-7645-2593-X

NETWORKING, SECURITY, PROGRAMMING & DATABASES

0-7645-6852-3

0-7645-5784-X

Also available:
- A+ Certification For Dummies
  0-7645-4187-0
- Access 2003 All-in-One Desk
  Reference For Dummies
  0-7645-3988-4
- Beginning Programming For Dummies
  0-7645-4997-9
- C For Dummies
  0-7645-7068-4
- Firewalls For Dummies
  0-7645-4048-3
- Home Networking For Dummies
  0-7645-42796

- Network Security For Dummies
  0-7645-1679-5
- Networking For Dummies
  0-7645-1677-9
- TCP/IP For Dummies
  0-7645-1760-0
- VBA For Dummies
  0-7645-3989-2
- Wireless All In-One Desk Referenc
  For Dummies
  0-7645-7496-5
- Wireless Home Networking For Dum
  0-7645-3910-8

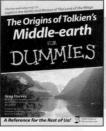